Skills for Success

Personal Development and Employability

Palgrave Study Skills

Other titles in this series by Stella Cotrell

Critical Thinking Skills
The Exam Skills Handbook
Skills for Success (2nd edn)
The Palgrave Student Planner
The Study Skills Handbook (3rd edn)
Teaching Study Skills and Supporting Learning

Authoring a PhD
Business Degree Success
Career Skills
Cite them Right (8th edn)
e-Learning Skills (2nd edn)
Effective Communication for
  Arts and Humanities Students
Effective Communication for
  Science and Technology
The Foundations of Research (2nd edn)
The Good Supervisor
Great Ways to Learn Anatomy and
  Physiology
How to Manage your Arts, Humanities and
  Social Science Degree
How to Manage your Distance and
  Open Learning Course
How to Manage your Postgraduate Course
How to Manage your Science and
  Technology Degree
How to Study Foreign Languages
How to use your Reading in your Essays
How to Write Better Essays (2nd edn)
How to Write your Undergraduate
  Dissertation
Information Skills
IT Skills for Successful Study

Making Sense of Statistics
The International Student Handbook
The Mature Student's Guide to Writing (2nd edn)
The Mature Student's Handbook
The Personal Tutor's Handbook
The Postgraduate Research Handbook (2nd edn)
Presentation Skills for Students (2nd edn)
The Principles of Writing in Psychology
Professional Writing (2nd edn)
Researching Online
Research Using IT
The Study Abroad Handbook
The Student's Guide to Writing (2nd edn)
The Student Life Handbook
Study Skills for Speakers of English as
  a Second Language
Studying Arts and Humanities
Studying the Built Environment
Studying Business at MBA and Masters Level
Studying Economics
Studying History (3rd edn)
Studying Law (2nd edn)
Studying Mathematics and its Applications
Studying Modern Drama (2nd edn)
Studying Physics
Studying Programming
Studying Psychology (2nd edn)
The Undergraduate Research Handbook
The Work-Based Learning Student Handbook
Work Placements - A Survival Guide for Students
Writing for Law
Writing for Nursing and Midwifrey Students
Write it Right
Writing for Engineers (3rd edn)

Palgrave Study Skills: Literature

General Editors: John Peck and Martin Coyle

How to Begin Studying English Literature
  (3rd edn)
How to Study a Jane Austen Novel (2nd edn)
How to Study a Charles Dickens Novel
How to Study Chaucer (2nd edn)
How to Study an E. M. Forster Novel
How to Study James Joyce
How to Study Linguistics (2nd edn)

How to Study Modern Poetry
How to Study a Novel (2nd edn)
How to Study a Poet
How to Study a Renaissance Play
How to Study Romantic Poetry (2nd edn)
How to Study a Shakespeare Play (2nd edn)
How to Study Television
Practical Criticism

Skills for Success

Personal Development and Employability

Second Edition

Stella Cottrell

First edition published 2003
Second edition published 2010

First published 2003 by
PALGRAVE MACMILLAN

Palgrave Macmillan in the UK is an imprint of Macmillan Publishers Limited, registered in England, company number 785998, of Houndmills, Basingstoke, Hampshire RG21 6XS.

Palgrave Macmillan in the US is a division of St Martin's Press LLC, 175 Fifth Avenue, New York, N.Y. 10010

Palgrave Macmillan is the global academic imprint of the above companies and has companies and representatives throughout the world.

Palgrave® and Macmillan® are registered trademarks in the United States, the United Kingdom, Europe and other countries

ISBN: 978-0-230-25018-5   paperback

This book is printed on paper suitable for recycling and made from fully managed and sustained forest sources. Logging, pulping and manufacturing processes are expected to conform to the environmental regulations of the country of origin.

A catalogue record for this book is available from the British Library.

A catalog record for this book is available from the Library of Congress.

10 9 8 7 6 5 4
19 18 17 16 15 14 13 12 11

Printed in China

Contents

Introductory notes for university staff

Since the first edition of *Skills for Success* was published in 2003, the landscape for personal development planning (PDP) within HEIs has changed almost beyond recognition. There has been a host of initiatives to encourage and support students to address the broader curriculum. These initiatives are variously linked to careers education and 'employability', to enriching the core curriculum, or to action taken to address issues indicated through the National Student Survey. PDP has been usefully applied to the arenas of student support, volunteering and community engagement, widening participation and school liaison, Enterprise and Knowledge Transfer (EKT), support for small businesses, and others.

Feedback from academic staff approached by Palgrave Macmillan indicated that, although graduate 'employability' was the key motivator for advocating PDP (or a version of this), PDP was also viewed as important in enabling HEIs to develop students as rounded people, creative individuals or 'radical thinkers'. The broad applicability of PDP to different agendas is reflected in the range of approaches to PDP adopted by HEIs and the way that it is presented to students, parents and funders.

The 'additional extra' aspect of PDP has been emphasised by packages offered to students such as 'University Plus' schemes. HEIs have been variously involved in mapping how skills taught through the curriculum could be applied in life and work, and redesigning programmes to broaden the range of skills that students could develop through the curriculum. Credit is offered for extra-curricular activities, opportunities created for work placements at home and abroad, research projects undertaken for business and the community, and a whole host of developmental activities provided. Elaborate on-line resources enable students to identify where on their programme or through other activities they can address personal skills gaps. The energy and support for PDP is already very different from that at the turn of the century.

What is Personal Development Planning (PDP) and what do we have to do?

The Dearing Enquiry (1997) recommended that progress files be introduced by universities as 'a means by which students can monitor, build, and reflect upon their personal development'. The Quality Assurance Agency (QAA) now expects all universities to use the progress file initiative to ensure that students undertake personal planning throughout their time as undergraduates. Progress files consist of three elements: (1) personal development processes, (2) student records that guide personal reflection and planning, and (3) the formal university transcript.

The processes of Personal Development Planning (PDP) are at the heart of the progress files initiative and are the most important aspect of it. PDP brings together the three concepts of personal development, 'improving learning and performance', and forward planning to achieve goals, whether academic, personal or professional. There are formal requirements for universities to deliver PDP. These include:

- informing students about PDP when they first make contact and at each stage of their learning;
- providing structured opportunities for reflection and PDP at all stages of university education;
- enabling students to keep records of their personal progress to aid reflection and planning;

- providing formal records of achievement (transcripts) that students can use to assist their planning as well as their job applications.

PDP refers to much more than career planning, although that is one important aspect of the initiative. It is about creating structured opportunities for students to develop a wider range of skills and personal qualities that will benefit them in life, work and study. These might include inter-personal skills, team work, problem-solving, self-management skills and similar skills. At its best, PDP develops rounded, reflective individuals who are responsible, emotionally mature, forward thinking, and capable of working well with others. Such skills and attributes take time, practice, support and encouragement to develop. Where possible, it helps students when these are made relevant and accessible by being provided through their programme and linked to the curriculum rather than left to occasional and last-minute sessions with the Careers Service.

How can this book help university staff to deliver PDP?

This book provides information and structured activities that assist universities in meeting QAA expectations for PDP. It includes a broad range of approaches so that lecturers and other staff can select those that they feel are most relevant. There are activities within the text that tutors have found useful when considering how to deliver PDP, either through workshops or tutorials. In addition, academic staff can direct students to materials within the book that:

- inform them about personal development planning;
- structure reflection on a broad range of PDP issues;
- help them to evaluate current levels of competence and confidence;
- include activities that develop specific skills and attitudes;
- relate PDP to academic study;
- enable aspects of PDP to be incorporated into the curriculum;
- enable them to record different kinds of goals and achievements for their personal records.

Over time, you will probably want to adapt some activities to suit your own programme. However, for those starting out in this area, activities are written in a generic way in order to enable time-pressured staff to use them with minimum alterations.

Using Skills for Success with students

The book is designed for use either as a key text to support PDP within a programme of study, or to be used as a stand-alone text. It is not designed for students to read from cover to cover. Not every aspect of the book will be relevant to all students for their particular programme or level of study. It is likely that many students will find it quite hard to think about their future in this way and to plan the development of their personal skills and qualities over a three- or four-year period unless they receive support. That is why Dearing and the QAA lay emphasis on 'structured opportunities' for PDP. Tutors can assist students by:

- identifying which materials and activities are most useful at their stage of the programme;
- creating workshop opportunities for students to undertake the activities in a supported way;
- providing opportunities for discussion, activities and reflection;
- if possible, developing skills and qualities (such as team work, problem-solving, self-evaluation and action-planning) through the curriculum over the length of the programme so that these are nurtured and reinforced over time.

The following activities are suggested for each level of an undergraduate programme. They are not exhaustive, and there are other activities in the book that you may wish to use at each level.

Level 1 PDP activities

Introduce PDP

The Introduction to the book (pp. 1–12) will help introduce the concept of PDP to students in line with QAA expectations. It specifies some of the benefits of PDP. Students can be invited to personalise these so that they see the relevance of PDP to themselves. At level 1, students may need lecturers to make explicit the links between PDP and their programme, clarifying how developing skills and personal qualities can assist academic progress on their particular programme.

Personal engagement

Some students find it difficult to grasp the importance of forward planning. 'The future' can seem a long way off. This book provides many activities to assist students to focus on themselves, their ambitions and their motivation from a number of angles. Some activities focus more on self-understanding, some on life planning, and some on learning styles and habits. Tutors can help students by guiding them towards activities from Chapters 1-4 that suit their programme, interests or personality.

Employability

Students who make the wrong choice of degree are the most likely to leave early and may not be preparing adequately for jobs that interest them. You may like to invite the Careers Service to offer a session about career options and subject choices. Students also need to be informed early on about the kinds of skills, qualities and experiences that employers are looking for, so that they can plan their development. These cannot usually be gained 'at the last minute': personal, inter-personal and task-management skills take time and experience to develop.

Identify local opportunities

Identify what kinds of structured activities students can expect from the university over their time as a student. Clarify what, if anything, will be offered through the programme and by academic staff, and the procedures for accessing this. Invite in representatives from central units that provide some of those opportunities, to make a brief introduction, or ask them to provide a flier. Students may have met some of these staff in an advisory capacity during induction, but they would have a different role from a PDP perspective.

Provide information about options that students can take to supplement their main subject or broaden their studies.

Link to study skills

It can be helpful to link PDP to academic development, especially at level 1. An initial PDP self-evaluation could be linked to the early identification of study skills needs. Students benefit from being involved in diagnostic and self-evaluation processes, even if objective testing is also used. Once areas for improvement are identified, these can be followed up by guidance and a plan of action. It is useful for staff to monitor student action plans where this is feasible. However, students should be able to show how they have monitored and evaluated their own development. Students could also support each other in achieving development plans, such as through the action sets described in Chapter 6. Materials for supporting specific study skills can be found in *The Study Skills Handbook* (Cottrell, 2008, 3rd edn, published by Palgrave Macmillan).

Introduce self-management

This can link quite easily with study skills such as time management and working with others. Some or all of Chapter 4, 'Successful self-management' and Chapter 6, 'People Skills', will be useful at level 1. Chapter 3 is also useful in helping students to understand the conidtions that impact on their performance and how they might take more responsibility for managing these in order to improve their performance.

Look forward

Mature students may be studying for a qualification for career reasons such as to progress to a particular professional status within their current occupations or to change occupation. Good personal planning can enable such students to apply what they have learnt on their programme to their employment – and vice versa – as well as considering their broader career and academic options. Gaining recognition at work and/or promotions whilst still working towards the qualification can be a real spur to motivation, especially for part-time students on longer programmes.

School-leavers may find it difficult to think ahead towards a career, even at level 3. The earlier this is raised, the more time students have to plan towards a job they will want. Activities in Chapter 1, 'The vision: What is success?', encourage students to explore what is important to them for their futures. It can be useful to discuss different concepts of success and achievement, especially if student retention rates are an issue. Not all students will be as academically successful as they would like. This can be difficult, especially in a university culture where the academic focus is a major part of everyday life.

For some students, aspects of personal identity and family duty, not to mention personal finances, are bound up with very specific ideas of what constitutes success. Whilst every attempt should be made to support improvements in academic performance, it is important that students think through what is really important to them beyond their degree, and the contribution that academic study can make towards achieving personal goals, irrespective of degree classification.

Start early with skills of reflection

Introduce the concept of reflection as early as possible. Many people find it takes time to develop reflective skills, so it is important to build this in early to ensure plenty of practice. Chapter 8, 'The art of reflection', gives examples of types of reflective activity. Draw attention to those used for your subject at each level. If possible, give brief examples of reflective writing from your subject discipline. Let students know from the outset whether reflective journals, logs or blogs will be seen by tutors so that they can make decisions about what to include and what is private. Realistically, if reflective materials do not count towards the completion of the module in some way or are not used actively as part of teaching, then students are unlikely to maintain them, however valuable they might be. Some ways of incorporating reflection into programmes are:

- set reflective activities drawn from various chapters of this book to discuss in class or tutorials;

- set a reflective essay or position paper for an assignment (see Chapter 8, 'The Art of Reflection');
- ask students to submit a summary from their reflective journal and copies of certain pages (by negotiation);
- ask students to reflect upon specific issues which they then discuss in class;
- make clear that reflective journals, logs or blogs are to be submitted and count towards the assignment mark (even if the journal itself is not given a mark);
- provide a reflective cover sheet for students to complete and hand in with assignments; examples of these are given in Cottrell (2001, pp. 237–8, 300–2, 319–21);
- make clear whether journals will be marked and what percentage of the mark is allocated to this;
- give time in class for comments to be recorded in journals after an activity has taken place;
- invite comments based upon reflective work, as relevant opportunities arise.

Record achievement

Encourage students to begin the process of recording achievement. This should arise naturally out of writing action plans, setting targets and monitoring these. At level 1, you may prefer to focus such action plans entirely on skills development or planning for a particular assignment. The aim is to help students to become systematic in thinking ahead, making plans, executing a plan and reflecting how the plan and their performance could have been improved.

Level 2 PDP activities

It is likely that the bulk of PDP activity will take place at level 2. At this level, tutors can usefully establish a base line. This could include:

- students identifying progress to date, based upon work undertaken at level 1 and outside of university study;
- updating personal goals and action plans;
- making specific links between academic skills and their application and adaptation to non-academic contexts.

Management skills

The four skills areas covered between Chapters 4 and 7 are loosely referred to here as 'management' skills as they enable students to:

- manage themselves;
- manage their working relationships;
- manage tasks, projects and problem-solving;
- manage their minds and their thinking.

These skills are mutually reinforcing, and together form the core of what is needed for the kinds of jobs graduates can expect to enter. A weakness in any one of these skills can impact upon the others. Together the four skills establish a solid basis for working in most situations with confidence, irrespective of the context. Students will be better prepared to address any problem from a strategic and creative standpoint, identify their own development needs, take responsibility, cope with pressure, and work with others to arrive at a solution. Material in Chapter 3, 'Understanding your personal performance', is also relevant.

Academic staff can assist students by creating opportunities to develop these four 'management' skills, using the materials in the book as well as subject-specific examples. The emphasis on each skill will vary depending on the kinds of careers usually associated with the programme and what it is feasible to cover either through the programme or alongside it. 'People skills', for example, will mean different things depending on whether the skills most frequently needed within the discipline are primarily for working on an individual basis with clients, working in a research team, managing other people's work, coping with the public and so on. Tutors can guide students to the appropriate skills within the chapter and use naturally occurring situations to evaluate, discuss and reflect upon relevant skills. It is worth noting that over 40 per cent of graduates enter professions that are not related to their subject discipline, and where 'management' skills are likely to be at a premium.

Career planning

In their penultimate year, which is usually HE level 2, students need to prepare more seriously for employment. Employers are now much less likely to offer intensive training after employment than was the case in the past. They prefer to take on graduates who already show relevant skills in areas they want. The skills required are especially those of self-management, working with others, and being able to 'hit the ground running' to solve problems, especially as part of a team. This means that students who lack experience of team working, employment culture, applied problem-solving or project work are likely to be at a disadvantage when they apply for jobs. Students need to be much more alert to career planning than was the case several years ago and need to be active in searching out opportunities to develop and apply skills.

The Careers Service is obviously the first port of call for guidance about career planning. As a personal tutor, you may identify those who have not yet seen a Careers Adviser and prompt a visit early in the penultimate year of study. Academic staff can also promote career planning by activities such as inviting alumni and professionals to talk to students about how they used subject skills in particular work situations. Assignments that focus on applying subject knowledge to work or 'real life' contexts can also encourage work-related reflection.

Experience

Students can be reluctant to take on extracurricular activities in case they affect their degree grades. It can be helpful if academic staff give guidance on this and encourage those who would benefit from broadening their experience to look for opportunities to do so. Increasingly, programmes have developed links with businesses, agencies, schools and community groups to generate work experience and placements that enable students to explore themes or develop skills relevant to their programme. These can be used to produce assignments for formal assessment, and provide opportunities for students to gain feedback on their skills from people other than their tutor.

Recording achievement and attributes

It is not enough for students to have developed skills and gained experience, they also need to be able to talk about these, drawing out their relevance to different contexts. HEIs are now much more aware that students, as well as gaining knowledge and skills, also need to understand the relevance of these and be able to articulate them in ways that make sense to employers and others. This is one reason for the emphasis on structured reflection: 'transferable skills' and 'transferable experience' are not always readily recognised. It is helpful if academic or careers staff make explicit the ways that skills developed within the programme could be transferred or adapted to the world of work.

In addition, employers are interested to know about personal qualities, how these have been acquired and demonstrated. They may be keen to see whether the student is aware of the relevance of their skills, qualities, experience and knowledge to the workplace, and how good they are at spotting and using opportunities. This means that 'recording achievement' is not simply about writing a list or even a curriculum vitae (CV). Many employers do not accept CVs any more. Useful records are now more analytical, evaluative and reflective. The materials provided in Chapter 9, 'Personal records: recording reflection and achievement', and the Resource Bank, encourage students to draw out the significance of their achievements. This puts them in a better position to address competence-based job application processes.

Level 3 PDP activities

Projects and dissertations

PDP at level 3 is likely to consist of fine-tuning and updating work undertaken at level 2. Some universities are linking level 3 PDP to the dissertation. For example, students are encouraged to map the development of their project planning skills when they undertake their dissertation. Students are sometimes introduced to dissertation skills at level 2, such as through early project planning. Chapters 5 and 7 are likely to help in developing these skills. These would need to be supplemented by materials relating to the research methodologies used for specific subject disciplines.

Recording achievement

Although, ideally, students would have been recording achievement throughout their programme, records will need to be completed and updated during level 3. The key time for interviews is early in the final year, so record maintenance should be encouraged at the end of level 2 and the start of level 3.

Applying for jobs

The Careers Service will provide the main support for job applications. However, if you are aware that students are soon to attend an interview or have not visited the Careers Service, you may wish to draw their attention to Chapter 10, 'Successful job applications'.

The future of PDP

PDP is still a mutable entity within higher education. It will take shape over time as different disciplines and universities adapt it in ways that are meaningful for their own students. The terminology used to describe PDP may vary from one HEI to another. However, universities and colleges are actively engaged. Indeed, they market themselves in terms of the skills sets and qualities that make their graduates distinctive. Themes of social responsibility, business readiness, and global citizenship are typical, and speak to a different kind of agenda than that of the past. Students will not only gain subject expertise, they will acquire a broader education that will enable them to progress with confidence into new positions once they graduate – if not before. This trend is likely to continue.

I hope this book will assist busy staff in higher education to deliver PDP more easily – and to help their students to achieve their ambitions.

Stella Cottrell

List of abbreviations

CEO   Chief Executive Officer

CPD   continual professional development

CV   curriculum vitae

CVCP   Committee of Vice Chancellors and Principals

HE   Higher Education

HEI   Higher Education Institutions

IiP   Investors in People

PDP   personal development planning

PI   performance indicators

QAA   Quality Assurance Agency

Acknowledgements

Acknowledgements and thanks are due to the many people who contributed to the development of activities and ideas presented in this book. In particular, very warm thanks are given to the reviewers, drawn from several universities, who made suggestions for improvements to the proposals and drafts of each edition. Their comments and guidance not only encouraged me to proceed, but also added considerably to the final version of this text, making it more relevant to a wide range of higher education contexts.

Thanks are also due to the lecturers and professional support staff at the (now) University of Bedfordshire for pioneering work in introducing personal development planning into the curriculum in 2002, especially Mark Atlay, Roger Woods, Valerie Shrimplin, Professor Kate Robinson, Dai John and all the staff who pointed out that lecturers needed materials from which to work with students.

I would also like to thank everyone at Palgrave Macmillan who contributed to the production of this edition, especially Suzannah Burywood for keeping the whole ship on course.

Finally I should like to thank my partner for countless good ideas, for kindly giving up weekends and holidays to get the new edition out, and, not least, the endless supplies of food and drink to keep me going.

Stella Cottrell
2010

Introduction

Think positively and masterfully with confidence and faith, and life becomes more secure, more fraught with activity, richer in achievement and experience.

Eddie Rickenbacker

What's it all for?

What do you really want?
Do you know what you want to aim for in life?
What skills and personal qualities will you need along the way?
What can you do now to put yourself in charge of your own future?

Create your own horizon

We all have dreams of what life might be like in the future and what we might become. Whilst for many of us these dreams remain distant and vague, for others they come true. It may feel as though good fortune smiles on certain individuals – and luck can certainly be one component of success. However, as we shall see in Chapter 1, successful people usually develop skills, attitudes and behaviours that anybody else could too. Your dreams are in your hands.

As a student, 'the future', when decisions need to be made, may seem to be a long way off. It is not uncommon for students to have little idea of what they want to do when they come to the end of their programme. Even if you are studying for a vocational degree, your ambitions may change during your course. If you don't know what you want, the answers rarely fall fully formed out of the sky.

The use you make of your time as a student, and the decisions you make then, will have an impact on the choices open to you later on. It is in your interest to use personal development planning so as to make the best possible choices along the way. It is never too early to start that process. You do not need to know exactly what you want, but it is useful to form a vision of the life you want to lead, the sort of jobs you wish to undertake, the kind of person you want to be – and then to map out the steps that take you in the right direction.

This book is designed to support you to:

- shape your own ambitions;
- identify the skills, qualities and attitudes needed to achieve your goals;
- develop skills, qualities and attitudes that will help you to find a good job as a graduate;
- make strong job applications;
- use your time as a student effectively;
- manage your personal development.

Personal Development Planning (PDP) as a student

More than just a degree

When students complete their programmes, they usually have a good understanding of their subject discipline and have developed skills associated with their course of academic study. This is good, but is only part of the story.

Being at university or college provides opportunities to mix with a wide range of people, to take part in new activities, to manage positions of responsibility and to broaden your outlook. Most of these opportunities lie outside of the taught curriculum although, increasingly, programmes are being designed with aspects of personal and professional development built into the curriculum. Students are being encouraged to adopt a broad-based approach to their time as a student and to use their time and the curriculum imaginatively.

Why is PDP actively encouraged for students?

The kinds of jobs that most graduates want to enter require a range of qualities and skills that take time, support and good planning to develop. These include people skills, problem-solving, project work and self-management. Such skills cannot be suddenly acquired in isolation or at the last minute. In the past, many graduates felt disappointed that they were not better prepared for when they left university. It has now been recognised that students need structured opportunities to think about, and plan towards, their future.

In Britain, the Quality Assurance Agency for Higher Education (QAA) requires universities and other Higher Education Institutions (HEIs) to provide PDP and 'progress files' for all undergraduates. This requirement consists of three parts:

1. A Personal Development Planning process (PDP)

2. Personal records of learning and achievement

3. A formal transcript provided by the institution

1. Personal Development Planning process (PDP)

The PDP process is something to be lived, thought about, discussed and experimented with over several years. The QAA describes it as:

> Structured and supported processes to develop the capacity of individuals to reflect upon their learning and achievement, and to plan for their own personal education and career development. (QAA, 2000)

2. Personal records of learning and achievement

These can contain details of personal goals, plans, reviews and achievements. They are a source of material for you to draw upon to monitor your own progress and to prepare job applications.

3. A formal transcript provided by the institution

The formal transcript is provided by the university or college, usually in addition to a degree certificate. It records more information about your learning and achievement than the traditional degree certificate.

The Benefits of PDP

When undertaken in supported and structured ways, PDP gives you a much deeper understanding of your performance. You develop abilities in evaluating this for yourself. Instead of being locked into a routine learning cycle, you enter into an upwards learning spiral. PDP puts you in charge.

Read through the potential benefits of PDP listed below. Tick any of these that you consider would be of relevance to you.

Benefits of PDP to academic performance

The advantages for me of taking a developmental approach to my studies are:

- ☐ a clearer focus for my academic work;
- ☐ more control over personal motivation – and the ability to direct this to achieve my goals;
- ☐ skills in self-management;
- ☐ greater independence and confidence through gaining a better understanding of how to improve my performance;
- ☐ more enjoyment and less stress from my academic studies as I become consciously skilled;
- ☐ greater awareness of how to apply what I have learnt to new problems and contexts;
- ☐ reflective, strategic, analytical and creative thinking skills that strengthen academic performance.

The personal planning approach presented in this book can have a positive effect upon your academic work, especially when combined with the development of study skills. Study skills for higher-level study form a separate but related area. These are covered in a companion volume, *The Study Skills Handbook* (2008). See also, *Critical Thinking* (Cottrell, 2005).

Benefits of PDP to professional life

The advantages to me of taking a PDP approach to career and professional life are:

- ☐ strategies for improving personal performance;
- ☐ a better sense of the life and work I want;
- ☐ more confidence in the choices I make;
- ☐ confidence in the skills, qualities and attributes I bring to the career of my choice;
- ☐ being in a better position to compete for jobs and to discuss my skills and competences with employers;
- ☐ the positive attitudes, creative thinking, and problem-solving approaches associated with successful professional life.

Benefits of PDP to personal life

The advantages of taking a PDP approach to my personal life are:

- ☐ gaining a better understanding of myself and how I 'tick';
- ☐ being in a better position to make appropriate choices to meet my aspirations;
- ☐ gaining a better sense of myself as an individual;
- ☐ greater awareness of my needs and how to meet these;
- ☐ greater awareness of the unique contribution I can make;
- ☐ developing a positive, forward-looking approach;
- ☐ developing skills such as reflection, strategic thinking, self-direction and self-evaluation, useful in most life contexts.

Activity

- Browse through the benefits you ticked in the three lists above. Which of these are most important to you?
- Choose between three and five of these and jot down in your own words what these mean for you.

What PDP do I want and need?

The following activities enable you to stand back and consider:

- what kind of personal development planning you might need,
- your priorities for PDP.

ⓔ Do I need Personal Development Planning?

Self-evaluation

For each of the following statements, rate your responses as outlined below.
Note that *strongly agree* carries no score.

Rating: *0 = strongly agree   1 = agree   2 = sort of agree   3 = disagree   4 = strongly disagree*

	Rating				
1. I am certain that I can keep myself motivated towards achieving my degree for the next few years	0	1	2	3	4
2. I am very clear what my goals are for the next seven years	0	1	2	3	4
3. I am confident that I have planned sufficiently to enable me to achieve my goals	0	1	2	3	4
4. I am very clear how my degree fits into my life plans	0	1	2	3	4
5. I am clear which skills employers are looking for	0	1	2	3	4
6. I am confident I have the skills employers are looking for	0	1	2	3	4
7. I am very clear about the importance of reflective activity to professional life	0	1	2	3	4
8. I am confident that I am able to undertake structured reflection without guidelines	0	1	2	3	4
9. I am confident that I can develop an effective strategy to meet most circumstances	0	1	2	3	4
10. I am confident that I can set well-formed targets	0	1	2	3	4
11. I have a clear understanding of how to evaluate my own performance	0	1	2	3	4
12. I am confident that I know how to improve my performance in most circumstances	0	1	2	3	4
13. I know how to apply my expertise in one area to a very different field	0	1	2	3	4
14. I am confident that I can see myself as others see me	0	1	2	3	4
15. I am confident that I have effective listening skills	0	1	2	3	4
16. I am an assertive person	0	1	2	3	4
17. I am a good 'self-starter'	0	1	2	3	4
18. I am aware of the best roles for me to fill for team work	0	1	2	3	4
19. I am confident at problem-solving	0	1	2	3	4
20. I am confident that I know how to make best use of my mind	0	1	2	3	4
21. I am confident that I will take a creative approach to most problems	0	1	2	3	4
22. I am confident about making competence-based applications for jobs	0	1	2	3	4
23. I am always very clear about which skills I am developing	0	1	2	3	4
24. I can see clearly how my skills apply to a wide range of other situations	0	1	2	3	4
25. I know where my own 'developmental edge' lies	0	1	2	3	4

Add up your score out of 100.   Total score _____

Although this is only a rough guide, you now have a personal development 'needs' score. If this is more than zero, then you would benefit from some personal development. The higher your score, the more likely it is that you need to undertake personal development. Even if you do not need any personal development today, this is likely to change within a few months or even weeks, as your circumstances change.

What are my PDP priorities?

- Identify in column A which aspects of personal development are important to you at present. Give a rating between 5 and 0, giving 5 for *very important* and 0 for *not important at all*.
- In column B, consider how essential it is that you develop this aspect soon. Give a rating between 5 and 0, giving 5 for *very essential* and 0 for *not essential at all*.
- By adding scores in columns A and B, you will gain an idea of where your priorities lie (column C).

Aspects I want to develop further I want to . . .	A How important is this to me? *Rate from 0 to 5*	B How essential to develop it now? *Rate from 0 to 5*	C Priority score *Add scores for columns A and B*	See chapter
1. Clarify my vision and goals for my life				1 and 11
2. Clarify my values				1 and 11
3. Identify a source of inspiration				1
4. Clarify what 'success' means to me				1
5. Clarify what I want to achieve from university				1
6. Strengthen my motivation				1
7. Understand myself better				1, 2, 3, 4 and 11
8. Understand what reflection is about				8
9. Identify ways of approaching reflection				8
10. Evaluate my learning goals				8
11. Develop a reflective journal				8 and wherever you see 📖
12. Write about my personal development planning				8 and 9
13. Develop a strategy for improving performance				4 and 5
14. Develop a strategy to address problems				5

Aspects I want to develop further I want to . . .	A How important is this to me? Rate from 0 to 5	B How essential to develop it now? Rate from 0 to 5	C Priority score Add scores for columns A and B	See chapter
15. Make sense of my life story				2
16. Understand the effect of my personal choices				2
17. Gain a sense of my strengths and areas for improvement				2, 3, 9 and 11
18. Make better use of my own expertise				2 and 9
19. Understand my personal performance profile and preferences				3
20. Identify personal qualities				2 and 9
21. Know how to make a SWOT analysis				4
22. Improve my time management				4
23. Develop more constructive attitudes to achieve my goals				2 and 4
24. Develop my self-confidence				3 and 4
25. Understand more about emotional intelligence				4
26. Manage change and uncertainty more effectively				4
27. Understand what prevents me from achieving my potential				2, 3, 4 and 7
28. Complete tasks more effectively				5
29. Improve my problem-solving skills				5
30. Know how to set effective targets				5
31. Be better at getting down to tasks				5
32. Become a good 'self-starter'				5

Aspects I want to develop further I want to . . .	A How important is this to me? *Rate from 0 to 5*	B How essential to develop it now? *Rate from 0 to 5*	C Priority score *Add scores for columns A and B*	See chapter
33. Develop project-management skills				5
34. Identify my 'competitiveness' in task management				5
35. Develop better rapport with others				6
36. Develop my listening skills				6
37. Develop team-work skills				6
38. Set up a support group (or action sets)				6
39. Be better at giving and receiving criticism				6
40. Be more assertive				6
41. Deal well with difficult people				6
42. Develop negotiating skills				6
43. Develop leadership skills				6
44. Develop creative thinking skills				7
45. Understand more about the brain and how to use it				7
46. Develop skills in applying for jobs				9 and 10
47. Make use of personal records when applying for jobs				9 and 10
48. Develop my personal records				9 and 10

Development priorities
- Look back over the priorities table above.
- Identify the three aspects that you gave the highest scores. If there are more than three with the same score, select three.
- Write the three priorities in words that are meaningful to you.
- If you are ready to start on these, you may find it helpful to use the Action Plan on p. 119.

What kinds of PDP opportunities do I want?

A broad range of opportunities for personal development planning is now made available at most institutions of higher education – though each approaches this differently. Browse the websites of universities that interest you in order to see what they offer and the approaches they take; make sure these suit you. Before going to the websites, consider first what you would want your chosen university to offer, using the lists below.

Tick [✓] those opportunities that you would prefer to have made available to you:

Opportunities through the curriculum

☐ PDP as a core subject or as optional modules;
☐ credit-bearing career-planning modules;
☐ credit for work experience or projects undertaken at work;
☐ credit for voluntary work;
☐ training and credit for mentoring others;
☐ skills development built into the curriculum;
☐ 'electives' or subsidiary subjects that enable me to broaden my perspective by learning about something outside of my main subject.

Jamila's efforts at personal development knew no bounds.

Opportunities provided through programme staff and support services

- [ ] personal tutors: interviews or tutorial sessions on an individual or small group basis;
- [ ] academic guidance: specialist advisers who give advice on academic choices;
- [ ] careers advisory services with a range of individual, paper and on-line resources;
- [ ] job-shops and information about work opportunities;
- [ ] learning development units: support for academic or language skills;
- [ ] voluntary work experience organised through the university or college;
- [ ] skills programmes offered by the student union or a central department;
- [ ] employer-led skills sessions;
- [ ] chances to meet with employers;
- [ ] Web-based resources and tools.

Other opportunities

- [ ] entrepreneurship prizes or awards;
- [ ] positions of responsibility such as student representative for the programme, posts within the student union or for student clubs;
- [ ] contributing to a student magazine or radio;
- [ ] mentoring other students;
- [ ] mentoring or coaching children in local schools;
- [ ] setting up my own club or support group;
- [ ] taking part in activities in the local community;
- [ ] projects for employers undertaken by undergraduates;
- [ ] graduate schemes with employers.

The approach taken by this book

Personal Development Planning

PDP is here interpreted as a structured, reflective process which gives individuals greater insight into their own development. Activities and resources are provided to enable that process. These include materials that help you to:

- [ ] explore what is valuable to your own development;
- [ ] achieve personal goals;
- [ ] undertake the processes of reflection, planning, recording and evaluation;

> **Activity**
>
> Look through the items that you have ticked as important. Check whether these are available at your university or college.

- [ ] articulate your abilities to employers;
- [ ] develop the skills associated with success;
- [ ] make effective job applications.

A solution-focused approach

This approach is characterised by a belief that people are usually capable of arriving at their own solutions, even if this requires some guidance and support. People usually have far more knowledge and expertise than they believe. Guided reflection can encourage people to consider the same issue from many perspectives, allowing different insights and personal solutions to emerge. This book provides practical strategies and guidance for addressing problems and managing tasks, in both the short and long term, and tools to assist you in arriving at the best solutions.

The contents of the book

Your success

Chapter 1 takes as its starting place the notion that all students want to experience success. Most make sacrifices to put themselves through college or university and expect a better future as a result. However, many students are very vague about how to plan for a future they really want. This chapter helps you consider questions such as:

- What does success mean to you?
- What motivates you?
- What are your ambitions, goals, values?
- Who or what inspires you?
- What kind of life do you want to find yourself living 10 or 20 years from now – and what would be your worst nightmare?

You can travel a long way if you have a good idea of who you are and what you really want.

Focus on you

Chapter 2 encourages you to look in detail at you – and what helps you to achieve. Use Chapter 2 to gain different perspectives on:

- your life story so far and the role you play in your own story;
- how you may be perceived by others;
- how you respond to opportunity and adversity;
- the impact of your learning history on your current performance;
- where your expertise lies – and how that could be applied to new contexts.

Understanding personal performance

We are each distinct in what helps or hinders us to perform at our best. In Chapter 3, you have the opportunity to:

- analyse in depth the conditions that have most impact on your performance;
- identify your 'personal performance formula';
- identify the optimum conditions for you when undertaking different kinds of task.

Taking charge

Success begins with knowing and managing yourself. Whilst the first three chapters focus on knowing yourself, Chapter 4 looks at successful self-management. Use this chapter to increase chances of personal success by improving:

- your emotional self-management;
- your time management;
- your 'emotional intelligence';
- your attitudes;
- how you manage change, confusion and uncertainty.

Managing solutions

Good problem-solving strategies will enable you to take on almost any task and will greatly increase personal confidence when you enter new situations. Use Chapter 5 to:

- organise time and tasks effectively;
- learn basic problem-solving strategies;
- select and apply problem-solving strategies to more complex tasks and problems;

- develop planning skills, such as identifying priorities, setting targets and finding good solutions;
- learn skills useful to project management;
- gain familiarity with concepts such as performance indicators and benchmarking;
- audit your personal 'competitiveness'.

People skills

How good are your 'people skills'? Good people skills mean that teams work better, and that individuals gain the consideration and support that they need. People skills create more effective and manageable work environments, which is why employers place such a high value upon them. Use Chapter 6 to consider ways of developing your people skills. It addresses such issues as:

- developing rapport;
- listening skills;
- team work;
- assertiveness and negotiation skills;
- leadership;
- giving and receiving constructive criticism.

Creative thinking

Creativity isn't simply for artists. The most elusive aspect of problem-solving and task completion is in the 'spark of creativity' that brings the right idea to mind at the right time. Chapter 7, 'Thinking outside the box', looks at ways of building confidence in your individual creativity. Use Chapter 7 to:

- develop confidence in your creative abilities;
- harness a basic knowledge of how the mind works in order to improve your thinking skills;
- try out a range of activities to develop creative thinking skills.

Reflection

Many professions require a 'reflective practitioner' approach. Lecturers may require you to 'reflect upon your performance'. But what is 'reflection'? How do you go about it? How do you write about it? As you work through the book, you will find many opportunities for structured reflection. Chapter 8 outlines different methods for structured reflection. You are unlikely to need all of these so browse through and select methods that suit you and your programme. Your tutors may direct you to certain kinds of reflection. The chapter also gives guidance on the structured reflection required for marked assignments.

Personal records

Chapter 9 outlines the rationale for keeping personal records for diverse purposes. It is linked to a *Resource Bank* of materials from which you can select pro-forma for recording key information and reflections. These can be photocopied for updating by hand or are available electronically at www.palgrave.com/studyskills/pdp. There are structured opportunities to reflect upon what you have learnt from different experiences. When completed, these records will provide an invaluable resource when applying for positions and preparing for interviews.

Just the job

Surveys of students show that their main goals in entering university are associated with finding a graduate job or improving their work prospects. The skills developed throughout the book are those associated with graduate careers. Chapter 10 focuses on the process of job application. It looks at such issues as:

● what employers are looking for;
● choosing a job that suits you;
● using the PDP process to plan towards a career;
● making successful job applications;
● preparing for interviews.

The chapter aims to equip you to make good choices and strong applications for the jobs that interest you most.

Raise your game

Finally, Chapter 11 draws together and updates the learning and reflection undertaken throughout the book. If you have followed through on the skills development introduced throughout the book, you will have noticed changes in yourself. The chapter encourages you to recognise personal change and to review your values and goals. It

encourages you to build connections between different skills, areas of expertise and personal development so that you can more easily transfer your skills from one context to another. You are invited to assess your readiness for taking higher risks and are challenged to identify your own 'working edge' for future development.

How to use this book

Experiment

The strategies and skills developed in this book can be applied to a wide range of circumstances.

● Combine and adapt these to suit you;
● experiment with applying the different strategies to your studies, job and personal life;
● find out what works best for you.

Keep a journal

This book uses self-evaluation questionnaires, question-based activities and other activities in order to structure personal reflection. Spaces have been provided in the text where brief and immediate responses are most useful. For more detailed responses, find a light notebook that is easy to carry around. The book refers to this as a 'reflective journal', but you may prefer to use a diary, log, blog, notebook, 'ideas book' or whatever suits you.

Thandi struggled under the weight of an active imagination, carefully noted on a daily basis.

Use the journal to develop ideas, capture your insights and inspiration, work through your thoughts, identify helpful and unhelpful responses to events, and so forth. If you find something is puzzling you, write out your thoughts or feelings. You will probably find that giving the matter attention in this way helps to clarify what is going on. Put time aside regularly to make entries in your journal, and to look back over previous entries. Note the changes in your thinking and personal development.

This symbol reminds you to note down your reflections in your journal when working through the book. Alternatively, you may prefer to record your reflection electronically using the e-Resource Bank that accompanies this text.

Be selective

Each chapter contains a wide range of activities. Don't feel you have to undertake them all. Different activities will appeal to individual students. Select those that look most relevant to you. On another occasion, you may prefer a different set of activities. However, do notice whether you resist undertaking particular activities. The personal development activities we resist are often those that we need the most.

Read out of sequence

Browse through the book and identify chapters and sections that are relevant to you. It is not important to read the chapters in the order presented, except for parts of the last chapter.

- Use Chapter 10 if you are applying for a job now.
- If you feel uninspired about life or study, try Chapters 1, 2 or 7.

- If you are struggling with an assignment, look at Chapters 3, 5 and 7, and use these to supplement a study skills book.
- If you are finding it difficult to deal with a particular person or group setting at present, use Chapter 6.
- If you feel your life or study needs better management, look at Chapters 3, 4 or 5.

However, most aspects of personal development, improving performance and problem-solving are closely interlinked. What you need for any particular situation may be spread across several chapters.

Keep records

Chapter 9 and the competence sheets in the Resource Bank provide a wide range of resources to record your experiences. Look at this early on rather than waiting until you have read the other chapters.

Students may photocopy blank sheets such as self-evaluation questionnaires and planners for their personal use. This will enable you to compare your responses to the same activity at different times and to monitor your own development.

The e-Resource Bank

A selection of materials has also been provided electronically at www.palgrave.com/studyskills/pdp. These can be copied, e-used or adapted for your own personal use. You can use these to take short cuts for working out your own strategies, models, planning tools and prompts.

Do it again!

Return to the activities at different times throughout your studies, and even beyond. The basic concepts covered in this book are applicable to many circumstances. When you enter a new situation, you will interpret the material differently.

Enjoy the book and good luck with all your ambitions!

Chapter 1

The vision: what is success?

To accomplish great things, we must dream as well as act.

Anatole France

Learning outcomes

This chapter offers opportunities to:

reflect upon the nature of success
understand the importance of personal vision to successful outcomes
formulate a personal definition of success
gain insight into personal motivation, inspiration and values, and see how these assist current study
refine your vision of the future and consider how current study contributes towards that vision.

Introduction

Everybody wants to be successful – and in their own way. Everybody has their own version of what 'success' means for themselves and for others. The kinds of success characterised by Barack Obama, Beyoncé, David Beckham or Indira Ghandi, are all very different but no less valuable to the people concerned.

Our concepts of success can be rather vague and open to change. This is especially the case for students – even if some objectives appear clear cut. Embarking on a programme in higher education is, typically, a time of transition – a time for leaving behind the worlds of school and family, or barriers to progression at work, or perceived gaps in knowledge. It is an exciting time, full of potential. As a student, you are exposed to new ideas, new perspectives on the world, new people and opportunities. It is likely that your horizons will be stretched, your values challenged, your ambitions changed. Anything might be possible, all kinds of paths may open up to you.

Being at university is about more than gaining a qualification – important though that is. Students today expect their time in higher education to be a passport to other kinds of success: to a good job, a career, longer-term financial security, more interesting work, management level opportunities, specialist skills and knowledge required for particular professions, a different lifestyle.

Competition for such opportunities is generally great- and a degree alone is unlikely to make you stand out from the crowd. As a student, you will be making decisions that will have an impact on your future opportunities, such as in:

- the options you select;
- the way you approach your studies;
- the projects you undertake;
- the way you apply your learning in work settings if you are already employed;
- the skills and qualities you develop through activities you undertake outside the curriculum;
- and the chances you don't use too.

The activities in this chapter aim to sharpen your thinking about your aims, ambitions and the versions of success you most value. That, in turn, should help you in making decisions that will help you to achieve that success.

Defining success

There are many ways of looking at 'success'. Some people define success in terms of objective material criteria (how much money, how high a position in a company, how big a house?).

However, successful athletes may win world records, even fame, without earning a great deal of money. Successful artists may measure their success by how true they are to their artistic endeavour. Others judge success by the integrity they brought to a task: the confidence that they did their best in honest ways and can live with their conscience. It used to be a sign of success to still have your own teeth at an advanced age!

In other words, 'success' is a very subjective matter. It depends on what is meaningful to you and the people around you.

> ### Activity: Successful people
>
> - Jot down, as quickly as you can, the first ten people you think of as 'successful'.
> - Do these have anything in common?
> - What makes you think of them as 'successful'?
> - How do you think your list might differ from somebody else's? You could compare your list with that of a friend.

> ### Activity: Symbols of success
>
> - Jot down quickly the first ten things (or symbols) you associate with success.
> - How important is each of those symbols to you personally? Are these things that you want very much from life?
> - How do you think your list would differ from somebody else's? Compare your list with a friend's.

> ### Activity: Spectrums of success – or knowing what you want
>
> Below are pairs of statements, each of which relates to different points on a spectrum of opinion about what is successful. For each statement, mark on the spectrum where you would wish your own success to lie.
> For example, _____ X _____
>
> | | | |
> |---|---|---|
> | Being immensely rich | _____ | Having enough to survive |
> | Having high expectations | _____ | Being content with little |
> | Being a world expert | _____ | Knowing enough to survive |
> | Gaining higher degrees | _____ | Passing part of one degree |
> | World fame | _____ | Recognition by colleagues and peers |
> | Achieving high goals | _____ | Achieving something |
> | Seizing big opportunities | _____ | Being aware of some opportunities |
> | Winning on a world stage | _____ | Taking part in any activity |
> | A very high profile job | _____ | Having some work, paid or unpaid |
> | Being very popular | _____ | Having some good friends |
> | Being a world leader | _____ | Living a quiet life |
> | Being important on a world stage | _____ | Being recognised for personal achievements |
> | Having a close family life | _____ | Escaping the family |
> | Outstanding physical appearance and physique | _____ | Minimum interest in personal appearance |
> | Material wealth | _____ | A strong spiritual life |
>
> - Is there another aspect of success which is more important to you than any of those listed above? If so, what is that?
> - If you could be successful in only one area, what would that be? Why is this so important to you? What would it mean not to have this in your life?
> - What do your responses tell you about your own concept of 'success'?

💻 *Activity: A personal definition of success*

Complete the sentence below. In doing so, consider what personal success would be in your own case. Don't worry if you find this much more difficult than you imagined. You will be asked to return to this statement later in the chapter, when you may wish to change or refine it.

For me, being successful means . . .

Personal influences

Some of the definitions of success that you use were probably adopted originally to please other people – or are those you have inherited, or picked up from peers and the media. This is not necessarily a bad thing: these may be influences that you respect or that matter to you. External influences can be very valuable and help us to form our sense of who we are.

However, sometimes, we live out ideas of success that we pick up from other people, without thinking through what they really mean for us. It can be easy to lose ourselves in the values and interests presented by others, especially if we are surrounded by these for much of the time. We can 'forget' that there may be alternatives that are better suited to our personal circumstances, character and beliefs.

💻 *Activity: Personal ambitions*

Sometimes we come up with different answers if we frame the question differently. This activity invites you to give some initial thought to your ambitions for different areas of your life. Later activities explore this in more detail.

My ambitions for my academic work are:

My ambitions for my professional life or career are:

My ambitions for my personal life are:

As so much personal investment is likely to be involved in working towards your concept of success, it is worth considering how your own view of success has been influenced by others – and how far you can say 'This is really me.'

© Stella Cottrell (2003, 2010), *Skills for Success*, Palgrave Macmillan

Activity: Personal values 1

What I value most is . . .	Important to me (✓)			Important to me (✓)
1. A good car	☐	22.	Leadership and authority	☐
2. Challenge	☐	23.	Leaving something for posterity	☐
3. Contributing to society	☐	24.	Making a difference to the world	☐
4. Feeling I am in control of my life	☐	25.	Money	☐
5. Creativity	☐	26.	New experiences	☐
6. Fairness	☐	27.	Personal qualities such as kindness	☐
7. Fame and celebrity	☐	28.	Physical appearance	☐
8. Family and home life	☐	29.	Popularity	☐
9. Friendship	☐	30.	Good-quality possessions	☐
10. Having a good time	☐	31.	Power	☐
11. Health	☐	32.	Being needed	☐
12. Help received from others	☐	33.	Security	☐
13. Helping others	☐	34.	A feeling of self-worth	☐
14. Honesty	☐	35.	Social Life	☐
15. A big house	☐	36.	Solitude	☐
16. Independence	☐	37.	Spiritual life	☐
17. Influence	☐	38.	Sporting ability	☐
18. Integrity	☐	39.	Being wanted	☐
19. Intellectual abilities	☐	40.	Other things: (*state what*)	☐
20. A good job or career	☐			
21. Justice	☐			

Activity: Personal values 2

Select the ten items you value most and list these in order of importance, where 1 is the most important, 2 for the next in importance, and so on.

1.   6.

2.   7.

3.   8.

4.   9.

5.   10.

Consider the top ten items that you valued. What themes can you identify? For example, do your choices suggest you place a high value on any of the following:

● personal qualities (character);
● control over something;
● people;
● material objects;
● power and influence;
● mind and body;
● personal recognition.

Are you comfortable with your responses or do you feel you 'ought to' value other things? If so, what does this response tell you about yourself?

Identify a time when your values were put to the test. In your reflective journal, jot down:

● What happened?
● What did you find out about yourself on that occasion?
● What did you learn about your personal values from that occasion?

Life qualities

The following quotation refers to a number of qualities that one person, Gordon H. Taggart, wished to develop in his life.

I wish I were honest enough to admit all my shortcomings:

– brilliant enough to accept flattery without it making me arrogant;
– tall enough to tower above deceit;
– strong enough to reassure love;
– brave enough to welcome criticism;
– compassionate enough to understand human frailties;
– wise enough to recognise my mistakes;
– humble enough to appreciate greatness;
– staunch enough to stand by my friends;
– human enough to be thankful of my neighbour.

Gordon H. Taggart

📖 *Reflection*   Life qualities

● Which of the qualities identified by Taggart do you most value?
● Which do you make a conscious effort to develop?
● Which three of these qualities would be of most relevance in achieving your goals or vision?
● If you were asked to add another line to the quotation, what would you add that is relevant to your own values?

🖰 *Activity: Feeling Valued: Compliments*

Our values are also relected in what we want others to think about us- such as the comments we do or don't want made about us and the compliments that we treasure.

What three compliments do you most want to hear from other people?

(1)

(2)

(3)

📖 *Reflection*   Valued compliments

In your reflective journal, jot down:

● What do these suggest about what you value?
● What do you do to make it possible to receive such compliments?

© Stella Cottrell (2003, 2010), *Skills for Success*, Palgrave Macmillan

The vision: what is success?

Vision

It helps to get to the top of a mountain if we have seen the pinnacle and know where we are headed.

This does not necessarily mean that we should have very clear life goals, with every detail planned out. Successful people seem to be characterised by not having very rigid life plans (Taylor and Humphrey, 2002).

However, it is important to have a vision of the general direction in which we are going, the kind of life we want to lead, and the levels of personal investment we want to make in different kinds of activity. It is this vision that keeps us going when the inevitable unexpected setbacks occur. If we are assembling a bookcase or doing a jigsaw puzzle, it helps to have the picture before us of what we want to achieve, so that we can see the end goal as a realistic possibility. A vision of what we want to achieve is even more important when we are undertaking a project that lasts for several years, such as working towards a degree or a career.

Ambitions

An obvious starting place is to clarify your current sense of what your ambitions might be. Some people have very clearly formed ambitions and goals by the time they enter university. However, many students have given little thought to what they want after university. It is not necessary to have clearly defined goals, but it is useful to start clarifying personal ambitions, so that you can check both how important these really are to you – and how far you are working towards what matters to you.

The dream

Dream lofty dreams, and as you dream so shall you become. Your vision is the promise of what you shall at last unveil.

John Ruskin

When we are young, we are often told to stop day-dreaming. However, many great inventors and scientists attribute success to the combination of their analytical work with the inspiration that came through dreams or day-dreams.

Activity: The dream

This activity is linked to the activity, 'The Long-Term Vision', page 21.

First, undertake an activity that uses up any surplus energy and leaves you alert and awake. Taking a walk or doing housework is ideal, but any moderately strenuous activity will do. This will get the blood flowing to your brain (so you think better) but work off excess adrenalin (so you are open to being creative rather than defensive).

Then, find a comfortable seat where you will not be disturbed. Read the quotation by Ruskin (above) a few times and let your mind wander over what this means for you.

- What dreams have other people had for you (if any)?
- What are the dreams and ambitions of people you know well?
- How are your dreams different from those of people around you?

Your 'dream' does not have to be the same as anyone else's, and it does not need to be well defined. It may be something as simple as 'happiness'.

Clarifying the dream

To gain a clearer view of the 'dream', come back to the 'Dream' activity and repeat it from the beginning once you have undertaken the 'Vision' exercise below.

You may find that the more analytical nature of the 'Vision' activity focuses the mind. Let go of particular details when you return to the 'Dream' activity.

Your mind will automatically play with the ideas you had and feed them back, either straight away or at some time in the future. However, as our relaxed brain likes to play with images and metaphors, it may return the ideas to you in a way that is hard to recognise at first.

Whatever images come to mind on this second occasion, however unexpected, hold them in mind for a few days, and see what emerges.

The long-term vision

For the activity on pp 21-2, imagine yourself travelling forward into the future, to a time approximately 10 or 20 years from now. This activity is not about laying down a rigid plan for your future but, rather, is to help you form a general idea of what you would like to experience, as far as you can tell now. The aim is to gain a sense of the type of life you want, so that you can make the right kinds of choices to achieve it.

Activity: The Long-Term Vision

Ten years from now, I see myself . . .

Aspect	Write your own vision of this aspect below	How important is this aspect to me?
Living in which part of the world?		
Living in what kind of place (city, town, village, countryside, by the sea, etc.)?		
Considering the most important things in my life to be . . .		
Solitary? Or surrounded by people?		
Working with colleagues who are . . . artistic? intellectual? practical? caring? down-to-earth? active? thoughtful? kind?		
Working to stress levels which are . . . Pressurised? Reasonable? Very low level?		
Enjoying privacy? Public attention? Celebrity?		
Working 20, 30, 40, 50, 60, 80, 100 hours a week?		
Taking a lead? Being a good second in command? Happy to be part of a team? One of a large crowd?		
Wanting to 'get by' unnoticed? Gaining reasonable recognition for my work? Being top management? World-famous?		

Activity: The Long-Term Vision (continued)

Ten years from now, I see myself . . .

Aspect	Write your own vision of this aspect below	How important is this aspect to me?
Based mostly in an office? On the road? In the field?		
Working for myself? Working for a large company? Working for a small company?		
Doing work which is very varied? Very routine? Predictable?		
Likely to stay in the same job for years? Changing job occasionally?		
Living with a large/small/minimal family. With strong/weak/some family connections?		
Considering my work to be central/ important/not very important in my life?		
My contribution to my community or society will be through . . .		
My time outside work will be spent doing . . .		
My friends will be the kinds of people who . . .		
I will be the kind of person who . . .		
My main achievements in life are likely to be . . .		
Other important aspects of my vision of the future are . . .		
The main influences, inspirations and values on this vision of my future derive from . . .		

Look again at the third column of the activity, *How important is this aspect to me?* (pp. 21–2). Consider what this tells you about the kind of lifestyle and career that you are likely to enjoy?

If you found it difficult to answer many of the questions above, this suggests either that you are very flexible or that you need to spend more time thinking through what sort of things you want from life. This will help you to make certain decisions about programme options, work experience, extracurricular activities and early job applications.

Return now to p. 20 and complete 'The Dream' again.

Using the vision and the dream

- In what ways can you make use of the 'Vision' or 'Dream' that emerged through these activities to motivate you further?
- In what ways do your current study and extracurricular activities help take you forward towards your 'Vision'?

Activity: What do I want to gain from my time at university?

On the table below, indicate with a (✓) if the item is something that you want to gain from your time at university. Put more than one tick if you feel this is very important. (✓✓✓)

Go through the items you ticked and rate them in order of importance (1 for the most important, 2 for the next in importance, and so on).

From my time at university I want to:	Important to me?	Order of importance	From my time at university I want to:	Important to me?	Order of importance
'Get the piece of paper' (the qualification)			Develop technical skills		
Achieve a good classification of degree			Develop a wide range of skills		
Gain a deeper understanding of my specialist subject			Work with a wider range of people		
Enhance my thinking ability			Develop problem-solving skills		
Broaden my mind			Develop people skills		
Stretch myself intellectually			Try out new things		
Know myself better			Develop a broader set of interests		
Learn to believe in my own abilities			Gain work or volunteering experience		
Gain the confidence to speak in public			Make friends		
Experience student life			Make contacts for my career		
Enhance my career opportunities			Take on positions of responsibility		
Be able to get a well-paid job			Other things:		

Goals

The long-term vision gives us a sense of how well we know ourselves and a goal at which we can aim. Some people are very good at 'deferring gratification': that is, at making personal sacrifices in order to achieve a goal many years down the line. They usually have a very clear vision of what they want to achieve.

However, it is not easy to 'defer gratification' unless there are lots of small successes along the route. It is difficult to put effort and energy into study, work, research or exercise if we do not have mini-goals, or milestones towards which we are working. Success at these spurs us on to greater triumphs. If we are not successful, this can also be valuable, providing time to take stock and re-evaluate how important something really is to us.

Smaller goals or targets enable us to experience success along the way and test us in the short term. For example, we can:

● perform in concerts whilst training to become a professional musician;
● put on exhibitions if we wish to be an artist;
● publish material if we want to be a writer;
● make a speech at a wedding if we are likely to work in the public eye;
● take on voluntary work if we are anxious about working after graduation.

Assessed coursework and exams offer the experience of 'being tested' and can develop a range of qualities that go with such 'testing'.

Universities and colleges offer many opportunities for developing a more rounded portfolio of experience and broadening horizons. It is difficult to over-estimate the number of ways that extracurricular activities can be of benefit. The activity on p. 23 encourages you to take stock of the ways that you could make best use of your time as a student, depending on your circumstances and what is important to you.

Motivation

Success is associated with high levels of motivation. For this reason, it is useful to be clear about what is likely to motivate you the most. Each of us is motivated by different things. Below are some techniques people use to keep themselves motivated.

Being realistic

Little is achieved without setbacks, effort and hard work, and even moments when you feel like giving up. Although positive thinking is an asset, unrealistic thinking sets you up for failure as you will be unprepared to meet hurdles that are set in your way. Think through what setbacks you may face and make plans to deal with these. Take them in your stride as part of the natural process, rather than as disasters which mean you will fail.

Setting high expectations

Success is linked to high expectations. These may take the form of very specific things which you wish to achieve, or a more general vision or ambition. If you set low expectations, you will probably achieve very little. Once you set high expectations, you need to plan accordingly, making sure you create the right opportunities for yourself. If your expectations are low, you are likely to be unprepared for opportunities that arise.

Setting realistic milestones

The section above, on goals, refers to the importance of setting milestones so that you can chart your progress. The more challenging the overall goal, or the longer it takes to achieve, the more important it is to set yourself intermediate targets to check you are moving in the right direction.

Rewarding achievement

Promise yourself a reward for reaching your intermediate targets – something you would really appreciate but which is appropriate to the size of the task – and then make sure you really do take that reward when you reach the target. You can set rewards such as a break, a coffee, a special meal, a phone call to a friend, for small targets on a single day.

Ⓔ Activity: Short-term goals

Select the three items to which you gave the highest rating in the previous activity. Consider what short-term goals you can set in order to give yourself an initial taste of success. You may need several short-term goals for each item you select. These goals are 'milestones' along the road to success. Copy this table and keep it where it will remind you to complete the goal. An alternative action plan can be found on p. 119.

Item	Short-term goals	When I will do this	How I will know I have achieved this
1	(a)		
	(b)		
	(c)		
2	(a)		
	(b)		
	(c)		
3	(a)		
	(b)		
	(c)		

Harnessing support

If you feel it will be difficult to keep yourself on track, ask a friend or mentor to check at set, regular intervals that you are keeping to plan. You may work better if you set up a support group to encourage you to keep going. These can work best if you set clear targets and your support team is given a specific date on which to check whether targets have been met.

Recording success

It is easier to monitor and reward your successes if you keep a record. This can be useful for the task in hand and also in retrospect when you reflect back upon what you achieved. A record of past successes can be very motivating for future enterprises.

Hunting out the interest

It is much easier to succeed at a task if we find it engaging. We often react towards things we find

difficult as if they were inherently boring. However, we can make something appear interesting even if, at first, we do not think it is. For example, we can make it a personal challenge to complete the task, or set up challenging time targets for each stage. Perhaps paradoxically, if we find out more than we need to know about something, we are more likely to find it interesting: feeling we have expertise can increase our interest.

The important thing is to know what kinds of motivational spurs work for you.

Personal investment: benefits, costs and commitments

Put your heart, mind, intellect and soul into even your smallest acts. This is the secret of success.
Swami Sivanandi

The person who makes a success of living is the one who sees his goal steadily and aims for it unswervingly. That is dedication.
Cecil B. DeMille

You can be an ordinary athlete by getting away with less than your best. But if you want to be great, you have to give it all you've got, your everything.
Duke P. Kahanamoku

📖 **Reflection**   Commitment

● Do you agree with the comments quoted above?
● What, if anything, are you willing to commit to in such dedicated ways?
● What phrase would you find more motivating than those in the quotations?

For some people, success is measured by the achievement of a goal at any cost. For others, success is measured by overall outcomes. For example, the building of a new dam may be regarded as a successful outcome (it got built). On the other hand, some may view the event as a limited success or even a failure (it was built but at too great a cost financially, or to local inhabitants, or to the environment).

Activity: Sources of motivation

When the going gets tough, I am most likely to be motivated by . . .
(*tick all that apply to you*)

☐ my long-term vision
☐ lots of short-term goals
☐ my values
☐ my belief system
☐ my will to win
☐ my sources of inspiration
☐ people who are close to me
☐ my desire to do good for others
☐ my desire to prove something
☐ achieving lots of small successes along the way
☐ giving myself a reward for completing a stage
☐ enjoyment of the activity
☐ finding something in the activity to interest me
☐ the support of other people
☐ having another person monitor my progress
☐ recording my successes

Identify one personal goal. Using the chart below, consider what a successful outcome would mean to you. What is it really worth to you? Write your responses in the boxes on the right.

Your goal	
Perceived personal benefits of achieving this goal?	
Perceived benefits to other people if the goal is achieved?	
What would you need to invest to achieve this goal (time, money, possible loss of self-confidence, friendship, etc.)?	
What level of such costs would you consider unacceptable?	
What costs would there be to others (time, money, possible loss of trust, etc.)?	
What level of such costs would you consider unacceptable?	
How would other people's opinion of you change if you were successful? Would this differ if the 'costs' were different?	
Would other people's opinion matter to you?	
How would your opinion of yourself change if you succeeded? Would this be different if the 'costs' were different?	
At what point would the benefits outweigh the costs for you? (Or at which point would the costs outweigh the benefits?)	

Success to some people (those who benefit from the dam) may be a loss to others. This is an extreme example, but it illustrates the point that each act is accompanied by benefits and loss. Each of us has to weigh up, for ourselves, what 'costs' we are willing to bear in order to achieve what kind of outcome. Often, we proceed without even considering the full picture – without considering what we already have, really want and value.

In planning for success, it helps to know certain things about yourself, such as:

- What you really want – 'no matter what!'
- Your assets: what you have to bring to the task in hand, that you are willing to 'invest' or risk. This includes such things as time, effort, money and material resources, friends and family, practice, endurance, willingness to wait or to try again.
- Your limits: what sacrifices you are really prepared to make and where your limits lie. In this respect, the cost to others, the opinion of others, your values and your sense of self may all be relevant.

Ingredients of success

Taylor and Humphrey (2002) analysed interviews made with 80 UK and US business leaders, drawn from a wide range of businesses. They identified the skills and attributes which were most common amongst those who had been successful at chief executive level. Although most (91 per cent) had a degree and relevant technical skills, success was not closely linked to a level or type of knowledge: few had business degrees or outstanding technical ability.

Characteristics of successful chief executives

The Chief Executive Officers (CEOs) worked very long hours – but loved their work. They enjoyed leadership and recognition. They were noticeably self-confident, good at communicating with others and putting the interviewers at their ease. Their excellent inter-personal skills included patience and tolerance, often learned through the job itself. They were energetic, but took care to manage

stress levels and stay healthy. Male directors were more sensitive to variations in their emotional lives and needed emotional stability in order to succeed. Most had a wide range of interests and part of what they brought to a company was 'breadth of vision developed from a wide range of experience'. Most of these are self-management and people skills rather than unusual abilities or technical skills.

Attributes associated with success

The surprising outcome of Taylor and Humphrey's survey was that the range of personal skills and qualities associated with success were ones that most people could nurture. The researchers wrote: 'Board directors are not a race apart . . . we found ourselves in the presence of bright, hard-working people, but not creatures from another planet. They had a variety of IQs, expertise, and backgrounds. In other words, directors are just like the rest of us – and their positions are up for grabs.' The skills and attitudes of successful people can be developed by others. The main skills valued by the CEOs included:

- self-knowledge and self-awareness – this was especially noticeable, and the directors were frank about their skills and their shortcomings;
- inter-personal skills, especially the ability to work with, and lead, teams;
- problem-solving ability, using creative approaches and positive attitudes;
- a desire to win, especially on behalf of the company or team;
- a willingness to work very long hours and to 'do what it takes';
- emotional intelligence, especially when relating to others;
- the ability to manage stress and to take care of their health;
- a love of change;
- confidence;
- a broad range of personal interests;
- readiness to seize opportunities rather than making rigid personal plans.

Many of these skills have long been recognised as essential in the caring professions. It may be surprising to find this list associated with business success. However, similar skills are likely to be required across a very wide range of professions. Increasingly, employers expect employees to be able to work in project teams on complex problems. This requires many of the other skills listed: good people skills, emotional intelligence, self-knowledge, a positive attitude, a willingness to put the team's interests first. Negative-thinking, selfish people who lack confidence, who get easily stressed, fear change or who are not aware of how they are coping with their own emotions, are unlikely to be a great asset to a team.

However, the qualities needed for different kinds of success may vary from the above list. Academic success requires a willingness to refine analytical thinking skills. Successful relationships may require a willingness not to work very long hours outside of the home, but are still likely to require a willingness to 'do what it takes' to achieve a successful outcome for the relationship. High levels of success in any field tend to require long hours, hard work, practice, and a willingness to keep going towards achieving the goal even when you do not feel like it, or when you are tired or want to give up. There are few areas of life where an individual is unlikely to benefit from the characteristics associated with chief executives, as listed above.

Activity: Self-evaluation of personal qualities associated with success

	Good	Wish to improve	Not relevant to me	See chapter
Self-knowledge and self-awareness	☐	☐	☐	1 and 2
Problem-solving ability	☐	☐	☐	5 and 7
A creative approach	☐	☐	☐	7
Positive attitude	☐	☐	☐	4
People skills	☐	☐	☐	6
Team-working	☐	☐	☐	6
Leadership	☐	☐	☐	6
Negotiating skills	☐	☐	☐	6
A desire to succeed	☐	☐	☐	1
A willingness to 'do what it takes'	☐	☐	☐	4 and 5
Emotional intelligence	☐	☐	☐	4 and 6
The ability to manage personal stress	☐	☐	☐	4
The ability to cope with and/or promote change	☐	☐	☐	4
Self-confidence	☐	☐	☐	4 and 6
A broad range of personal interests	☐	☐	☐	1
Self-knowledge (reflection, self-analysis)	☐	☐	☐	1, 2 and 3
Risk management	☐	☐	☐	5
Ability to cope with uncertainty	☐	☐	☐	4

Activity: Attributes needed to achieve a particular goal

The goal or ambition analysed here is:

To achieve this goal or ambition, the following attributes will probably be needed:

Attribute	Highly relevant	May be relevant	Not relevant	Don't know
Self-knowledge and self-awareness	☐	☐	☐	☐
Problem-solving ability	☐	☐	☐	☐
A creative approach	☐	☐	☐	☐
Positive attitude	☐	☐	☐	☐
People skills	☐	☐	☐	☐
Team-working	☐	☐	☐	☐
Leadership	☐	☐	☐	☐
Negotiating skills	☐	☐	☐	☐
A desire to succeed	☐	☐	☐	☐
A willingness to 'do what it takes'	☐	☐	☐	☐
Emotional intelligence	☐	☐	☐	☐
The ability to manage personal stress	☐	☐	☐	☐
The ability to cope with and/or promote change	☐	☐	☐	☐
Self-confidence	☐	☐	☐	☐
A broad range of personal interests	☐	☐	☐	☐
Good health	☐	☐	☐	☐
Self-knowledge (reflection, self-analysis)	☐	☐	☐	☐
Risk management	☐	☐	☐	☐
Ability to cope with uncertainty	☐	☐	☐	☐

Other skills needed to achieve this goal or ambition:
1.

2.

3.

Personal qualities needed to achieve this goal or ambition:
1.

2.

3.

Any other attributes needed to achieve this goal or ambition:
1.

2.

3.

Where are you now? Self-evaluation of personal qualities associated with success

On the chart above (p. 29), identify whether each of the personal qualities associated with success are ones that you already possess, or wish to develop or are not relevant. The final column of the activity indicates where in the book you can find out more about this skill or aspect.

Skills and qualities needed to achieve your goals

It is worth comparing the list of the attributes associated with successful outcomes at chief executive level with the attributes you regard as necessary to achieving your goals and ambitions. You may find that your personal goals call for a very particular set of skills and qualities. However, it is important to think through all the kinds of situations and problems that you may have to address in order to achieve your goals. What qualities would help you in those circumstances?

Is there a good skills 'match'?

At this point, it is useful to compare the attributes that you identified as necessary for achieving a successful outcome of your goal (p. 30) with the attributes you ascribed yourself in the activity on p. 29. Is there a good match? If not, which skills and qualities will require further development? What will you do to develop these?

If you added further skills, goals and attributes to your list, which of these would benefit from being further developed whilst at university? What will you do to develop these?

Breadth of vision and experience

In the section on successful CEOs above, Taylor and Humphrey (2002) identified 'breadth of vision developed from a wide range of experience' as an important characteristic of successful people. It is easy to see why this would be the case. Experience gained from many different settings brings you into contact with a more diverse range of people. This provides opportunities for learning about people, developing inter-personal skills and net-

working. Each context provides knowledge, skills, opportunities to develop personal qualities, as well as new perspectives and information.

> **📖 Reflection**   Extending experience
>
> In your reflective journal, jot some thoughts on the following questions.
>
> - In what ways do you already have a breadth of experience drawn from different contexts?
> - In relation to your current goals and career aspirations, what opportunities are open to you for extending your breadth of experience? Consider, for example, your job, work experience, travel, taking on a position of responsibility, joining a student society, community or voluntary work, sporting activity, mentoring schemes, etc.
> - What opportunities are offered through the curriculum for designing a personal programme that extends your range of skills and experience?

Congruence

'Congruence' refers to consistency in our thoughts, actions, behaviours and beliefs. It is about all our energies flowing in the same direction. It takes less effort to achieve goals if there is a high level of congruence between the different factors that influence, inspire and support those goals. If you are struggling to see the way towards success, it is worth checking whether there is a high level of congruence (or a 'good fit') amongst the following:

- your vision;
- your motivation;
- the 'influences' you value;
- your sources of inspiration;
- your short-term goals, targets or milestones;
- your values and beliefs;
- the attitudes of the people around you;
- your means and resources;
- your current situation.

In particular, it is worth checking that your 'vision' is still relevant to you. New experiences can change your vision, either reinforcing it, modifying it, or making it irrelevant.

Are your vision, ambitions, values and inspiration in alignment? Where might there be sources of internal conflict that could be undermining your efforts? On the chart below, jot down a response to the questions, using the space boxes.

Goal (e.g. what I want to achieve from my time at university)?

What is my vision of success in relation to this goal? What would success look like?	
How does this goal fit into a bigger 'vision' for my life and my longer-term ambitions?	
What motivates me to pursue this goal – what do I want to gain from achieving this goal?	
What has influenced me, perhaps over many years, in forming this goal?	
What inspiration can I call upon to help me achieve this goal?	
What are my short-term goals? How do these support my main goal?	
How does this goal fit with my beliefs and values?	
How do the attitudes of people around me support me in working towards my current goal?	
What resources do I have, to support me towards my current goal?	
What else in my current situation supports or undermines me in working towards my goals?	
Conclusions	

'Goal inertia'

If you have 'vision inertia' or 'goal inertia', you continue to work towards a vision that may seem appealing but, in reality, no longer inspires or motivates you – there is no longer congruence between what you are doing and what you really want to do. This is especially true if your values change in the light of your experience. If this happens, tasks can seem to be more difficult or tiring. You may feel it more of a struggle to complete tasks, that you are looking for excuses to put tasks off, or even that you don't want to do anything at all. If you experience goal inertia it is time to recoup, to reconnect with your initial ambitions in at least some way, or else to change direction.

The preceding activity, 'Does it all add up?' can help identify the congruence of your own position.

Opportunities

Forks in the road

If you know what you want, either generally or in fine detail, are you taking and making opportunities that advance your aims? Are you somebody who looks for the opportunities in whatever comes your way or are you more likely to wait, hoping for the perfect moment to arrive? In every moment of the day, we make decisions that create a 'fork' in the path of our life. By acting one way or another, or by not acting at all, we make a choice to move in one direction and not another.

In the example shown on the flowchart below, at 15, Paulette decided to leave her part-time job at a local shop and work part-time in an electronics company. At the time, she just wanted a 'change of scene' that allowed her more flexible hours. From that decision, she met new people, overcame a fear of 'technical things', and travelled to China. These changes affected her choice of subject and friends at university.

What if I . . . ?

What ideas emerge if you keep asking yourself the same question and have to give a different answer each time? The obvious answers tend to get used up after a while so that you draw more on your imagination to find new responses. Some of your responses may become rather far-fetched. However, sometimes, unexpected and useful responses can emerge. For the 'What if I . . . ?' activity on p. 34, let your mind range broadly. Avoid censoring your thoughts, even if an idea seems unlikely. Be imaginative. See what emerges.

Example   Paulette's decision

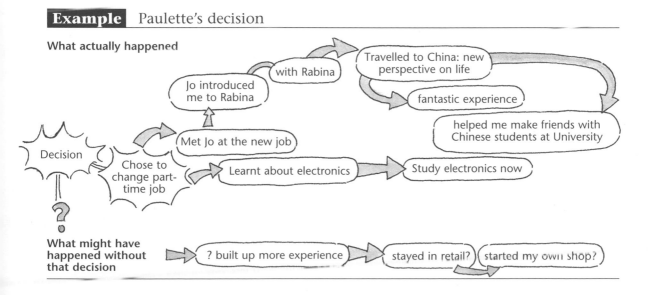

Activity: The road walked

Take approximately three minutes to jot down choices you have made that you look back on and feel good about. This may include significant friendships, work, how you dealt with difficult situations, saying or doing the right thing, presents given, offers that you accepted or turned down, your dedication to your learning or to resolving a problem, the benefits from learning a new skill, acts of kindness, and good decisions you made. Focus on your role – what you did or did not do – rather than on what others did to you.

Read through your list and select your best use of an opportunity. It may appear small, such as giving somebody a card and seeing their face light up, or it may have been a major event such as saving a life.

Take a piece of paper and write the example at the top of the paper, as in the example above under 'Paulette's decision'. Spend a few minutes jotting down the various impacts of that one occasion on other aspects of your life. What opportunities, large or small, arose for you from seizing that first opportunity?

Activity: The road unwalked

Now take approximately five minutes to brainstorm all the decisions you look back on and feel less good about. This may include opportunities that were present that you did not recognise at the time. For example, as well as the items on the above list, you may consider the things you did not do, say or learn. Focus on your role – what you did or did not do – rather than on what others did to you.

Read through your list and select the one opportunity that you feel you missed that has had the greatest impact upon your life.

Take a piece of paper and write down this decision as in the example above under 'Paulette's decision' (see p. 33). Spend a few minutes brainstorming all the ways that that one occasion has had an impact upon your life since. What other choices could you have made then? What might have been the consequences of making each of those other choices?

Activity: What if I . . . ? *(from p. 33)*

In your reflective journal, jot down at least thirty times:

📖 'What if I . . . ?'
'What if I . . . ?'
'What if I . . . ?'
etc.

Take about five minutes to write responses to the whole set of 'What if I . . . ?' statements. For example:

> 'What if I . . . spoke Japanese?' (I'd apply for a job in Japan)
> 'What if I invented a toy?' (I could set up a business)
> 'What if I rode a pogo stick?' (I would be fitter)

Make rapid replies so that you do not have time to check how sensible your responses are.

Look through your responses.

- Which ones surprise you?
- Which ones provide useful information?
- Which one would be the most interesting to put into action?
- Consider what the answer to some of these questions might be? Where does that line of thinking take you?

Closing comments

When engaged upon a long-term project such as gaining a degree or developing a career path, it is important to stay focused on what you want to achieve. This may be very different for each person. It is for you to decide what 'success' means for you, what you would consider to be an 'achievement', and what you want to gain from the experience. For some, the 'travelling' is as important as arriving: the journey may be the goal.

This chapter has encouraged you to think deeply about the future and the things that influence, motivate, inspire and guide you. Long-term goals such as gaining a degree and working towards a career require commitment. Though it would be lovely if everything ran smoothly, this is unlikely always to be the case over a period of several years. When things feel difficult, it is quite common to feel like giving up. It is then important to find ways to keep going until the path gets easier and to keep yourself motivated. Motivation is the key to success. It provides the energy and the drive. That is why the goal or 'vision' must contain something within it that really motivates you.

It is also important that you are true to what you really believe. The obvious reasons for personal goals are not always those that motivate us the most. This chapter has encouraged you to look more deeply below the surface and examine what is really important to you. You should now have a much clearer idea of your visions for your life, your goals, your targets, values, motivation and skills.

In the next chapter, you will have a chance to look more closely at further aspects of what makes you unique. Chapter 2 provides an opportunity to look back over your life journey and the events that have most significance for who you are now and how you make decisions. It will also enable you to consider how you construct your personal narrative and perception of yourself, and the impact this may have on the choices you make. By identifying expertise you may have hidden in your repertoire, you can consider how you do things now – and how you might do things differently in the future.

Further reading

Cottrell, S. M. (2007) *The Exam Skills Handbook: Achieving Peak Performance* (Basingstoke: Palgrave Macmillan).

Covey, S. R. (2004) *The Seven Habits of Highly Effective People: Powerful Lessons in Personal Change*, 15th Anniversary edn (London: Free Press).

Taylor, R. and Humphrey, J. (2002) *Fast Track to the Top: Skills for Career Success* (London: Kogan Page).

Chapter 2

Start with yourself

Self-knowledge is the beginning of self-improvement.

Spanish proverb

Learning outcomes

This chapter gives you the opportunity to:

consider the impact of your own life story upon your current life and performance

analyse how you construct your personal narrative and perceptions of yourself

analyse your learning journey and the impact of this upon your current approaches to study

identify areas of personal expertise that can be applied to new tasks and areas of learning

make use of your experience.

Introduction

This chapter focuses on how your life story so far, and the narratives that you construct to make sense of your experience, contribute to your uniqueness. It encourages you to investigate how your personal history, attitudes and beliefs about your ability might be influencing the way you do things now and your currrent achievement.

If you undertake the activities in this chapter with different goals in mind, you are likely to gain different sets of responses. If you find that a particular type of task is proving especially difficult for you, go through some of these activities again but with only that task in mind. You may uncover unexpected hindrances that you can then address.

Your life narrative

Personal narrative is used more and more in professional fields as a way of helping practitioners to understand the way they operate in the workplace. It is one of a number of tools that help individuals, by gaining a deeper understanding of themselves, to:

- make sense of their current reactions and responses in specific contexts;
- understand why their responses might be different from those of colleagues;
- reconnect with the feelings of significant events, so as to enable greater empathy with others;
- value their own experiences and those of others;
- identify where issues from the past might be having a negative effect now, so that these can be addressed.

It does take time to work on personal narratives, but the experience can be rewarding.

The 'true story'?

Each time you review your life story, it changes. The events may be the same, but different aspects become significant. If you write out your story every few years and look back at past versions, you may be surprised at how much your attitudes, responses and the themes of your story change over time.

In this chapter, you can consider your life story from different angles so as to gain different perspectives on yourself – rather than assuming there is one fixed version or interpretation.

The life metaphor

Before you launch into your story, it is helpful to stand back from it and take a snapshot of how you view it overall. One way of doing this is to consider the metaphors that you use – that is, the ways you describe your life, or events within it, in relation to other things. Some people regard life as a journey, or as a mission or a battle. Others think of it as a burden, a gift, an adventure, a lesson to be learnt, a trial, a treasure trove, a bottomless pit, a walk in the dark. These are their personal metaphors for their own lives.

Maybe you catch yourself using expressions such as: 'My life is a disaster waiting to happen . . .' or

'it's all part of life's rich tapestry . . .'. If so, these may indicate your metaphor for your life. By identifying and analysing the metaphors you use currently, you can gain insights that you might not have noticed before about how you view life – and how this might come across to other people.

Significant components in the plot

To produce the narrative for your life story, the first step is to work out key components of the plot.

Activity: Life metaphor

- What is your personal metaphor for your life? You may need to give some thought to this. If you do not think there is *one* metaphor, just select one for this exercise.
- What words do you use, if any, to express that metaphor in daily life?
- How does it help you to make sense of your life?
- In what ways, if any, does this metaphor offer a constructive way of approaching your life?

Activity: A new life metaphor

After the previous activity, you may feel that you would like to create a new metaphor for your life, to inspire you for the future. If so:

- Choose an item that inspires a postive reaction in you.
- Jot down the words: *My life is a ...* (or *My life is like a ...*).
- List as many points of comparison as you can between the item and your life.
- Continue with different items until you find one that is satisfying. Pin this up for a while as a reminder.

Activity: Components in the plot

Take five minutes to make a list of the people and events that you regard as most significant in your life. For example:

The most signficant events
- 'first times' you did something;
- successes;
- crises;
- challenges;
- opportunities that arose;
- important events in the family that were significant in their impact upon you;
- happy memories;
- school memories;
- holidays that were important in some way;
- friendships and relationships;
- work experience;
- other things (*state which*).

People who had the most influence or impact
- parents, carers, guardians, relatives;
- siblings and cousins;
- teachers, school staff, pupils, students;
- friends;
- romances;
- people you met on holiday, at social events, etc.;
- professionals such as nurses, doctors and dentists;
- neighbours; people who lived locally;
- employers or work colleagues;
- people who acted kindly or unkindly;
- chance encounters who made a difference;
- someone you didn't know well but who said, did or experienced something that affected you.

Your lists will be used for further activities in this chapter.

Life Chart: Plotting the journey

Now that you have identified the main components of your story, the next stage is to lay these out in such a way that you can work with them, plot out your life journey and draw connections between events. The visual and motor/kinaesthetic aspects of this task are important.

Activity: Life Chart: Plotting the journey

Using the items on your lists for 'Components in the plot' (p. 37):

- Use a large sheet of paper or card.
- Separate out each event and person on your list (such as by cutting up the list).
- Organise these into the order in which they occurred.

Arrange these so that you can 'see' the events in the order they occurred, leaving space to write and draw around them. Alternatively, work directly onto the card.

- Fix these lightly so you can change them round later or add new material if you choose.
- Add in the people where they played most significant roles.
- Build the visual aspect, using drawings, photographs or symbols to represent an occasion (such as a symbol of an ice-cream for a holiday, a dark cloud for a significant argument, etc.).

Activity: Find the links

On the chart you made for 'Life Chart: Plotting the journey':

- Give the date of each event (an approximate date will suffice).
- Using different colours, indicate whether each event or person was, overall, positive, negative or neutral for you.
- Write a brief commentary next to each item: a few details of each event and person, what you felt about them then, and what you feel now.
- Use arrows or other signs to draw connections between the events, and between people and events. Who or what influenced later stages in your journey?
- Circle just a few people and events that have the most significant impact on your life and performance now.

Create the narrative

You have gathered and ordered the raw material of your story. Now all you have to do is to write it out – or tell your story aloud and record it. It is tempting to cut out this step – but it is important to let the narrative develop. This will not only draw together your thinking, it will develop it.

Find the links

Once you have plotted out the key events and players in your story, the next stage is to draw out the connections between these. You may already have had to do this at a superficial level in order to work out the sequence in the plot.

Now, consider more deeply, if someone was significant in your life, what was their influence? How did that influence affect particular events? This may generate new material to add to your chart. Which events involved you meeting or losing someone who was significant in your life? In effect, you are looking for broad areas of 'cause and effect'.

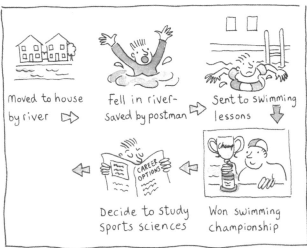

Moved to house by river ➡️

Fell in river – saved by postman ➡️

Sent to swimming lessons ⬇️

Decide to study sports sciences ⬅️

Career options ⬅️

Won swimming championship

Activity: Create the narrative

Write out your story. Make sure you include how you feel about your experiences. Be honest. This copy is just for you – so you don't need to worry about writing a good introduction or about your writing style. Just tell it.

Once you have completed your story, leave it for a few days and then go on to the next activity.

Themes in the tale

We noted above that each telling of a story, and especially our personal narrative, is likely to be different in some respects. There may be differences in terms of detail, the links made between events, interpretations, emphasis, and so forth. To this extent, our story is always a construction. By analysing what we choose to include and exclude, what we emphasise or brush over, the themes that run through our story of events, and changes in our interpretations from one telling to another, we can gain clues about ourselves that we might otherwise miss.

Reflection   Themes in the tale

Read through your 'narrative' or 'story' considering the following points:

- Have you included more positive or more negative experiences and events for your story? Could you have included more positive items? Are you avoiding negative or difficult issues that throw light on your experiences?
- What themes or patterns emerge from the story? For example, is the story full of adventures? Disasters? Effort and reward? Disappointment? Seizing and creating opportunities? Meeting and losing people? Solitary achievement or collaboration with others?
- What is the general tone of your story? Is it a sad or a happy story? Does it contain either much praise or much blame?
- What do the themes in your narrative tell you about the way you view your life? Is this the most helpful view you can take? Does this view further the 'vision' you identified in Chapter 1?

Activity: The Hero

Consider the roles you have given yourself in your narrative: what part do you play in the plot? Are you active, taking the lead, and making things happen? Do you sit back and wait for things to happen? Are you the passive recipient of other people's actions? Maybe you sound like you are forever in battle, holding your ground? Overall, have you written the narrative so that you sound mainly like:

- the Warrior stepping into battle and fighting your own or others' wars;
- the Saint who is always doing good and in the right;
- the Martyr who has to suffer so others can benefit;
- the Adventurer, looking for new experiences;
- the Scapegoat, carrying the blame for others;
- the Ruler, commanding the troops or the people;
- the Sportsperson, playing a good game;
- the Villain, who has been lucky or clever enough not to be caught;
- the Wounded Soldier, who needs time to heal;
- the Conjuror, pulling unexpected rabbits out of hats;
- the Dragon, the Knight, or the Maiden awaiting rescue;
- a different kind of hero? (*Identify what type*)

Yourself as Hero

You are the key player in your story, its 'hero'. One way to make sense of your life is to analyse the role you give yourself within your life story. This can give you insights not only into your character, but also into how other people may perceive you. For this to be helpful, you need to be honest with yourself and about what kind of character comes across.

> 📖 **Reflection**   You as 'hero'
>
> - Do you feel comfortable about the kind of hero that comes across in your story?
> - How far does the hero you have chosen represent the way you really think, feel and act?
> - What does this choice tell you about the way you view your life or yourself as an active agent in your own story?
> - Do you play very different roles depending on who you are with, where you are or what you are doing?

Caricature

Self-recognition is notoriously difficult to achieve. However, one way of gaining perspective on the self is through use of a 'caricature' technique.

A good caricaturist helps us to recognise a character by exaggerating particular features. These are often the characteristics that make the person more individual and distinctive. By exaggerating our own personality traits, behaviours, speech patterns, or events that seem to recur in our lives, we can stand back and take a look at these with a fresh eye. This may bring home certain aspects of ourselves more clearly. We gain a great deal from such insights – although self-recognition can involve a certain degree of embarrassment or discomfort.

The activity below allows you to stand back for a moment from your main narrative and work with some emerging themes. This is intended as a light-hearted activity that can, nonetheless, enable useful personal insights to emerge.

Activity: Create a personal caricature

If you feel you are up to the task, jot down your narrative again – or selected sections from it. This time, deviate from your memory of actual events in order to exaggerate certain key themes. Select personal traits, mannerisms, behaviours, speech, and/or themes in your life that you think are typical of you. If you are not sure about what these might be, ask a friend. For example:

- If the first draft of your story (or your life in general) contains many examples of 'beginning' and 'starting' activities, exaggerate this theme, adding in many more things that you 'started' (real or imaginary).
- If it contains many examples of meeting people, then flood your next draft with meetings, inventing meetings that never happened.
- If there are a number of accidents or disasters in your story, invent a whole lot more.
- If you think a particular comment is very typical of you, write it out seven times each time you introduce it:

> I was just about to do that.
> I was just about to do that.
> I was just about to do that.
> I was just about to do that.
> I was just about to do that.
> I was just about to do that.
> I was just about to do that.

Next:

- Read through your story, aloud. What does it tell you about yourself?
- Are you comfortable with your personal caricature – or do you want to change it?
- Were you able to laugh at your caricature?
- What do you think is the value of using this 'caricature' or 'exaggeration' technique for personal development?

Choices

Sometimes, it can feel that other people, events, history or 'destiny' rule the plot of our lives. Whilst it is true that we are all only part of a much bigger story, and that there are many influences on our lives over which we do not exercise control, it is also the case that we are agents in our own tale. There are choices that we make every day, some of which turn out to be more significant than others.

Activity: The choices made

Look again at your life chart and mark in all the occasions when you made a choice that had an impact upon your life. You may need to add new material to your chart as as result. Then consider,

- What kinds of choices have you faced?
- What opportunities have you taken or not taken?
- What were the effects of the choices you made on later events?

Visualise at least two different scenarios of how your life might be different now if you had made different choices. If possible, select one choice that you consider to have been a bad choice, and one that is a good choice.

📖 Reflection   Re-evaluating choices

- In retrospect, were all the outcomes of the 'choice' good ones you would still welcome?
- In what ways did the 'bad choice' provide different opportunities for you that, in retrospect, could be regarded as positive in some way? The examples on p. 34 ('The road unwalked') may serve as a useful prompt.
- What do you think characterises a 'good choice'?

Evaluating the opportunities

All experiences offer opportunities to learn and to develop strengths – no matter how wonderful or awful they may have been. Your story will contain examples of where there were experiences, welcome or not, that have given you opportunities to develop as a person. The way in which you responded to these may have had a significant impact on your personality and the way you view the world now. This may be apparent from your personal narrative.

Activity: Evaluating opportunities

Look again at your story.

- What things happened to you that would not be typical of everyone's experience? Identify at least one way that these provided some advantage (such as the people you can communicate with easily as a result, the realism they bring to your life, the different range of skills they developed, etc.).
- What were the most difficult things you had to face? What lessons did you learn from those events that can be of advantage to you either in completing your current programme or in achieving the 'vision' you identified in Chapter 1?
- How easy or difficult do you find it to regard experiences and challenges as 'opportunities'?

The 'next chapter'

Having written the narrative of your story to date and analysed it from various perspectives, it is time now to think about what the next chapter in your story might be.

💻 Activity: The 'next chapter'

Consider now:

- How do you want the plot of your life to unravel over the next 10–20 years? What kind of story do you want to be telling in 20 years' time?
- What kind of role do you wish to play in this next chapter of your life?
- What would need to change in your life now in order for you to play that role successfully?

Your top forty

Look again at your life story. Count how many examples of personal success you included. Was there at least one for every year of your life? If not, consider writing in some more.

Our personal success is rather like breathing: we rarely notice it on an everyday basis. However, it is hard to ignore 'hiccups' – the things that go wrong. Beaver (1998) argues that we do not spend enough time thinking of all the things we *can* do and spend too long focusing on what we cannot do. She encourages us to draw up very long lists of what we can do – and much shorter ones of things we cannot!

🖳 *Activity: Top forty strong points*

Make a list of your strong points, successes, qualities, attitudes and attributes. List at least forty things. If that sounds like too many, you are underestimating yourself. Draw stars by the ten that are your greatest assets. Draw circles around the seven of which you are most proud.

1.	21.
2.	22.
3.	23.
4.	24.
5.	25.
6.	26.
7.	27.
8.	28.
9.	29.
10.	30.
11.	31.
12.	32.
13.	33.
14.	34.
15.	35.
16.	36.
17.	37.
18.	38.
19.	39.
20.	40.

In your reflective journal, jot down your thoughts on the following questions.

- What is the ONE thing that you do best?
- What is it like to recognise so many strong points in yourself now? How often do you stop to value them?
- Are these strengths appreciated by the people around you? If not, how do you account for this? Is it, for example, because you are embarrassed about showing your strengths?
- Do you surround yourself with people who do not appreciate you? If you want to gain realistic recognition for your attributes, it is up to you to make that happen. What could you do to change the situation?

💻 *Activity: Seven areas for improvement*

List a maximum of seven areas for improvement in your life.

1.

2.

3.

4.

5.

6.

7.

- What is it like to recognise these weaker areas?
- What do you do to cope with them or to work around them on a day-to-day basis? Do you hide them, develop strategies, blame other people or find help and support?
- Who or what can help you to manage better in these areas?

Your learning history

In writing out your life story, you may already have included some events that had an impact upon the way you approach learning. Our early learning experiences are amongst the most profound influences upon our attainment and current levels of performance. They shape our approaches to learning itself, shaping our belief in ourselves and our ability to see opportunities for improving our performance.

This aspect of our story is a particularly important one, and this section provides a focus for considering its impact on you.

Activity: Learning history

- List the incidents that have had the most significant **positive** impact on the way you now approach study and learn new things. This may be anything from times you were happy at school, unexpected success in a subject, support provided over a long period of time, or even just a few words that appeared insignificant at the time but left a lasting impression on you.
- List the incidents that have had a significant **negative** impact on the way you now approach study and learn new things. In what ways do these affect you now? Now you have identified these, what could you do to reduce their effect on you?

Activity: Positive learning experiences

Think back to your time at school. Call to mind occasions when your learning seemed to flow, when it was fun, when you enjoyed learning and felt a sense of accomplishment. Make a list, now, before reading on, of all the conditions that gave rise to such positive learning experiences for you. If you find this hard, keep returning to the sentences:

'My best learning experiences were when . . .'

or

'I got most out of learning when . . .'

Common responses

Below is a list of common responses to the activity above. The list is typical of responses drawn from diverse groups of people within educational contexts. Check your list against it. You can add items to your own list if you think they are true of your experience.

My best learning experiences were when . . . (✔)

Nature of the task

- [ ] I felt the task set was interesting, worthwhile or of value to myself or others
- [ ] the learning was relevant to the real world or had practical uses
- [ ] the work was going to be seen and appreciated by somebody other than a teacher
- [ ] it was clear what was expected from me
- [ ] I could move around or there was movement built into the activities
- [ ] there was a creative aspect to the task
- [ ] there was personal choice in some aspects of the task
- [ ] there was a 'teaser', mystery or puzzle to be solved

Feelings and emotions

- [ ] there was praise and appreciation which came across as genuine
- [ ] I was treated like I mattered or my opinions and ideas counted

With whom

- [ ] I could work with my friends
- [ ] we did small group work or worked in pairs
- [ ] we taught each other

The teacher

- [ ] the teacher was fair
- [ ] the teacher thought of interesting ways of introducing new material
- [ ] the teacher worked beside us and inspired rather than preached at us

Timing

- [ ] I had time to finish what I was doing without rushing
- [ ] I had time to take it in
- [ ] there were lots of breaks so I didn't feel overloaded

Mastery

- [ ] I felt I understood one thing before moving onto another
- [ ] the tasks set were manageable but challenging so that there was a sense of both competence and achievement

Assessment

- [ ] I felt the way it was marked was fair
- [ ] I felt I had a fair chance of handing in what was expected
- [ ] my hard work was recognised
- [ ] I knew I couldn't get away with not doing my best

Special features

- [ ] we went on field trips or visits
- [ ] we had guest speakers or celebrity visits
- [ ] we showed our work to parents or visitors

📖 *Reflection*   How typical are your experiences

In your reflective journal, jot down responses to the following questions.

- Is the list you completed about positive learning experiences, on p. 43, similar to or very different from the general trend outlined on this page? If your list is considerably different from that given here, what reasons might there be for that?
- At school, you may have been dependent upon other people to create the right conditions for your learning. Which of the items on this list could you put in place for yourself now, to enhance your current learning experience as far as possible?

The impact of educational experience upon performance

> 📖 **Reflection**   The impact of your educational experiences

In your reflective journal, jot down responses to the following questions.

- In what ways do you consider your educational experiences have had an impact upon your performance generally?
- What positive things did the educational experience give you that you carry through life (this may not be classroom learning)?
- Look again at the items you identified as beneficial to your learning in the activity 'Positive learning experiences' (p. 43). Which of these could you bring into other situations, such as work or personal life, in order to enhance your performance, enjoyment or sense of satisfaction there?

Responding to setbacks

In your narrative (page 39) and in your consideration of your learning journey, you may have identified certain setbacks on your path. Setbacks can produce feelings of disappointment, discouragement or even 'denial' – a pretence that nothing went wrong. Whilst we would all rather that everything flowed well and without problems, when that doesn't happen, there are still benefits to be gained even from disastrous experiences – though such benefits may require some rooting out or take time to become apparent.

Setbacks and difficulties contain the seeds of our future success. As they hold the secret to 'what went wrong', they also contain valuable information about what could be done differently. Indeed, successful people often claim that they learnt more from their failures than from their successes, or that they are 'better people' because of them.

Apparent failure often brings us face to face with realities that we otherwise try to avoid. Setbacks can make us stop and take stock, follow new paths, meet new people, learn new skills, try things out

that we wouldn't have done. In particular, they tend to build personal qualities such as resilience, coping skills and empathy.

Turn it to advantage

Many people ascribe their success, relative or actual, to the way they responded to bad news or to adversity. We can make the decision to use our experience:

- as an excuse for not doing something;
- to 'prove' something;
- to keep going as before;
- to learn and move forward.

It is noticeable that the stories of many successful people include a critical experience when they were dismissed, belittled, ignored, suffered discrimination, or suffered a serious setback. Paradoxically, dealing with such events, whether at the time or later in life, can become the driving force that leads to unexpected successes.

This is very noticeable amongst students who face the most extreme difficulties or complex circumstances. Students with serious disabilities or mature students with multiple responsibilities find ways of completing their degrees and developing careers when those with fewer difficulties turned

> 📖 **Reflection**   The 'best failure'

In your reflective journal, jot down responses to at least five of the following questions:

- What, on the surface of it, was the best 'mistake' of your life?
- What happened? What was your role in the event?
- What characterised this event as a failure?
- What bad choices did you make?
- When did you first realise you had made a mistake? How did you find out?
- What lessons did you learn?
- What benefits resulted from learning those lessons?
- What opportunities arose out of this event?
- How did the event spur you to action that you might not otherwise have taken?
- What does this event tell you about the nature of success and failure?

back at lesser hurdles. Typically, they learn to use the apparent disadvantage as an advantage – developing skills in managing time, applying technologies, negotiating, multi-tasking or prioritising. Anybody can make use of difficulty in order to emerge stronger – but not everybody does.

> ### 📖 *Reflection* Make setbacks work for your goals
>
> In your reflective journal, consider:
>
> - What are the potential setbacks that you are likely to face in achieving your current goals?
> - What things might make it difficult for you to achieve these goals?
> - What kinds of things might be preventing you from achieving the 'vision' you identified in Chapter 1?
>
> - Consider how you can turn these setbacks 'on their heads', so that they become sources of strength, inventiveness, motivation or contact with others.
>
> Copy this and attach it where you are likely to see it on a regular basis.

Expertise metaphor

When confronted with new tasks, people often say things such as:

- *I don't know where to start.*
- *I can't cope with this.*
- *I am no good at things like this.*
- *I am not good enough.*

Sometimes, the gap between previous experience and the current task can make the task difficult to achieve. Sufficient time and support may make it more achievable.

However, we can take on challenges more easily if we can recognise, value and draw upon an area of personal expertise. This can happen even if the area of expertise seems to bear little relation to the task in hand, as the examples below illustrate. Conversely, failing to recognise the similarity between problems with which we are faced and those that we can solve already, is a key obstacle to performance.

Read through the examples below, looking at the ways that each of these three students made effective use of their current expertise in addressing apparently very different problems they had had with their studies. As you read, consider how you might draw on their general approach in order to make use of your own expertise.

Examples of expertise transfer

Victor and car maintenance

Victor's challenge was in producing academic writing. He had little writing experience because he entered university from a foundation programme that did not use formal written assignments. He was very reluctant to write and was convinced that he lacked the logical, sequential skills needed for continuous prose. On the other hand, Victor identified a strong interest and practical experience in car engines – which he used as his 'expertise metaphor'.

Victor listed all the processes and skills he used when working with car engines, and those he used to write an essay. He then looked for significant points of comparison between the two sets of lists. He analysed the ways car mechanics use skills in:

- finding out information (about the engine)
- sequencing the order of tasks
- planning time to meet deadlines
- weighing up options
- forming a theory about what is wrong
- testing out ideas (about how to fix it)
- selecting between options using the appropriate methods for the job
- prioritising tasks
- testing out results
- re-evaluating the work done
- reflecting on performance.

Victor found that the most helpful approach for him was to compare the factors that make an engine run with those needed for writing an essay. He wrote these out as a list of key points which he could look at whenever he found academic writing difficult. His list is reproduced below.

This may not be how other people view an essay: the important point is that the metaphor worked for Victor. It released his potential, not simply to write essays, but to write *good* essays. This was

Victor – My Engine

When I first started university, I had not worked at the academic level required by university before. When I visited the learning development unit . . . [it was] suggested that I treat an essay like a car engine. When I broke the metaphor (analogy) down, this is what I came up with:

1. Fuel – this supplies the necessary stored kinetic energy to power the engine – research at the library, lectures, seminars.
2. Battery – this stores the electrical energy – research notes, essay outline.
3. Oil – this lets the engine run smoothly – spelling and grammar.
4. The alternator – supplies electrical energy necessary for the engine to run – the essay question, unit guide, using aims etc.
5. Engine ignition system – supplies the spark to ignite the fuel, and the sequence in which the cylinders fire. Paragraphs.
6. Introduction – where this essay is going.
7. Main body – critical discussion of main points.
8. Conclusion – insights gained and mileage from essay, i.e.: 'What I have learned'.
9. Tool box – this is where the necessary tools are bought, borrowed or acquired, and stored – dyslexia workshops, English workshops, Accelerated Learning seminars, etc.

This can be broken down even more . . . When all the elements of the essay are integrated successfully then it should flow like a smoothly running engine.

Victor B.

---

because the process of writing now made sense in terms of things he really knew about.

Roger and aircraft assembly

Roger consistently failed to produce written work. He wrote well but was too much of a perfectionist. He evolved his ideas well during the process of writing and this also meant that, in practice, he would need to produce more than one draft. However, he always approached each draft as if it were the last, starting the whole of his work 'in neat' and editing beautifully as if this were the draft he would hand in. This meant he never reached the end; for all his hard work, he never had anything to hand in. In effect he was fine-tuning his work too early in the process.

Roger's area of expertise was assembling light aircraft that arrived from overseas as 'flatpacks'. He analysed the process of assembling a plane and how this might be similar to or different from assembling an essay. At this point, he recognised that if he tried to build a plane as he did an essay, it would also be impossible. If he tightened all the nuts and bolts, sanded it down, painted it and so forth on one part of the plane before going on to the next part, it would be impossible to manoeuvre the pieces into place. Nuts and bolts should be tightened, and the final touches added, only when the whole plane is in place. Roger could easily see the comparison with fine tuning an essay too early.

Once he had drawn the initial parallel, Roger saw many comparisons between aircraft assembly and academic problems. He used his previous expertise to address these. When introduced to new information, for example, he felt he should play around with it, like pieces of the flat pack, observing roughly how to structure these: '*As you bring them closer together, you are working quite globally – with an eye on how it all fits together. Then you can home in and complete sections.*' Similarly, he could see how good planning and structure was like 'glue' that held writing together: '*Keep an eye on how the sections will link. Aircraft glue is like a linking sentence, or a logical sequence that dovetails into the next item.*'

Luzia and dressmaking

Luzia also had difficulties with essay writing. She had extremely low self-esteem and was very reluctant to identify any area of expertise. Finally, she settled on dressmaking skills. She brainstormed all the processes that go into dressmaking, and drew parallels between these and essay writing.

For example, she saw that both dressmaking and essay writing required a clear vision of the final product. She couldn't set about choosing a pattern or buying materials until she had a sense of what she was trying to achieve. She compared this to interpreting the assignment title and having a strong argument: '*Your vision is your interest in it – without this, you just wouldn't get it done.*'

Similarly, both newly made clothes and essays need structure. Before she began to make a new item, she would decide whether it was to have a collar, cuffs or pleats and use this to guide her choice of pattern and material. For Luzia, laying out a pattern was like drawing up an essay plan: '*the pieces of a dressmaking pattern have to be laid out in a precise way so that the cloth falls properly*'. Similarly, in a well planned essay, all the pieces of the argument fall logically into place.

She made further comparisons between tacking a dress together before the final sewing and writing drafts before a final write-up. Trying a dress on to check for 'final flaws' was compared to proofreading. For Luzia, the most important element of dressmaking was having 'equal seams'. She compared this to treating different schools of thought equally when writing an essay: '*you must ask the same questions of each*'. The dressmaking analogy enabled Luzia to make sense of essay writing, calling upon her own expertise.

Make it 'make sense'

Just as Donaldson (1978) showed that young children are capable of performing tasks well above their supposed developmental level if the task is presented in a way that 'makes sense' to them, so Victor, Roger and Luzia were able to demonstrate that this is also true of adult expertise. They were able to use their own areas of relative expertise to address tasks that they had previously considered too difficult for them. They used extended metaphors – or an analogical thinking process – to accomplish this. If they can do this, so can anybody else.

It is very common for students to resist the idea that they are an 'expert' in anything. The first task, therefore, is to identify an area of expertise. This won't make you 'arrogant', as some people fear. Rather, it will provide you with a useful problem-solving tool. There will be one, or many, things that have several different stages or aspects to them and that you:

● perform with relative ease;
● can complete without supervision;
● feel comfortable doing – and may even enjoy.

Applying the Expertise Metaphor

Important aspects of working with the Expertise Metaphor are:

● Don't worry too much about the apparent difference between your area of expertise and the problem you are addressing;
● You don't need to be Olympic standard to consider yourself an 'expert' for this exercise;
● Expertise in everyday or mundane tasks can also work;
● Find out whether it works better for you to use features or component parts (as Victor did), processes (like Roger) or skills (Luzia);
● Where possible, aim to find points of similarity in the underlying structure of the tasks in which you are expert and those you are learning;
● Don't rush this – the obvious links can emerge if you allow yourself time to mull over the points of similarity;
● If the match in the points of comparison isn't exact, but still helps you understand what you need to do, that is the most important thing. This is a personal problem-solving approach not a literary exercise!

Activity: Identifying personal expertise

Select *one* task that you feel you can complete in the way described above (with ease, without supervision, etc.). This may be an item identified in the 'top forty' activity (see p. 42). It could be making a cake, dancing, playing pool, swimming, painting a picture, fixing a computer, etc. Consider this to be your area of expertise.

● Use the table below to list key components, processes and/or skills that go into completing typical activities in your area of expertise, as in the examples of Victor, Roger and Luzia above. Include the way you 'visualise' the task at the start. Pay special attention to the way you elaborate the problem at the beginning, working out what needs to be done.
● List all the skills and qualities that are needed to complete typical activities in your area of expertise.

(a) Area of personal expertise (*state which*):

Components (parts or features – see Victor)	Processes (the way things are done: see Roger)	Skills used in this area of expertise (see Luzia)

Analyse the Task
Use the table below to list key components, processes and/or skills for a task or problem that you need to address and which is proving tricky.

(b) Task or problem to address (*state which*):

Components (parts or features – see Victor)	Processes (the way things are done: see Roger)	Skills needed for this task (see Luzia)

Activity: Identifying personal expertise (continued)

Apply your expertise

Now, use the table below to draw parallels between your area of expertise and the area for improvement. Extend the metaphor as far as you can, so that you are really using your area of chosen expertise to assist you in the area for improvement. Think of all the ways that the second activity can be compared with the first.

For example, if your area of expertise was 'playing computer games' and your area for improvement was 'speaking in public', keep completing the following sentence: '*Speaking in public is like playing computer games because . . .*'. When you run out of ideas, go for a walk and come back and complete the sentence a few more times.

(c) Applying expertise

List below all the points of comparison between your area of expertise and the task you want to address

Area of expertise (component, process or skills)	Task (component, process or skills)

Select the best
- Read back over your responses.
- Highlight the points of comparison that you think will be most helpful.

This chapter has provided structured opportunities to reflect upon the way your experiences contribute to who you are now, the way you respond to challenge, and your approach to learning. It invited you to engage in a wide range of activities to explore personal experiences, choices, strengths and expertise. In this chapter, you commenced with a broad metaphor of your life and the sweep of your personal history. You then analysed aspects of that narrative, and looked more specifically at your learning history. Finally, you narrowed your focus to an area of personal expertise and considered how you could use this, and your approach to adversity, to enhance future performance. Chapter 3 looks in more detail at the theme of managing personal performance.

When we write and explain our life story with integrity, it may seem as though there could only be one possible way to tell it and that we have been true to the 'facts'. However, if you work through activities that explore your experiences from diverse angles and at different times, you are very likely to find that your responses change. The main events may remain similar, but the way you write about them, the details you choose to emphasise, the way you interpret them over time, will change as your experience, attitudes and perspectives change.

It is because our personal narratives and their interpretation are open to change that we can take our story at any one time and look to see what it tells us about our approach to life. Some people have very extreme sets of life experiences, yet when they tell their stories, they emphasise the unexpected benefits or the people they met or the characteristics they developed as a result. Another person may have less challenging experiences and yet respond as if one of these has the power to control their life for ever. We are the writers of our own story, we shape its narrative, we provide the interpretations. The interpretations we make can be a source of energy and motivation that carries us towards our vision of success.

Further reading

Beaver, D. (1998) *NLP for Lazy Learning* (Shaftesbury, Dorset, and Boston, MA: Element).

Cottrell, S. M. (2008) *The Study Skills Handbook*, 3rd edn (Basingstoke: Palgrave Macmillan).

Chapter 3

Understanding your personal performance

There is only one corner of the universe you can be certain of improving, and that's your own self.

Aldous Huxley

Learning outcomes

This chapter gives you opportunities to:

identify the impact of previous learning and performance styles on your current performance
identify conditions that most suit your learning and performance
gain an understanding of personalised approaches to learning and performance
identify your personal formula for easier and more successful performance
apply your personal performance formula to different contexts.

Introduction

In the previous chapter you thought about your own life journey and how you characterised yourself within this by using metaphors such as 'the hero' or by exaggerating elements of your story to form caricatures. This chapter is about deepening your understanding of what you need in order to 'get things done' – that is, to perform at all, to perform well and in ways that best suit you. It encourages you to take a personalised approach to learning and performance and provides a toolbox of resources to help you identify your personal preferences.

The activities enable you to consider the key factors that help and hinder you in achieving your best. From these, you will be able to derive your own personal formula for success and put this to the test. Activities also encourage you to consider how to work with your preferences – or, if necessary, how to work around them.

Learning or performance?

Anything we do depends partly on what we have learnt and partly on how we put that learning into action.

1. *Learning* includes such things as underlying theory, background information, on-the-job experience, and finding out 'how to . . . '

2. *Performance* includes learning, but it also involves putting knowledge, skills, personal qualities and experience into practice.

We may be better at one of these than the other, at either learning or performance. We may, for example, have learnt a speech well but not be able to deliver it in a public setting, or find it hard to learn a speech yet be good at public speaking once the pressure is on. In general, people judge us by how well we perform – not by what we think we have learnt. This means that it is well worth considering the conditions that enable us to perform at our best.

Types of learner

In recent decades, there has been much consideration of types of learner and styles of doing things – such as *visual* or *auditory* or *kinaesthetic* learning styles. There is a chance to identify your own learning style in this chapter too.

As performance includes learning, the information gained from such exercises is relevant to understanding your overall personal performance. You will probably find that what you discover about your performance preferences can also inform your approach to study.

Unique individuals

Although there are trends in preferences, which suggest 'types' of person or learner, this book takes the position that we are each unique in the particulars of:

● how we learn;
● how we respond to new tasks, circumstances, people and challenge;
● what we need in order to perform at our best.

Those particular details can be what really counts – if not all the time, then at least for specific activities or for significant tasks and occasions.

We all have preferences in the way we work and study. One of countless things may have a profound effect upon your performance. Dunn and Dunn, for example, isolated 21 different factors that affect learning. They found that some people are very sensitive to particular conditions, and they can under-achieve if these are not in place. Sometimes, changing something as small as your seating position, the light, or the way you study can have a dramatic effect (Dunn et al. ,1995). This chapter enables you to study your own learning preferences in detail.

Taking a personalised approach
More than just 'getting by'
Much of the time, we can 'get by' doing things in broadly the same way as other people or using strategies that have worked in the past. However, if we wish, we can take action that enables us to achieve more than just doing 'OK'.

We can benefit from considering what really works for us as individuals, from gaining an in-depth knowledge of ourselves and the conditions that enable us to perform well with maximum ease. The importance of attention to detail, even details that appear to be superficial, is recognised by those for whom success is important.

The example of top athletes
Top athletes look at how making fine adjustments to their training, equipment, and technique can give them an advantage, sometimes even of just a fraction of a second or point. They and the teams that support them look at every angle – the weather, features in the physical environment, diet, clothing, and so forth, both during training (whilst learning) and for the day of the competition. What is needed for training may be different from what is needed for competing.

Select the occasion
We do not need to pay minute attention to each aspect of every activity we undertake unless the stakes are very high. However, it is useful to be aware of what impacts upon our performance so that we can call on that self-knowledge on those occasions when we want to do well, have a competitive edge or conserve time and energy.

Personal performance factors

The activities below are designed to help you analyse the impact of different influences and conditions upon your personal performance. For those activities that use scored ratings, a high score in one area does not necessarily mean that you are a certain 'type' of learner or person; it suggests that you have habits, styles or preferences that may influence successful performance.

Personal Performance and Learning S.H.A.P.E.

SHAPE stands for Style, Habits, Attitudes, Preferences and Experience. All of these combine to make us each distinctive in how we learn and perform.

Style

There is not general agreement on what is a *style*, a *habit*, a *preference*. Some people believe that learning styles are like personality traits – that they are part of you and that you cannot really change them. If that is the case, you have to adapt your learning and performance to fit your own style. Others consider learning styles to be more like deeply seated preferences that indicate your general 'comfort zone'. In that case, you would have more control in moderating your style to achieve success in a broader range of contexts.

- Do you feel that your style of learning is so deep-seated and fixed that it cannot be changed? (In answering this, you may find it helpful to look back over your responses to the activities in Chapter 2 that looked at influences on your learning.)
- Do you feel that you have a 'learning style' that is a reflection of your personality?

Habits

When we are doing well, it can seem logical to keep doing the same things even if that behaviour may not fit new circumstances. It is generally easier to do what is familiar rather than risk trying out new strategies. Consider whether the way you approach *your* learning and performance is the result of past habits.

- Are you over-attached to habits and patterns of study behaviour that do not really help you as an adult learner?
- If so, what would happen if you changed those habits?

Attitudes

Our attitudes have a powerful effect on our behaviours and emotions, as well on how others perceive us and react to us. That is true of academic contexts just as in everyday life. Whether you are conscious of it or not, your learning and performance are affected by the attitudes and beliefs that you bring to them.

- What are your beliefs about why you do or do not do well academically?
- What are your beliefs about what makes a good student? Do you feel happy thinking of yourself as that kind of person?
- Do you feel comfortable about all aspects of academic success? If not, do you allow yourself to underperform as a result?

Preferences

This chapter helps you to identify and make use of personal preferences. Working in ways that suit us means we are not struggling against our own wishes, which is generally helpful. However, sometimes our preferences can be a hindrance.

- Which of your preferences, if any, are more of a hindrance than a help? Would you be able to change these preferences if you wanted to?

Experience

The previous chapter looked in detail at your learning experiences.

- How far do you feel your past experiences are shaping the way you approach the notion of 'being successful' in your current studies or work?

> **📖 Reflection**   Put to the test?
>
> - Which of these aspects do you consider to be having the greatest effect upon your current learning and performance?
> - How do these different aspects interact to form your own 'learning SHAPE'?

Personal Performance Factors

1. Structure

The following set of questions looks at how far you prefer to work in structured or unstructured ways. Rate each pair of statements only once. **Rating**: select from a scale where 3 = 'True and extremely important for me' and 1 = 'True but not particularly important for me'. A rating of 0 would mean 'no preference'.

Less structure									**More structure**
1.	I enjoy creative chaos	3	2	1	0	1	2	3	I enjoy being very organised
2.	My desk/workspace is a mess	3	2	1	0	1	2	3	My desk is always neat
3.	I never plan my work	3	2	1	0	1	2	3	I always plan my work in detail
4.	I remember things in my head	3	2	1	0	1	2	3	I write lots of lists
5.	I never use bookmarks	3	2	1	0	1	2	3	I always use bookmarks
6.	I leave my papers out overnight	3	2	1	0	1	2	3	I tidy my papers away at night
7.	I work whenever I find the time	3	2	1	0	1	2	3	I work to a strict routine
8.	I study what interests me that day	3	2	1	0	1	2	3	I work to a strict timetable
9.	I have a relaxed approach to time	3	2	1	0	1	2	3	I always meet deadlines
10.	I am happy to 'go with the flow'	3	2	1	0	1	2	3	I need a clear sense of the end goal

Score for less structure _____

Score for more structure _____

Total score: [＿＿＿＿]

Interpreting your score
- Total score: **0–10** suggests you are flexible for this factor.
- Total score: **20–30** suggests you have very strong preferences, though these may not form a particular pattern.
- A score of **20–30** for the 'Less structure' column suggests you have a strong preference for working or studying in your own way at your own time. This can be a very creative and independent way of working. It is worth considering whether a more organised and structured approach would help. Danger points to watch for are missing deadlines and not fulfilling the requirements for an assignment.
- A score of **20–30** for the 'More structure' column suggests you have a strong preference for working or studying in an organised and systematic way. This can be a very productive way of working, and you are likely to be someone who gets things done and in an organised and timely fashion. It is worth considering whether more flexibility and openness to new ideas would benefit your performance. Danger points to watch for are over-rigid ways of thinking and working.
- Scores of **10–20** for either column suggest moderate over-dependence on your personal preferences. It may be useful to experiment with features of the opposite column.

© Stella Cottrell (2003, 2010), *Skills for Success*, Palgrave Macmillan

2. External direction

The following set of questions looks at how far you prefer to work with or without external direction. Rate each pair of statements only once. **Rating**: select from a scale where 3 = 'True and extremely important for me' and 1 = 'True but not particularly important for me'. A rating of 0 would mean 'no preference'.

Less external direction								**More external direction**

I prefer . . .

1.	lectures to be unpredictable	3	2	1	0	1	2	3	to know what to expect in lectures
2.	a lecture just to unfold	3	2	1	0	1	2	3	an outline or agenda at the beginning of lectures
3.	to develop my own projects	3	2	1	0	1	2	3	to be given set assignments
4.	to invent my own assignment titles	3	2	1	0	1	2	3	tutors to set assignment titles
5.	to explore topics for myself	3	2	1	0	1	2	3	tutors to guide my thinking
6.	to develop my own reading list	3	2	1	0	1	2	3	tutors to give the reading list
7.	to do things my own way	3	2	1	0	1	2	3	to be told exactly what I have to do
8.	to pick up how to use computer software as I go along	3	2	1	0	1	2	3	to go on a course to learn new software
9.	to just get on with study for myself	3	2	1	0	1	2	3	the lecturer to give an early overview of the subject
10.	to work out how to solve new problems	3	2	1	0	1	2	3	clear guidance on how to approach new problems

Score for less external direction _____   *Score for more external direction* _____

Total score: [   ]

Interpreting your score

- Total score: **0–10** suggests you are flexible for this factor.
- Total score: **20–30** suggests you have very strong preferences, though these may not form a particular pattern.
- A score of **20–30** for the 'Less external direction' column suggests you have a strong preference for taking control over how you work. This can be very useful in developing as an independent, autonomous learner, capable of taking on new projects and setting targets for yourself. It is worth considering whether you need to be more open to ideas from others. Danger points to watch for are possible weaknesses in team working and not fulfilling the requirements for an assignment.
- A score of **20–30** for the 'More external direction' column suggests you are very open to direction and leadership from others. This can be useful in ensuring that you are going in the right direction, for using time economically and for team working. It is worth considering whether you need to take more control over your own learning and be more open to exploration and risk-taking. Danger points to watch for are reliance on others to do your thinking and planning, and underdeveloped personal independence and leadership.
- Scores of **10–20** for either column suggest moderate over-dependence on your personal preferences for study. It may be useful to experiment with features of the opposite column.

3. Working with others

The following set of questions looks at how far you prefer to work with or without other people. Rate each pair of statements only once. **Rating**: select from a scale where 3 = 'True and extremely important for me' and 1 = 'True but not particularly important for me'. A rating of 0 would mean 'no preference'.

	Preference for working with others								**Preference for working alone**
1.	I prefer group work	3	2	1	0	1	2	3	I prefer to work on my own
2.	In a library, I prefer to sit near others	3	2	1	0	1	2	3	In a library, I prefer to sit on my own
3.	I like to go through lecture notes with a friend	3	2	1	0	1	2	3	I prefer to keep my lecture notes private
4.	I value hearing other people's ideas	3	2	1	0	1	2	3	I prefer to develop my own ideas
5.	I enjoy the interaction in group work	3	2	1	0	1	2	3	I enjoy thinking through an idea in quiet reflection
6.	I learn more through discussion than reading	3	2	1	0	1	2	3	I learn more from reading than discussion
7.	Groups come up with more ideas	3	2	1	0	1	2	3	I come up with more ideas on my own
8.	For me, team working is really useful	3	2	1	0	1	2	3	For me, team working is a waste of time
9.	I like to discuss assignments with others	3	2	1	0	1	2	3	I prefer working alone on assignments
10.	I would find a study support group helpful	3	2	1	0	1	2	3	I work best if left to myself

Score for working with others _____   *Score for working alone* _____

Total score: [   ]

Interpreting your score

● Total score: **0–10** suggests you are flexible for this factor.
● Total score: **20–30** suggests you have very strong preferences, though these may not form a particular pattern.
● A score of **20–30** for the 'working with others' column suggests a strong social preference when working or studying. This can be very useful for gaining a wide set of perspectives and ideas, for developing social skills, for team working and for developing mutual support. It is worth considering how far you would benefit from more time studying independently. Danger points are possible over-reliance on others and not developing your own ideas in an independent way.
● A score of **20–30** for the 'working alone' column suggests a strong preference for solitary working. This can be useful for avoiding distractions, for achieving goals, and developing independence. It is worth considering in more depth what can be gained from working with others and the skills that emerge from reconciling different sets of opinions and personalities. You may lose out by not gaining access to a wide set of perspectives, especially in real-life or 'applied' settings. Danger points may be failure to appreciate the work of others and under-developed inter-personal skills.
● Scores of **10–20** for either column suggest moderate over-dependence on your personal preferences. It may be useful to experiment with features of the opposite column.

© Stella Cottrell (2003, 2010), *Skills for Success*, Palgrave Macmillan

Understanding your personal performance

4. Level of physical stimulus

The following set of questions looks at how far physical factors may affect the way you work. Rate each pair of statements only once. **Rating:** select from a scale where 3 = 'True and extremely important for me' and 1 = 'True but not particularly important for me'. A rating of 0 would mean 'no preference'.

	High stimulus								**Low stimulus**
1.	I need to work in a very bright room	3	2	1	0	1	2	3	I need to work in a very dim light
2.	I need music or TV in the background	3	2	1	0	1	2	3	I need absolute quiet to work
3.	I work well when there is a lot going on in the background	3	2	1	0	1	2	3	My attention is very easily distracted
4.	I always eat when I am studying	3	2	1	0	1	2	3	I can't think about food when I am studying
5.	I need to drink a lot when studying	3	2	1	0	1	2	3	I never drink whilst studying
6.	I work best when it is either very hot or cold	3	2	1	0	1	2	3	I prefer a moderate room temperature
7.	I tend to fiddle with things as I work	3	2	1	0	1	2	3	I am quite still when I settle down to work
8.	It helps me to think if I walk about	3	2	1	0	1	2	3	I can't think if I am moving about
9.	Doodling helps me to listen in meetings and lectures	3	2	1	0	1	2	3	I focus on listening and making notes in meetings and lectures
10.	I prefer to work on several things at once	3	2	1	0	1	2	3	I need to finish one thing before starting another

Score for high stimulus _____   *Score for low stimulus* _____

Total score: [   ]

Interpreting your score
- Total score: **0–10** suggests you have a high tolerance for working in most conditions.
- Total score: **20–30** suggests you have very strong preferences, though these may not form a particular pattern.
- Scores of **0–1** for any item suggests that you have a reasonable tolerance for working without that stimulus being present.
- Scores of **2** for any item suggests that your performance might be affected if that stimulus is not present.
- Scores of **3** for any item suggests your performance might be seriously affected if that stimulus is not present. You may need to think creatively about how you can make it possible to provide that stimulus for most study contexts (for example, if you are light sensitive, by using bright lamps to increase the lighting or by wearing hats or sunglasses to dim light).
- A score of **20–30** for either column suggests a very strong overall preference for working either with or without stimulus. Given this preference, it is possible that if these stimuli were not present when you were being taught in childhood, learning may have felt difficult for you. High scores may also indicate a high level of stress. It may be helpful to speak to a counsellor or adviser about this.

Experiment
It is worth experimenting with studying with different kinds of stimuli present or absent. Monitor how far these do affect your performance. For example, many people have been surprised at how far they follow a pattern set down when they were at school as if that were the only 'right' way to study or work when alone. You will find that you learn more easily if you find the stimulus combination that suits you best.

5. Global or serialist

The following set of questions looks at how far your learning responds to 'global or 'serialist' approaches. Rate each pair of statements only once. **Rating**: select from a scale where 3 = 'True and extremely important for me' and 1 = 'True but not particularly important for me'. A rating of 0 would mean 'no preference'.

Which of the statements in each pair is more true of you? How does this affect the way you study?

	Global styles								**Serialist styles**

When studying or working on a project, I prefer to . . .

	Global	3	2	1	0	1	2	3	Serialist
1.	start off by gaining a broad overview	3	2	1	0	1	2	3	start off from interesting details
2.	have the whole subject mapped out in a diagram or description	3	2	1	0	1	2	3	find the logical sequence
3.	work from fully rounded examples	3	2	1	0	1	2	3	work from a clear list
4.	use mind maps, 'picture' notes or a recorded discussion	3	2	1	0	1	2	3	use headings and bullet points or a recorded list of key points
5.	launch in at the deep end	3	2	1	0	1	2	3	plan things out carefully first
6.	use my intuition	3	2	1	0	1	2	3	adhere strictly to the facts
7.	use my imagination	3	2	1	0	1	2	3	reason things out
8.	search for connections between things	3	2	1	0	1	2	3	classify and categorise information
9.	search for similarities	3	2	1	0	1	2	3	search for differences
10.	draw things together	3	2	1	0	1	2	3	analyse the detail

Score for global styles _____   *Score for serialist styles* _____

Total score: [   ]

Interpreting your score
- Total score: **0–10** suggests you are flexible for this factor.
- Total score: **20–30** suggests you have very strong preferences, though these may not form a particular pattern.
- A score of **20–30** for the 'Global style' column suggests you have a strong preference for taking a holistic approach to work or study. This can be very useful for synthesising information, and making creative links. It is worth considering whether you need to bring more order and system to your activities. Look for possible weaknesses in managing clarity, detail, order and sequence in your work or writing.
- A score of **20–30** for the 'Serialist styles' column suggests you take a logical, analytical approach to study. This can be very useful in ensuring clarity and structure in your work. It is worth considering whether you need to create opportunities for developing your imagination and intuition. It may help to experiment with searching out links and connections between ideas. Possible weaknesses may be in drawing together your ideas into a strong whole and in making connections between what you are studying and the bigger picture.
- Scores of **10–20** for either column suggest moderate strengths for that style of working. It may be useful to experiment with features of the opposite column.

© Stella Cottrell (2003, 2010), *Skills for Success*, Palgrave Macmillan

6. Pressure

The following set of questions looks at how far you prefer to work with or without pressure. Rate each pair of statements only once. **Rating**: select from a scale where 3 = 'True and extremely important for me' and 1 = 'True but not particularly important for me'. A rating of 0 would mean 'no preference'.

	Prefer high pressure								**Prefer low pressure**
1.	I complete tasks in one go	3	2	1	0	1	2	3	I break tasks into manageable sections
2.	I get everything done	3	2	1	0	1	2	3	I select certain things to do
3.	I want to please everyone	3	2	1	0	1	2	3	I know I can't please everyone
4.	I adapt well to the time available	3	2	1	0	1	2	3	I need plenty of time to do things properly
5.	I work best when multi-tasking	3	2	1	0	1	2	3	I work best if I do one thing at a time
6.	I work best with tight deadlines	3	2	1	0	1	2	3	I work best if there is no deadline
7.	I need to feel a sense of urgency	3	2	1	0	1	2	3	I need to feel very relaxed when working
8.	I work best without support from others	3	2	1	0	1	2	3	I work best with support from others
9.	I catch meals when I can	3	2	1	0	1	2	3	I always take a break for meals
10.	I need the final result to be perfect	3	2	1	0	1	2	3	I am happy if the final result is 'good enough'

Score for high pressure _____   *Score for low pressure* _____

Total score

Interpreting your score

- Total score: **0–10** suggests you are flexible for this factor.
- Total score: **20–30** suggests you have very strong preferences, though these may not form a particular pattern.
- Scores of **20–30** for 'high pressure' suggest that you are likely to respond well to exams, competition and targets. You need to take care to manage stress levels and check carefully that they are not adversely affecting performance, behaviour and health without your realising. You may need to set your own targets for activities that you find boring or of low importance.
- Scores of **20–30** for 'low pressure' suggest that you may be good at protecting your health and well-being, and at producing good work even when there isn't external pressure to do so. You need to beware of over-sensitivity to stress and to external requirements and conditions.
- Scores of **10–20** for either high or low pressure suggest moderate preferences for that way of working. It may be helpful to experiment with features of the opposite column.

7. Method

When you have something completely new to learn, how do you set about learning it?
Tick the boxes that are true of you.

I find it easier to learn through . . .

☐ listening
☐ personalising the material
☐ watching others
☐ picturing it in my head
☐ writing about it
☐ turning it into a picture
☐ turning it into headings
☐ categorising and labelling it
☐ day-dreaming about it
☐ recording myself talking about it

☐ reading
☐ asking questions
☐ adapting the task to suit myself
☐ writing it out
☐ making a chart
☐ colour-coding it
☐ talking it through with others
☐ linking it to what I know already
☐ describing or explaining it to others
☐ thinking about it whilst I do housework or similar tasks

- Which of the above methods are you not using at present that might be of use to you?
- Are there other methods you could use that you are not using currently?
- Highlight the methods that you feel are the most important in helping you to achieve well.

---

8. Honey and Mumford learning styles

Honey and Mumford (1992) developed a questionnaire that divided people into four main types. A broad outline of their learning types is given below. Which of the following are generally true of you (there may be more than one)? Which is the most true?

☐ **'Activist' learning style**. I prefer to work in intuitive, flexible and spontaneous ways, generating ideas and trying out new things. I usually have a lot to say and contribute. I like to learn from experience, such as through problem-solving, group-work, workshops, discussion, or team work.

☐ **'Reflector' learning style**. I like to watch and reflect, gathering data and taking time to consider all options and alternatives before making a decision. Lectures, project work and working alone suit me.

☐ **'Theorist' learning style**. I like to learn by going through things thoroughly and logically, step by step, with clear guidelines, and to feel I have learnt solidly before I have to apply what I know. I prefer to learn from books, problem-solving and discussion.

☐ **'Pragmatist' learning style**. I like to learn by 'trying things out' to see if they work, just getting on with it, getting to the point. I like to be practical and realistic. I prefer to learn on work-based projects and practical applications.

- Do you think you might benefit from choosing certain types of study module or programme in order to ensure the teaching and assessment match your preferred learning type?
- Could you organise your study or your work to suit your learning type?
- Do you think it is helpful to see yourself as a 'type' of learner? How does this impact upon your performance in different circumstances? What might be the disadvantages of identifying too closely with one method or style of learning?

9. Visual, auditory and kinaesthetic learning styles

Rate each of the following statements, depending on how true you think it is of you, by drawing a ring round the number.

Rating: *4 = yes, this is very true of me   3 = yes, it is true of me   2 = sort of true/don't know*
1 = hardly ever true   0 = not true of me at all

1.	When I'm reading, I picture the scene in my head	4	3	2	1	0
2.	I have a good memory for conversation	4	3	2	1	0
3.	I will remember something better if I have seen it written down	4	3	2	1	0
4.	I remember things best if I get up and move about	4	3	2	1	0
5.	I use my hands a lot when I'm speaking	4	3	2	1	0
6.	I like to picture what I am learning	4	3	2	1	0
7.	I remember phone numbers by the movement I make to dial to them	4	3	2	1	0
8.	I repeat things out loud or over and over in my head to remember them	4	3	2	1	0
9.	I doodle whilst I am listening	4	3	2	1	0
10.	I add up numbers out loud	4	3	2	1	0
11.	I can't add up unless I can see the numbers written down	4	3	2	1	0
12.	I'm good at remembering the words to songs	4	3	2	1	0
13.	I prefer to watch something being done before I try it myself	4	3	2	1	0
14.	I like to ask a lot of questions in class	4	3	2	1	0
15.	I find it easy to remember where I last saw something	4	3	2	1	0
16.	I write out words to see if the spelling feels right	4	3	2	1	0
17.	I have a good eye for colour	4	3	2	1	0
18.	I'm good at sport	4	3	2	1	0
19.	I am able to learn things off by heart quite easily	4	3	2	1	0
20.	I have a good ear for music	4	3	2	1	0
21.	I'm good at practical things	4	3	2	1	0
22.	If somebody gives me a set of instructions, I can remember them quite easily	4	3	2	1	0
23.	I tend to move around a lot on my chair when working	4	3	2	1	0
24.	I tend to fiddle and play about with my hands a lot	4	3	2	1	0
25.	I prefer to have instructions written down so I can see them	4	3	2	1	0
26.	I like to learn by doing	4	3	2	1	0
27.	I visualise a spelling to see if I have got it right	4	3	2	1	0
28.	I run a film in my head of what I have to learn	4	3	2	1	0
29.	I prefer to learn through discussion	4	3	2	1	0
30.	I like to hear exactly what I have to do	4	3	2	1	0
31.	I like to 'just try it out' rather than following instructions	4	3	2	1	0
32.	I like to learn by doing practical things	4	3	2	1	0
33.	I remember a phone number by the way it sounds	4	3	2	1	0
34.	I like to learn from slides and pictures	4	3	2	1	0
35.	I sing and hum a lot	4	3	2	1	0
36.	I like the tutor to use PowerPoint® slides and write on the board	4	3	2	1	0

Scoring

Each statement that you rated above indicates a preference for either a visual, auditory or kinaesthetic way of learning and performing.

- Visual learners find it easier to learn if information is presented so they can see it, and where they use their eyes or visual imagination to learn.
- Auditory learners learn best by hearing and recalling sound cues.
- Kinaesthetic learners tend to learn best where there is a physical sensation, such as movement, touch or a feeling.

Write down your scores for each statement and then add up your totals.

Visual scores	Auditory scores	Kinaesthetic scores
Statement 1:	Statement 2:	Statement 4:
Statement 3:	Statement 8:	Statement 5:
Statement 6:	Statement 10:	Statement 7:
Statement 11:	Statement 12:	Statement 9:
Statement 13:	Statement 14:	Statement 16:
Statement 15:	Statement 19:	Statement 18:
Statement 17:	Statement 20:	Statement 21:
Statement 25:	Statement 22:	Statement 23:
Statement 27:	Statement 29:	Statement 24:
Statement 28:	Statement 30:	Statement 26:
Statement 34:	Statement 33:	Statement 31:
Statement 36:	Statement 35:	Statement 32:

Total

Interpreting your score

No strong preference: If your scores for all three areas are similar, then you may not have a strong sensory preference for learning. If your scores are high (40–48 for each area), then you use all of your senses well to assist your learning. If scores are low (between 0 and 24), you may need to use your senses more consciously to assist your learning and experiment more with your learning.

A strong preference: The more marked the preference for one sense, the more you may need to ensure that you find ways of making good use of it, in order to make learning easier. Consider how you could incorporate into your study all the items listed above for that sense. Be creative. You might also like to consider whether you would gain from using the other senses more.

Personal Performance Profile

If you have worked through some or all of the activities in this and the previous chapter, it is likely that you have generated a great deal of information about what you need in order to get things done. The following activities enable you to pare that down to find the key factors in your performance profile.

Personal Profile: Chart

The chart below enables you to draw together your scores and ratings for the activities on pages (55–63) so that your preferences for each aspect stand out clearly.

If you notice that you feel energised when it comes to writing out some items, that already provides a clue as to your performance needs. However, if you feel your energy wanes when it comes to writing out certain items, this could indicate EITHER items you can omit as not significant to your performance OR items you know you should include as they work or are 'good for you' but which you don't actually like. If you need it, include it.

e Personal Performance Profile Chart

Aspect	Score	Level and direction of preference
Example: Structure (page 49)	*9*	*Very strong preference for 'more structure'*
Example: External direction	*27*	*No preference either way on 'external direction'*
Structure (page)		
External direction (page)		
Working with others (page)		
Physical stimulus (page)		
Global/serialist (page)		
Pressure (page)		
Visual, auditory, kinaesthetic (page)		

📖 *Reflection*   Personal Performance Profile Chart

Use your responses on the Personal Performance Profile Chart above to analyse your profile. Consider what this tells you about your preferences. In particular:

● Note the aspect for which you gave the highest rating(s).
● Note the aspect for which you gave the lowest rating(s).
● Note whether you tend to have all high, or all low, or all moderate ratings, or whether you have no preferences at all.

What do these trends suggest to you about what you need in order to perform at your best?

Select key factors

The Personal Performance Profile Chart above enabled you to gain one perspective on your performance profile.

However, you may have noticed that you have strong preferences for particular factors listed in the activities on pages 55–63 but not for every factor as a whole. For example, you may have a strong preference for one or two items listed for 'Less Structure' (page 55) but all your other preferences might have been for 'More structure'. You may have had an even number of strong preferences on each list so that this balanced out as no overall pattern of preference.

The profiling activity below enables you to draw together specific information from each activity, so that you can see your key information more clearly. Look back over your responses to the activities on pages (55–63). Consider what each tells you about your preferences for getting things done. Select those items that you feel stand out strongly for you and list these below. An example of how you might approach this is given in italics on the chart below.

---

e Activity: Personal Performance Profile

Previous activity *Example:* *Structure (page 55)*	Personal preference factors identified through previous activities *I generally need a lot of structure but I do need to structure things for myself. I need to personalise my workspace; I use lists a lot; I work to a strict routine and timetable.*
Structure (page 55)	
External direction (page 56)	
Working with others (page 57)	
Physical stimulus (Page 58)	
Global/serialist (page 59)	
Pressure (page 60)	
Methods (page 61)	
Honey and Mumford Styles (page 61)	
Visual, auditory, kinaesthetic (page 62)	
Learning history (pages 43–4)	
Expertise metaphor (pages 49–50)	
Other factors?	

Personal Performance Formula

The two previous activities enabled you to summarise a wide range of information about your personal performance. In the next activity, you can distil this information further in order to identify your Personal Performance Formula. This isn't a 'scientific formula' – it is your personal formula as identified through your own structured reflection, your analysis of how you do things, and your own selection of factors that are important to you.

Activity: Personal Performance Factors

From the factors you identified in the two previous activities (pages 64–5), select and list up to 10 that are the most significant for you. It is up to you how many you list, where you select these factors from, and how you word them so that they are meaningful to you.

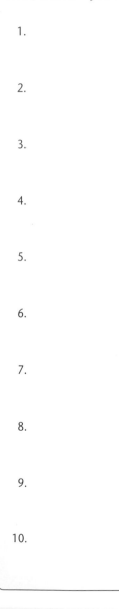

1.

2.

3.

4.

5.

6.

7.

8.

9.

10.

Name it!

It is likely that you have identified a unique combination of factors – which is why this is referred to as your *Personal Performance Formula* (PPF). As such, that unique combination, or formula, won't yet have a name. It is a good idea to give it one.

Naming your performance formula helps:

- to summarise the list of relevant performance factors;
- to make the formula your own;
- to remember it when needed.

That name will, of course, be personal to you – so the more individual it is, the better. It can:

- be as long or as short as you like
- summon up a sound, image or feeling that means something to you
- rhyme if you want it too
- include your name – or not
- hint at your performance preferences
- be based around a famous person or fictitious character
- be humorous – or not
- something entirely different!

ⓔ Activity: Name your Personal Performance Formula

- Read through the factors you listed for your Personal Performance Formula.
- Decide on a name that you feel sums up your personal performance preferences.
- Write it below – in a style that suits you!

Task-specific performance factors

When does the PPF work?

So far, you have identified a generalised performance formula. For some people, one broad set of factors, their Personal Performance Formula (PPF), is applicable to almost everything they do;

for others, factors that influence performance vary greatly from one task to another. Indeed, one reason why people underachieve is that they cling to factors that were successful in the past or to a specific context, and apply them to tasks or contexts where they do not have the same effect.

Now that you have identified your Personal Performance Formula, it is worth considering when and how this applies in practice, using the following activities.

ⓔ Activity: Test your PPF on different tasks

Test out your *Personal Performance Formula* (PPF) for constancy.

- Select two distinct tasks or activities that vary in scale, character, or both. Write brief details of these in the two tables provided below (pages 68–9).
- On the tables below, write out the list of up to 10 factors that you identified for your PPF (page 66). If you wrote down many details against each factor, then just summarise the information you gave.
- Jot down *how* each factor applies to the task or activity you identified.
- Decide whether, overall, the PPF does apply to the task or activity (circle YES or NO).

Don't worry! Hold out your hand to it. Cats like to sniff you first to make sure you're friendly

Test your Personal Performance Formula (PPF): Task 1		
Task (*short description of the task*)		
Your PPF factors (from your list on page 66)	How the PPF applies to Task 1	Applies?
1		YES/NO
2		YES/NO
3		YES/NO
4		YES/NO
5		YES/NO
6		YES/NO
7		YES/NO
8		YES/NO
9		YES/NO
10		YES/NO
	Total Number of 'Yes'	

Other factors or conditions that would enable me to perform best at this task:

Testing your Personal Performance Formula (PPF): Task 2		
Task (*short description of the task*)		
Your PPF factors (from your list on page 66)	How the PPF applies to Task 1	Applies?
1		YES/NO
2		YES/NO
3		YES/NO
4		YES/NO
5		YES/NO
6		YES/NO
7		YES/NO
8		YES/NO
9		YES/NO
10		YES/NO
	Total Number of 'Yes'	
Other factors or conditions that would enable me to perform best at this task:		

Did it apply?

If at least half of your PPF factors applied to both tasks, then you have identified a PPF with general applicability. The higher the number of factors that applied to each task, the stronger your formula is likely to be. This makes life relatively easy! It is worth noting your PPF and considering how you can apply it to tasks where you feel it will be helpful.

Could you have a stronger task-specific PPF?

Even though you have identified a personal performance formula that will work for you for different tasks, it is still worth checking whether a different formula might be even more successful for specific kinds of task.

You can do this by:

● evaluating the relative significance of each factor for particular tasks or contexts;
● considering whether other factors could make a difference for specific tasks or contexts.

If you do note such differences, then you have identified a task-specific PPF which may serve you better. Note it down. Consider a way of ensuring that you will recall this when it would be helpful, such as by giving it a name of its own.

If the PPF didn't apply

It is not unusual for people to identify different sets of factors that impact upon their performance in distinct tasks. For example, the factors that apply to successful study when working on a piece of coursework are very likely to be different from those that apply in the exam room or a work-based project.

If few of the factors you had identified applied to the tasks you selected for testing the PPF, then you haven't identified a generally applicable Personal Performance Formula; you have identified that your PPF would be specific to certain types of activity.

You are also likely to be more sensitive to context. Success for you may depend on how well you

think through your performance needs in relation to particular tasks and situations. If you are not achieving the outcomes you want, then it is especially important for you to plan significant tasks carefully, identifying what you need and how you will put that into place so as to maximise your chances of success.

You may benefit from identifying a Personal Performance Formula for each type of significant task or context. If you think this is so:

● list the key factors (in summary);
● devise a name for each PPF;
● consider a way of ensuring that you will recall this PPF when you need it – and the kinds of task or activity to which it applies.

Applying your Personal Performance Formula

Playing to your strengths

In the activities above, you identified how you *prefer* to do things and the conditions under which you prefer to take action. There is a lot of sense in working to your preferences as you are likely to be operating in ways that are most comfortable and familiar for you. If you are feeling at ease and happy with your conditions then, in general, you are more likely to:

- be 'playing to your strengths';
- be willing to engage with the task;
- be able to focus on the task in hand;
- avoid needless pressure and stress;
- avoid emotional states that detract from your performance;
- be less distracted by your surroundings.

If you have identified a PPF, then it makes sense to use it.

Making it work

Your performance preferences will sometimes be easy to accommodate where you work or study. Inevitably, on other occasions, there will not be an exact match between the way you want to work and study and the way that others teach or manage, or in terms of what is expected in the particular circumstances.

It is up to you to identify:

- what factors are essential to enable you to perform at your best;
- whether there is some way that these could be accommodated;
- how you can adapt either your needs or the task in order to work to your preferences;
- how you will work around the 'gaps' if your PPF cannot be accommodated.

In the next chapters, you will find further ideas and resources that can help you to manage your performance.

Finding a way

Although there will be times when you have to work in conditions that are not ideal, consider whether you could negotiate with your employer or tutor for more flexibility so you can better apply your Personal Performance Formula. It might be possible, for example, to:

- complete part of a task at home where you can adapt the conditions to suit you;
- work in a quieter room for tasks where you need to concentrate;
- defer the task until a time that suits your ways of working;
- have longer to perform one task if you can take less time on another;
- work with a colleague on parts of the task that play to mutual strengths;
- negotiate the deadlines on an aspect of the task;
- swap that task for another.

> ### 📖 *Reflection*   Find a way
>
> Consider one task that you are finding difficult at the moment. Which aspects of the task or your work/study conditions could you negotiate in order to be able to work on this more easily in line with your personal performance formula?

'What I like' versus 'what actually works?'

Check whether your preferences are helping or hindering! Although it can be beneficial to work to your preferences, it may be that you have selected a range of factors that:

- narrow your overall range of choices;
- make life more comfortable but offer too little challenge;
- reduce pressure but don't get the job done;
- reduce your chances of gaining something that matters to you;
- put too much pressure on other people to accommodate your needs.

This requires you to be very frank with yourself. You are likely to know whether you are fooling yourself that your preferences are working if they are not. If your work, marks or feedback from others are not improving, then it is likely that you need to reconsider – and identify the formula that really will work!

In this chapter, you have analysed in depth many features of your own learning and performance. The activities enabled you to gain an understanding of the conditions that you consider are important to have in place if you are to perform at your best. You have used this to identify your own Personal Performance Formula, and then considered how that formula might need to be adapted for specific tasks and situations. Whilst you are encouraged to use your preferences and to identify ways of making these work to your advantage, you also need to be honest with yourself in identifying where personal preferences might be a hindrance.

As adult learners, we can adapt conditions to suit our personal needs. We can find ways of making effective use of our physical senses in order to better absorb and remember information. We can give thought to the assumptions we make about our learning and the restrictions we place upon ourselves. Whilst we cannot control all the circumstances that affect us, we do have the power to shape our thinking so that we learn more from our experiences. We can choose to have more power over our minds and to take control over our learning and performance.

Further reading

Dunn, R., Griggs, S., Olson, J., Beasley, M. and Gorman, B. (1995) 'A Meta-analytic Validation of the Dunn and Dunn Model of Learning Style Preferences', *Journal of Educational Research*, 88 (6), 353–62.

Honey, P. and Mumford, A. (1992) *The Manual of Learning Styles Questionnaire* (Maidenhead, Berks: Peter Honey Publications).

Lawrence, G. (1993) *People Types and Tiger Stripes*, 3rd edn (Gainesville, FL: Centre for Applications of Psychological Type).

Chapter 4

Successful self-management

To conquer others is strong; to conquer oneself is mighty.

Lao-Tzu

Learning outcomes

This chapter offers opportunities to:

identify tools and resources for successful self-management
understand the importance of constructive attitudes to success in any field
evaluate and develop your emotional intelligence
identify factors that prevent you from achieving excellence.

Introduction

Self-management encompasses a very broad range of skills, qualities, attitudes and experience. It can include some or all of the following:

- being able to analyse your situation, identifying strengths, weaknesses, opportunities and threats;
- identifying resources and sources of support;
- managing your time;
- adopting attitudes that support your aims;
- taking a solution-focused approach to managing problems;
- managing your own emotions;
- coping when in distress;
- managing change, uncertainty and confusion.

These are usually demanded of students whilst at university or in their first jobs, and are addressed in this chapter. There are associated skills and strategies covered in other chapters. For example:

- being a self-starter (Chapter 5);
- being able to motivate yourself to finish what you start (Chapter 5);

- taking steps to improve your own performance (all chapters);
- being assertive (Chapter 6).

Intra-personal skills

'*Intra*-personal' refers to your own inner world, in contrast to '*inter*-personal', which refers to how you relate to other people. Intra-personal skills help us to manage our feelings, responses and actions, so that we are able to function at our best. Some branches of psychology have long recognised the importance of our emotional well-being to our capacity to perform well. You may have noticed this on occasions such as exams, if anxiety or personal matters prevented you from concentrating or remembering.

The world of emotions

The 'intra-personal' world has the most profound effect upon our responses, our thinking, our behaviour, our views of ourselves, our feelings and our achievement. It touches upon what is closest to our hearts and being. It is, especially, the arena of the emotions. When we work with emotions, we can expect to feel emotional at times. Most of us can find this quite challenging, and so there is a temptation to shy away from developing intra-personal skills. If we try to avoid any issue where emotions may be involved, it can mean we do not get to the heart of the issue, and so do not achieve all we could. On the other hand, when we understand more about ourselves, know our own triggers, and develop our emotional intelligence, we are more able to manage every situation we enter.

This chapter forms a brief introduction to a very wide-ranging subject. It does not go into detail about sensitive subjects but, given the differences in our life stories, it is to be expected that some activities may be emotionally sensitive for individuals. If you feel you need to talk something through as a result of any activities, it is worth noting that student counselling services were set up to deal with all kinds of matters, small issues as well as major ones. You do not need to be in a crisis to see them. Services are confidential and they may also be able to find support for you away from the university if you prefer.

Activity: Focus

For this chapter, identify a personal goal or a situation that you wish to think about more deeply, in order to give focus to your responses.

SWOT analysis

A SWOT analysis is a useful, quick tool for taking stock of your situation. It is a simple way of analysing your level of readiness for a new task. It can take you to the core of an issue very quickly. SWOT stands for Strengths, Weaknesses, Opportunities, Threats.

Activity: SWOT Analysis

- For the focus you selected in the previous activity, use the resource sheet on p. 75 to jot down as many examples of strengths and weaknesses as you can under each heading. Include personal qualities, skills, experiences, knowledge, resources and support.
- Under 'Opportunities', jot down any opportunities that could arise from achieving this goal. Include short- and long-term benefits.
- Under 'Threats', jot down the things that seem threatening, worrying, very challenging, or which are causing you some anxiety.

The Activities in this book, and especially those in this chapter, should help you to manage some of the 'threats'.

Emily prided herself on her emotional detachment.

SWOT Analysis Resource Sheet

Goal:

Strengths	Weaknesses

Opportunities	Threats

Successful self-management

Personal resources

Very few of us have the ideal resources, but none of us is without any. This is especially true for students. A wide range of services is offered through the university, college or community, and listed in various leaflets, books and directories.

Activity: Finding information

- Make a list of all the sources of support available through the Student Union and Student Services that are likely to be useful to you.
- Follow this up by making appointments – put these in your diary. Before appointments, read the literature provided so as to check the documentation or details you need to bring. Always take your student card or number.

📠 Activity: Sources of support

In the boxes below, list the sources of support available to you for each item. Put a tick in the box by those that you need to pursue in the next few weeks.

Academic advice and guidance ☐

Financial ☐

Careers/finding a job ☐

Meeting people ☐

Finding somewhere to live ☐

Emotional questions, needs and support ☐

Health issues ☐

Other resource needs:

Time management

Your time is one of your most valuable resources. How well do you use your time at present? Which of the following characteristics are typical of you?

Activity: Evaluating time management

For each item, identify which one response is most true for you, indicating this with a tick (✔).

Characteristic	Yes, a lot	Yes, sometimes	No	I don't know
I recognise the following characteristics as true of me:				
Being late	☐	☐	☐	☐
Not knowing where I am supposed to be	☐	☐	☐	☐
Delays because I can't remember where I put things	☐	☐	☐	☐
Missing appointments	☐	☐	☐	☐
Rushing at the end of a task	☐	☐	☐	☐
Missing deadlines	☐	☐	☐	☐
Not being clear what I need to do next	☐	☐	☐	☐
Taking too late a bus or train	☐	☐	☐	☐
Getting caught up in interesting diversions	☐	☐	☐	☐
Finding it hard to get started	☐	☐	☐	☐
Taking too long to complete a task	☐	☐	☐	☐
Running out of time	☐	☐	☐	☐
Not knowing how long it takes me to complete a task	☐	☐	☐	☐
Dashing around all day	☐	☐	☐	☐
Forgetting what I have to do	☐	☐	☐	☐

- If your response to all of the above was 'NO' you seem to have very good time management. Is it perfect, or are there areas where you could improve further?
- If your response to some items was: 'I don't know', then you would seem to lack awareness about your time management. Speak to people who know you well and find out what they think about your time management.
- If your response to any of the above was 'Yes', the following activities and guidance may help.

Activity: Factors in time management

For each item, identify which one response is most true for you, indicating this with a tick (✓).

Factor	Very true	Sometimes true	Never true
1. I use small pockets of time in the day to sort out minor tasks	☐	☐	☐
2. I get down to work quickly; I am well motivated to start	☐	☐	☐
3. I have timed myself completing the different aspects of larger tasks	☐	☐	☐
4. I know when I have done enough rather than aiming at perfection	☐	☐	☐
5. I say 'NO' when I lack time	☐	☐	☐
6. I delegate work to others when I can	☐	☐	☐
7. I ask for help where possible	☐	☐	☐
8. I have a go rather than worrying too much about getting things wrong	☐	☐	☐
9. I have strategies for starting a task rather than wondering where to begin	☐	☐	☐
10. I keep a diary and use it effectively	☐	☐	☐
11. I am well-organised so as not to waste time	☐	☐	☐
12. I plan my activities in a logical order	☐	☐	☐

Activity: Identify solutions

If you answered 'sometimes true' or 'never true' to any of the above time management factors, identify at least three you could improve.

● Some strategies for managing these time factors are given below. Which could you use to improve your time management?
● In your reflective journal, re-write these as positive 'I will…' statements. For example, 'I will keep an effective diary'
● Add specific details that make it more likely you will take action. For example, 'I will buy a diary today at the Student Shop after my Design lecture. I will carry it in my blue bag. I will check it every evening after dinner so that I can plan ahead for the next day.'

Managing time effectively

For each of the time management statements in the activity 'Factors in time management' (above), there are suggestions below about how to address that aspect.

1 Use small pockets of time in the day to sort out minor tasks

This is a key strategy for effective time management. Use time waiting in queues, on a bus or even waiting for the kettle to boil to recap on your learning, formulate lists, work out a problem, etc.

$E = a^2 + ...$

Keep a pencil and small notebook with detachable pages nearby to jot down your ideas. Make a mental note of the times in the day when you could multi-task in this way. This strategy also reduces the stress associated with queuing and tedious tasks.

2 Motivation to 'get going'

We saw in Chapter 1 how important motivation is to success. If you do not feel motivated, then be active in finding a source of motivation or inspiration. Focus on your long-term goals: check these are still important to you. Remind yourself of the benefits you expect. Write these where you can see them. Set short-term targets that you can manage, so that you get frequent tastes of success.

3 Time tasks

Time management requires you to know how long something takes. This is easier if you break a larger project down into smaller tasks. Often, one or two of these will take longer than you expect. It may be aspects of starting and finishing tasks that take longer than expected. Plan for all stages, and find out how much time you need to allocate for each stage.

4 Cost your time

Work out whether the amount of time you spend on each aspect of a task is 'cost-effective'. Usually the return (such as extra marks) decreases after a certain point. Academic work is hard to get perfect, as there isn't usually a single right answer. If you gain satisfaction from the additional study time, that is fine, as long as you have calculated what you are giving up in exchange.

5 Say 'no'

Identify what lies behind your difficulty in saying 'no'. It may be your beliefs, such as that 'a nice person' always helps out. If so, think what it means to be kind to yourself. Also, what are the negative

Of all the donkeys, Geoffrey found it the hardest to say 'No'.

consequences of always saying 'yes'? For example, does this give other people a chance to be kind or to take full responsibility? Alternatively, this might be a question of assertiveness or negotiation (see Chapter 6). There may be very long-standing or domestic issues which contribute to your difficulty in saying 'no'. If so, you should speak to a student counsellor.

6 Delegate to others

Identify what lies beneath a reluctance to delegate. For example, do you distrust others to do the job well? If so, what are the effects of this on your own time management, stress levels and personal efficiency? What would be the benefits to you and to others if you delegated more? How will others learn to do a job well if you do not delegate? Could you find a compromise where you share some tasks in the shorter term?

7 Ask for help

Recognise your own limits. Support services are set up because it is expected that people will need help. This is especially true for students. Asking friends and colleagues for help can contribute to their own personal development too. It can build their self-esteem and problem-solving skills. It gives them an opportunity to be helpful, which they may value.

8 and 9 Starting strategies

Use a basic starting strategy such as brainstorming or writing a list. Start with what you can do – and work from there. Often, a problem arises when we focus too much on what the end product should be rather than building from what we already know. Start small. Branch out. The ideas will come. If not, look for ideas in Chapters 5, 7 or 8.

10 and 11 Use a diary

A diary is an essential life tool. Some people prefer electronic organisers. Choose one that is light enough to carry around at all times. Check it at least three times a day. Develop the habit of writing everything in it to avoid double-booking. Enter all targets. Enter deadlines on the date of the deadline *and* the day you want to start work on that assignment.

Student Day Planner

Early morning (to do before I leave home)

Time	Task	Place/Room	With	Bring/Say/Do
8:00–9:00				
9:00–10:00				
10:00–11:00				
11:00–12:00				
12:00–1:00				
1:00–2:00				
2:00–3:00				
3:00–4:00				
4:00–5:00				
5:00–6:00				
Early evening				
Night				
Preparation for tomorrow (must do)				

12 Plan activities out in a logical order

Write a list of all the tasks you need to undertake during the day. Re-write the list, grouping the activities by place. Allow sufficient time to move from one place to another. Write the locations in your diary.

Student Day Planner

The Student Day Planner (shown on p. 80) divides time into sections most commonly used by students. Block in all your lectures, seminars, tutorials, workshops, lab-sessions, and assignment deadlines for each term or semester and then copy it. This saves writing it out several times. Indicate the room, the lecturer, and any materials you have to bring with you, so the information is easy to find.

Things that get forgotten

- The time it takes to travel between appointments – mark that in.
- The time when work for a deadline should begin – rather than just the deadline itself.
- New locations. These may be hard to find. Plan to leave time for getting lost.
- Queuing time.
- Transport delays. These are not usually accepted as excuses unless they are very rare with unusual circumstances.
- Information technology going wrong; waiting to use a shared printer, etc.

Time management for academic work is covered in more detail in *The Study Skills Handbook* (Cottrell, 2008).

Attitudes

Up to a point, every man is what he thinks he is.

F. H. Bradley

What's in a thought?

No two people respond in the same way to the same event. One person may be angry and determined to take action if something goes wrong; a second may shrug and forget it; a third may feel it is 'yet another example of why there is no point trying'. Our thinking about an event influences our response to it and the outcome. Our thoughts shape our experience, affecting what we feel physically and emotionally, how we interpret events, how we respond in a crisis and how we direct our lives.

Taking responsibility

One of the first steps in managing a situation is taking responsibility for oneself as an active, thinking, creative agent within the process. It may well be the case that 'someone' should have acted better, or may even be to blame for what happened. Taking responsibility does not mean excusing or taking the blame for somebody else's actions. It means moving beyond the 'blame' to find the most constructive outcome possible. The responsibility here is to yourself.

Often, the internal story that we create around events focuses on what went wrong and whose fault it was rather than on finding the best outcome. We run 'pre-recorded messages' about 'they' or 'it ', such as:

The Big Bad 'they'

- they make me . . .
- they should take the first step . . .
- they shouldn't put me in this position . . .
- they shouldn't set these deadlines . . .
- they should help me more . . .
- they started it . . .
- they design these so badly . . .

The Big Bad 'it'

- it is too difficult . . .
- it is too soon . . .
- it is too complex . . .
- it overwhelms me . . .
- 'it's doing my head in' . . .
- it won't work . . .
- it's a waste of time . . .
- it keeps doing this wrong . . .

> **Reflection**   The pre-recorded message
>
> - Which 'it' do you tend to blame (if any)?
> - Which 'they' do you tend to blame (if any)?
> - What other responses do you make when things go wrong that avoid taking personal responsibility for a constructive outcome?

Constructive messages

We can create alternative messages that lead to more productive outcomes. For example:

- I can do this . . .
- It's OK. There is a way of dealing with this.
- We can find a solution.
- In the circumstances, the best step is . . .
- The first step is . . .
- I take responsibility for my part in this.
- I'll have a go.

If we repeat these often enough, these become new 'pre-recorded messages' that will kick in automatically.

Activity: Change the message

- Write down five constructive responses you could use when things go wrong.
- Check that these enable you to take responsibility for yourself.
- Choose the *one* you like the most and write it where you will see it this week. Try it out and record what happens

Self-belief

Belief in oneself and one's own capabilities is essential. Low self-esteem creates stress, which makes the brain less efficient. It is also more likely to encourage a sense of defeat and a belief that there is 'no point'.

Self-confidence, a belief that one has the right to be and think and do what one wants, subject to reasonable limits and concern for others, enhances performance. It motivates and drives you forward.

Reflection   Self-belief critical incident

In your reflective journal, jot down a list of things you have done, no matter how small, that you are pleased about or proud of. Then, choose one to think about in more detail. Jot down:

- What happened? What did you do or say?
- What were the consequences? How did you or others benefit from this situation?
- What personal characteristics are demonstrated in this incident?
- What can you find in this incident that should make you feel good about yourself?

Activity: Self-descriptions

- Brainstorm a list of 30 things that you like about yourself.

1. tall
2. handsome
3. flexible
4. manages change well . . .

- Go through your list, and underline all those that contain a positive description: 'I'm a reliable person', 'I am kind', 'I am helpful', etc.
- If there are fewer than 30 such positive phrases, add more to your list until there are 30. Don't underestimate yourself. If any phrases contain the words 'I try to . . .' or 'I am quite . . .', reword these so they are more definite and positive.

Which three descriptions of yourself do you like the best? What reasons have you for believing that these descriptions are accurate?

It is also attractive to other people. This can bring more interest, resources and support, increasing the likelihood of success.

Self-permission

Sometimes, we are unable to move forward because we refuse to give ourselves 'permission'. It is as if we hear a pre-recorded message saying:

- 'I'm not allowed';
- 'I'm not good enough';
- 'I'm not worthy of the risk';
- 'I'm not deserving of the consequences';
- 'I'm not made for this sort of thing';
- 'I'm not strong enough to cope with failure';
- 'It's not me'.

This can be true of anybody, but it is especially the case if there were strong messages at school or in the family that encouraged low expectations.

Activity: Permission

Take three minutes each to complete the following two lists. Write quickly, without analysing your responses as you write.

List 1
I am allowed to . . . (write as many things as you can think of).

List 2
I am not allowed to . . . (write as many things as you can think of).

Check back over your two lists and see if you can spot any themes.

● What sorts of things are you 'allowed' to do?
● What sorts of things are you 'not allowed' to do?
● Which list is longer? What might be the reason for that?
● Who says 'you are not allowed to . . .'? Is it really true that you do not have permission to achieve in these areas?

From this activity, you may recognise messages from a long time ago that are still echoing in the present. Many of the 'permissions' we refuse ourselves today began a long time ago. These do not have to remain as barriers to achievement. Take a look at your list and identify those on the 'I am not allowed' list that you could transfer to the 'I am allowed' list. Write these down.

Taking a solution-focused approach

> *Whenever you are asked if you can do a job, tell 'em,*
> *Certainly I can! – and get busy and find out how to do it.*

Theodore Roosevelt

Solution-focused versus difficulty-focused thinking

Difficulty-focused thinking
Focusing on the difficulty usually produces negative responses: the problem can seem insoluble. It depletes your own and other people's emotional and physical energy, creating a sense of weariness, hopelessness or helplessness. The dominant message is that the problem is difficult, it will be hard work to find a solution, and solutions are unlikely. The difficulty-focused approach uses words and phrases such as:

● 'but . . .'
● 'I can't see how . . .'
● 'oh no!', 'not again!'
● 'it's hard to believe . . .'
● 'that won't work'
● 'I doubt it'.

At worst, difficulty-focused people tend to pick fault with every proposal, draw attention to flaws in the best possible solution, and discourage others from believing that there could be a sensible solution.

A solution-focused approach
A solution-focused approach describes the situation, identifies the points of difficulty, and

moves quickly to a search for the best possible resolution. It uses words and phrases such as:

- 'yes, and we could also . . .'
- 'what if we . . . ?'
- 'are there other ways of looking at this?'
- 'let's brainstorm ideas . . .'
- 'let's look again at our options . . .'
- 'let's see if we have missed any options . . .'
- 'let's check whether we can make this work . . .'
- 'what could we adapt?'
- 'who else would know about this . . . ?'

The dominant message is that a solution of one kind or another will have to be found eventually, even if it is an interim one, so it is better to focus energies on finding the solution sooner rather than later. A solution-focused approach is often expected of those in managerial roles. As most graduates enter jobs with managerial responsibilities, it is worth developing this approach. If you have been surrounded by people who take a difficulty-focused approach, you might find this a useful challenge.

> ### 📖 *Reflection*   Solution focus
>
> - Do you tend to use the words and phrases associated with a 'difficulty-focused' approach or a 'solution-focused' approach?
> - Which words and phrases are typical of you when faced with a complex situation?
> - Do you tend to employ a solution-focused approach?
> - What could you do to develop a more solution-focused attitude?

Ways of addressing a new challenge

Lazarus (1999) identifies two main strategies for approaching a difficulty: 'problem-focused coping' and 'emotion-focused' coping:

- problem-focused: looking outwards to the external, concrete problem and its circumstances;
- emotion-focused: looking inwards at personal attitudes and emotions that impact upon your individual reaction to the situation.

A solution-focused approach can use either approach, adopting a constructive and positive attitude for either. The solution-focused approach takes the position that there is a solution to every problem and that we have that solution within us. Sometimes, we arrive at the solution more easily if we talk to others or use a particular strategy. The 'solution' is the best constructive outcome that can be found for the situation in the circumstances. This may not be everything that we would like, but it directs energy in a positive way so that the best outcome possible is achieved.

A solution-focused approach requires very little, beyond an attitude of mind.

Changing your environment

A negative, blaming, 'can't be bothered' environment is not inspiring. A few people with such approaches can spread negativity very easily. They can even create a culture which is self-defeating. You can probably think of the people around you who create an aura of negativity. (Maybe you are that person?)

As adults, we can monitor the impact of our environment on our responses, taking note of what leaves us feeling encouraged and what does not. We can take action to create an environment around us that supports what we want to achieve.

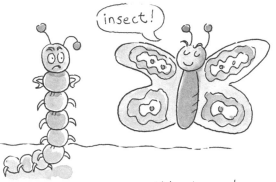

It wasn't what Cuthbert said as much as the way he said it.

Identify positive inputs

- Identify the people around you who leave you feeling positive about your goals, direction or programme of study.
- What is it about them that seems to increase positive responses?

- What other things in the environment support your goal? Competition and constructive criticism can be included as positive inputs.

Jot down these factors, starting with 'I . . .', and identifying how you could increase the positive aspects of your environment. For example:

I appreciate the way Busola makes a point of saying she enjoys good seminars. I could identify the things I find positive about each seminar.

I find it useful that the library is open until 8:00 p.m. I could use it more in the evening.

Identify negative inputs
- Which people leave you feeling dejected, anxious, tired, despondent?

- What do you feel or do when you are in the presence of negative attitudes?
- What factors in your current environment could undermine or sabotage your goals?
- What can you do to reduce the impact of such factors upon you?

Emotional intelligence

Evaluating your emotional intelligence

The following activity enables you to evaluate your emotional intelligence. This is not a scientific test: emotions do not lend themselves easily to such testing. However, it gives you an opportunity to reflect upon your emotional life through a structured activity.

Activity: Evaluating your emotional intelligence

1. Emotional management (self)

For each item, identify which one response is most true for you, indicating this with a tick. ✓

Item	Always true	Usually true	Occasionally true	Not true	Don't know
1. I know which emotions I am experiencing	☐	☐	☐	☐	☐
2. I am aware of my emotions	☐	☐	☐	☐	☐
3. I allow myself to feel emotional	☐	☐	☐	☐	☐
4. I take notice of my emotions	☐	☐	☐	☐	☐
5. I can name the emotions I am feeling	☐	☐	☐	☐	☐
6. I tell other people what I am feeling	☐	☐	☐	☐	☐
7. I take responsibility for my own feelings	☐	☐	☐	☐	☐
8. I know what triggers different kinds of emotion in me	☐	☐	☐	☐	☐
9. I can respond without being overwhelmed by emotion	☐	☐	☐	☐	☐
10. I can express the right amount of feeling for the circumstances	☐	☐	☐	☐	☐
11. I can be assertive rather than aggressive or passive whilst feeling emotional	☐	☐	☐	☐	☐
12. I know when my feelings are not being expressed	☐	☐	☐	☐	☐
13. I make opportunities to express my feelings after an event, if needed	☐	☐	☐	☐	☐

Activity: Evaluating your emotional intelligence *(continued)*

Item	Always true	Usually true	Occasionally true	Not true	Don't know
14. I know the ways that my feelings affect my performance	☐	☐	☐	☐	☐
15. I regularly talk about my feelings to somebody I trust	☐	☐	☐	☐	☐
16. I reflect upon my feelings					
17. I allow myself to feel 'small' or vulnerable at times	☐	☐	☐	☐	☐
18. I cry if I need to					
19. I will allow myself to withdraw from a situation in order to experience my feelings, where feasible	☐	☐	☐	☐	☐
20. I am aware of how my feelings are affected by the people around me	☐	☐	☐	☐	☐

2. Emotional management (others)

For each item, identify which one response is most true for you, indicating this with a tick. ✓

Item	Always true	Usually true	Occasionally true	Not true	Don't know
1. I know which emotions other people are experiencing	☐	☐	☐	☐	☐
2. I am aware of other people's feelings	☐	☐	☐	☐	☐
3. I allow other people to feel their emotions	☐	☐	☐	☐	☐
4. I take notice of other people's emotions	☐	☐	☐	☐	☐
5. I can name the emotions other people are feeling	☐	☐	☐	☐	☐
6. I speak to other people about their feelings	☐	☐	☐	☐	☐
7. I take responsibility for my own feelings when other people are feeling emotional	☐	☐	☐	☐	☐
8. I know what triggers emotional responses in people I see regularly	☐	☐	☐	☐	☐
9. I am aware of my own responses to other people's emotions	☐	☐	☐	☐	☐
10. I allow others to express what they feel is right for the circumstances	☐	☐	☐	☐	☐

Item	Always true	Usually true	Occasionally true	Not true	Don't know
11. I can be assertive when other people are being aggressive, passive or emotional	☐	☐	☐	☐	☐
12. I am aware when other people are not expressing their feelings	☐	☐	☐	☐	☐
13. I make opportunities to enable other people to express their feelings	☐	☐	☐	☐	☐
14. I am aware of how I let other people's feelings affect my performance	☐	☐	☐	☐	☐
15. I regularly listen to someone I know well talking about their feelings	☐	☐	☐	☐	☐
16. I reflect upon the way feelings are experienced and expressed in groups	☐	☐	☐	☐	☐
17. I allow other people to feel 'small' or vulnerable	☐	☐	☐	☐	☐
18. I am comfortable when others cry if they need to	☐	☐	☐	☐	☐
19. I understand when other people withdraw from a situation in order to experience their feelings	☐	☐	☐	☐	☐
20. I am aware of how my feelings affect the people around me	☐	☐	☐	☐	☐

3. Emotions in action

For each item, identify which one response is most true for you, indicating this with a tick.

Item	Always true	Usually true	Occasionally true	Not true	Don't know
1. I feel comfortable even when people disagree with me	☐	☐	☐	☐	☐
2. I can allow other people their own opinions	☐	☐	☐	☐	☐
3. I can feel angry without taking it out on others	☐	☐	☐	☐	☐
4. I can accept criticism without getting angry	☐	☐	☐	☐	☐
5. I can voice my own opinions	☐	☐	☐	☐	☐
6. I am able to remain positive even when the situation looks gloomy	☐	☐	☐	☐	☐

Activity: Evaluating your emotional intelligence *(continued)*

Item	Always true	Usually true	Occasionally true	Not true	Don't know
7. I can allow myself to be sad – and to experience the sadness without pushing it away	☐	☐	☐	☐	☐
8. I can make decisions and act upon them	☐	☐	☐	☐	☐
9. I can stop and assess a situation before I act or speak	☐	☐	☐	☐	☐
10. I feel comfortable working with people from very different backgrounds to mine	☐	☐	☐	☐	☐
11. I can enjoy diversity in the people around me	☐	☐	☐	☐	☐
12. I will speak out for what I believe is right	☐	☐	☐	☐	☐
13. I ask for help when I need it	☐	☐	☐	☐	☐
14. I can let myself feel emotions without taking a drink, cigarette, drug, or comfort eating	☐	☐	☐	☐	☐
15. I am calm in a crisis	☐	☐	☐	☐	☐
16. I can identify when my behaviour is unreasonable – and stop it	☐	☐	☐	☐	☐
17. I can manage uncertainty without having to have an answer straight away	☐	☐	☐	☐	☐
18. I can manage my emotions under pressure	☐	☐	☐	☐	☐
19. I take responsibility for my own part in events	☐	☐	☐	☐	☐
20. I can admit a mistake and apologise	☐	☐	☐	☐	☐

Scoring your responses

For each item on the above sets of questions, allocate to yourself the following scores: Always true (4); Usually true (3); Occasionally true (2); Not true (1); Don't know (0).

1. Emotional management (self):   Score _____

2. Emotional management (others): Score _____

3. Emotions in action: Score _____

Total score: _____

Interpreting your scores

150–200   If your answers are accurate, this suggests that you have a sophisticated approach to emotional life. You seem capable of managing your own emotions as well as coping with the emotions of other people. You seem able to make the kinds of responses that accompany emotional intelligence. Your emotional intelligence should provide you with an asset in almost any situation.

100–149   This is a good score. If your evaluations are accurate, you have a very good foundation for developing your emotional intelligence further. Emotional intelligence is an asset in most situations so this is very much worth doing. Look at the responses which have high scores: what do these tell you about your strengths? Are there any themes evident in the questions that received lower scores? It is worth noting whether one of the three sections had a lower score than the others. Identify which of these is your priority for further self-development.

50–99   This is a reasonable score, especially if you entered university straight from school. However, it suggests that you have lots of room to develop your emotional management skills. If your evaluation is accurate, you would benefit from making emotional self-management a priority area. Identify which areas are your strengths. These are the assets you take into most situations. Look for themes in the lower scores. Which types of issues are most relevant to the achievement of your goals? Identify which of these is your priority for further self-development.

0–49   If your evaluation is accurate, you may have a real challenge on your hands. Remember that this is not a scientific test. There may be many areas of emotional intelligence in which you excel that are not covered by this activity. For example, some people are exceptional in crises – but there is only one question related to managing a crisis above. Other people are emotionally sophisticated with particular types of people, such as children, the elderly, sick people, etc. In addition, your evaluation may have been harsh. On the other hand, you may really feel that the emotional world is rather a tricky one. You may feel that people misunderstand you or your motives much of the time. You are not alone if you feel that. However, it is not necessarily a very comfortable position to be in. The good news is that emotional intelligence is an asset that can be developed. The student counselling service at the university will probably be able to give you confidential advice if you are at all concerned.

What is emotional intelligence?

'Emotional intelligence' is a term made current by Goleman (1995). It is slowly becoming recognised that it isn't simply what we do and what we think that affects our ability to cope, manage and succeed, but also how we manage our feelings.

Emotional intelligence involves:

● knowing the appropriate feelings for the circumstances;
● experiencing the appropriate feelings for the circumstances;
● expressing feelings appropriate to the circumstances;
● making opportunities to express feelings that cannot be expressed fully in the original circumstances.

This may sound easy. However, your reflections above may have indicated to you that emotions often get in the way of a rational interpretation of a situation. They tend to prevent us from working towards the best or most constructive solution to the issues. In general, people tend to over-express their feelings (excessive anger, passivity, distress and so forth) or to bottle up their feelings in order to cope. Different circumstances permit a different level of expression. We need to consider such matters as:

● What response will lead to the most constructive outcome?
● How will other people respond?
● What are other people's needs?

Example ABC model for dealing with distress

A *Activating event*   The 'activating event' might be that a student, Gareth, has not read the course handbook. As a result, he did not realise that two essay deadlines fell on the same day. He asked for an extension, but was refused as it was not possible in the circumstances. Gareth must complete both essays in five days. If not, he will need to retake a module. The situation is not easy.

B *Beliefs*   Gareth can make a decision to work flat out to produce two essays, possibly accepting lower marks, or he can defer one of the modules and increase the possibility of higher marks for both in the long term. This would take a few months longer, but is feasible. However, Gareth argues that he is 'totally stupid' to have got into this situation and that this is typical of the mess he makes of his 'whole life'. He links the current problem with difficulties he experiences elsewhere so that the issue is no longer a missed deadline (which can be managed) but everything about his life. He does not believe he can write the essays as he has convinced himself that nothing he does will work.

C *Consequences*   The consequences are that Gareth's beliefs lock him into inaction. All of his energies are diverted into self-blame and hopelessness. He feels very small and is too embarrassed to talk to his friends. Instead of using his time to write the essays, he wastes time worrying or drinking, trying to push the problem away. Because he is stressed, he finds it difficult to concentrate. He can't study or make sense of what he reads. He misses his shift for his part-time job, making his overall situation even worse – convincing him further that his 'life' is a problem.

D *Dealing with it*   What could you do if you found yourself in a similar situation? In this case, it is beliefs that are fuelling the distress and leading to unhelpful consequences. You could either focus on the problem so as to divert yourself from the beliefs, or change the beliefs.

If you focus on the problem, you can:

● Describe the activating event, reducing it to the basics. Acknowledge what went wrong and what has been learnt. Yes, Gareth should have read the handbook. However, he is unlikely to make this mistake again, and this could be a critical lesson from which he learns and gains in the longer term. He is far from being the only student to get into such a position.
● Consider what has to be done. List all your options. Find out what these are and write them down. Write the advantages of each option. Then consider the feasibility and consequences of each.
● Move as quickly as possible into 'problem-solving mode', using a problem-solving strategy (see Chapter 5). Brainstorm options for solving the core problem. Evaluate these and choose one.
● Make a decision – and then stick to it and accept the consequences. The consequences might not be ideal, but they can be the 'best possible' for the situation. They are not life-threatening or catastrophic in the larger picture.
● Develop an action plan and follow it.

To challenge unhelpful beliefs:

● Write down words that motivate you, such as: 'there is a solution' or 'I can do this'.
● List your negative thoughts (beliefs). Go through the list, undertaking a 'reality check'. Ask 'Is this belief going to help me find a solution?'
● Challenge all beliefs that start with 'I should have . . .' or 'I always . . .'.
● Challenge all beliefs that refer to any other situation except the current problem.
● Cross out, with a thick line, all beliefs that do not help achieve a solution to the current situation.
● Brainstorm constructive phrases or messages until you find at least one that seems both helpful and true to you. Underline that belief or idea three times. Put a line through all the others.
● Speak to a friend or counsellor to put the situation into perspective.

Managing change, confusion and uncertainty

Activity: Approaches to change

For each item, identify which one response is most true for you, indicating this with a tick.

Characteristic	Always true	Usually true	Occasionally true	Not true
1. I enjoy change	☐	☐	☐	☐
2. I look for the opportunities in new situations and circumstances	☐	☐	☐	☐
3. I feel comfortable meeting new people	☐	☐	☐	☐
4. I am confident about coping in new surroundings	☐	☐	☐	☐
5. I welcome new perspectives on an issue or problem	☐	☐	☐	☐
6. I ask people for feedback	☐	☐	☐	☐
7. I can change my plans at the last minute without feeling stressed	☐	☐	☐	☐
8. I can study reasonably well in a wide range of circumstances	☐	☐	☐	☐
9. I enjoy starting new subjects or projects	☐	☐	☐	☐
10. I will work early or late at short notice	☐	☐	☐	☐

Scoring your responses

For each item, allocate to yourself the following scores:
Always true (3);   Usually true (2);   Occasionally true (1);   Not true (0)

Score _____

Reflecting on your score

24–30 This suggests you have a very strong and positive approach to change. What beneficial characteristics does this enable you to bring to study? How would this be of benefit in a work context? Do you look for change at the expense of continuity?

16–23 This suggests you have a positive approach to change. What beneficial characteristics does this enable you to bring to study? How would this be of benefit in a work context?

8–15 This suggests that you have an ambivalent approach to change. You can be positive about change. What benefits could you gain from developing a more positive approach?

0–7 Your score suggests a strong preference for continuity. You may need to be creative to find work and circumstances that enable you to maintain this level of continuity. It may be helpful to talk through your resistance to change with a counsellor. What disadvantages does your resistance to change bring you? Is there one area where you could develop greater flexibility?

Position 2: Relativism stages (Approaches 3 and 4 on the activity above)

4.   Acceptable uncertainty: 'Everyone has a right to their own opinion', despite what teachers or leaders might think. For assignments, it is important to find out the lecturers' opinions.

5.   'All knowledge and value are contextual and relative.' For assignments, students should enquire: 'What is required of me in this context?'

Position 3: Commitment stages (Approaches 5 and 6 on the activity above)

6.   Personal orientation: you feel it is necessary to make a commitment to certain viewpoints (out of a range of possibilities) with an understanding of, and tolerance for, other viewpoints.

7.   You have made a commitment to certain viewpoints.

8.   The implications of your commitment have been experienced and you realise the responsibilities this brings.

9.   You regard your commitment to your views as 'an on-going, unfolding activity' through which your lifestyle and identity are expressed.

📖 *Reflection*   Managing uncertainty

● What are your expectations of your lecturers? Do you expect them to provide, or lead you towards, a 'right answer'?

● How comfortable do you feel with the idea that there may not be 'right answers' to questions that are important to you?

● How open are you to hearing opinions that contradict your own?

If this subject interests you, ask your tutors for literature that discusses the nature of 'truth' or 'fact' or 'right answers' in your subject area.

Changing position

Perry found that it can take years for students to feel comfortable at stages 7–9 of this hierarchy. You may find you are in very different positions on the hierarchy depending on the issue.

You do not have to agree that Perry's hierarchy applies to every question. However, the hierarchy can be a useful tool for evaluating the nature of your own responses to issues, and your readiness to accept uncertainty on an issue. You will know how comfortable or uncomfortable you feel about applying any particular stage to your own ideas. You may need a greater knowledge of all the issues and the consequences of taking a particular position in a wide range of circumstances in order to change position on the hierarchy.

It can be hard to feel comfortable at levels 4–9 on some issues unless your sense of self, your beliefs or

your values also change. There isn't a 'quick fix' to changing the way we think. However, being aware of how we are thinking and responding can help the process of development.

You can also use Perry's hierarchy to help you understand where other people are in their thinking. It is important to be sensitive to where people are situated: you cannot force people into a different set of beliefs.

Transitional learning and 'disequilibrium'

Issues discussed in higher education may not have 'right' answers. There may be several answers or it may depend on how particular evidence is assessed, or there may be insufficient evidence to come to a firm conclusion. Some issues discussed at this level will directly challenge what you have learnt before, or seem to contradict views that you or people close to you hold as valuable. This can be unsettling or confusing.

📖 *Reflection*   Confusion

● Do you feel that you are finding it harder to learn since starting university level study?

● Do you ever feel that you are more confused about what an issue involves when you find out more about it?

● Do you feel you are going backwards the more you learn?

● How does this make you feel? Do you think you are really 'going backwards'?

'Equilibration'

Saven-Baden (2000) uses the term 'transitional learning' to refer to 'shifts' that occur when students' frames of reference, or 'life world' are challenged by their learning, especially as the result of critical reflection. You may feel this at certain times when you move onto a higher level of learning. Saven-Baden decribes this state as: 'characterised by frustration and confusion, and a loss of sense of self'.

This suggests that we can interpret some confusion as a healthy sign. It indicates that we are pushing ourselves, our learning, our knowledge, our skills beyond their former level. In other words, we are not stagnating. Piaget (1975) regarded this process of 'equilibration' as essential to our development. Equilibration occurs in three stages:

1. Equilibrium: first there is a state of satisfaction with our current ways of thinking and doing.

2. Disequilibrium: then we gain a sense of growing dissatisfaction and an awareness of the limitations of our existing ways of thinking and doing. This is the stage where confusion and worry can set in.

3. A more stable equilibrium: finally, if we persist in our enquiries, we can move to a more sophisticated way of thinking that overcomes the limitations of our previous thinking and performance.

Siegler (1991) cites the example of a child who thinks that only animals are living things. When she hears plants referred to as being 'alive', she becomes uncertain of what 'alive' means. This uncertainty, although temporarily uncomfortable, is a necessary stage in opening up to a new understanding of the world. Dissatisfaction begins an internal questioning which then opens us up to exploring new options.

For students to progress to more sophisticated ways of thinking, they need to be receptive to disequilibrium and to be able to manage or 'contain' short-term confusion. Otherwise, they may cling to the 'security' of their former equilibrium.

📖 Reflection   Coping with disequilibrium

- Think back to a time when you felt you would never learn something – but did. What was it that was difficult to learn?
- How did you manage to work through the 'confusion' or disheartened stage to the stage where you had achieved your goal?
- What was it like to be successful in the end?
- How well do you feel you can manage the 'disequilibrium stage' as a student? What kind of support would help?

Holding the uncertainty

When we feel uncertain or confused, we lose our sense of equilibrium. Naturally, this makes us want to find our 'balance' again. The temptation is to act too quickly, rushing in to find a solution so that we feel better. Often, this leads to hasty action which limits our possibilities.

Although it may feel uncomfortable, it is important to learn to experience the feelings of discomfort and to 'sit with them' for a while, whilst we find out more about the situation. We need to:

- acknowledge the feeling of discomfort or anxiety;
- allow ourselves to wait before rushing into action;
- find help and support if we need it – talking to somebody can help;

- find out more about the idea or situation that challenges us;
- aim to understand what it is that we find so challenging – and look for potential opportunities;
- consider our options, preferably within a problem-solving strategy;
- act when we have weighed up the options.

Not everyone appreciated Gary's capacity to sit with uncertainty until he had weighed up all options carefully

---

📖 *Reflection*   Managing uncertainty

In your reflective journal, jot down your responses to the following questions.

- What kinds of uncertainty have you been faced with recently?
- What was your response?
- In retrospect, do you think you could have managed this uncertainty differently or more constructively?
- Did you look for any support in managing this uncertainty? If not, what stopped you?
- What could you do to improve the way you manage uncertainty?

Using Motivators and Inhibitors to manage personal performance

We are all subject to influences that either enhance our performance, or else inhibit our progress. You have already had the chance to identify a number of such factors in Chapter 3, 'Understanding your personal performance'. Here, you have an opportunity to build upon that understanding by applying a framework for analysing a broader set of influences. This can provide further insights that you can use to help manage aspects of personal performance.

Dilts et al. (1990) offered a six-level framework for exploring factors that can inhibit or promote learning. The framework below adapts Dilts's model, using eight levels to analyse performance.

Levels of inhibition and motivation (adapted from Dilts et al., 1990)

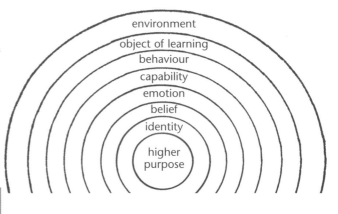

The 'Eight Levels' framework

The Eight Levels framework enables us to look at performance from different perspectives. Items nearer to the core, such as 'higher purpose' and 'identity', are considered to have greatest impact and are referred to as 'higher level'. If positively engaged, these higher level motivators can go a long way towards overriding negative impacts, or 'inhibitors', at lower levels. It is as though the 'core' has a greater gravitational pull on our energies. By analysing your experience in this way, you can identify for any task (or in general):

- at which level you feel the 'inhibitors' lie for you;

- at which level the 'motivators' lie for you;
- ways of managing inhibitors so as that your experience is better and/or personal performance improved.

1. Environmental (where? when? with whom?)

As we saw in Chapter 3, 'Understanding your personal performance', the context in which we learn and take action can have a profound effect . 'Environment' *here* can refer to the wider social, cultural or ideological context or the immediate physical environment such as the lighting or background distractions. If you are strongly motivated or inhibited on a task at the environmental level, this may be evident in what you emphasise when speaking (as in the italics below):

'I love doing this/I can't do it *in this room*, with *this light, with people like these, at an institution like this*.''

Managing performance at the environmental level

If this sounds like you, consider what you can do to change the environment to suit your needs. Your responses to the activities in Chapter 3 may be useful in considering this issue. Environmental sensitivity can be caused by past trauma or current stress, so investigating those issues could also help.

> **Reflection** Environmental motivators and inhibitors
>
> - How relevant do you think environmental factors are to your own performnance in a particular area, either in motivating you or in preventing excellent performance?
> - In what ways do these affect your performance?
> - How can you better manage any negative impact or make more use of positive impacts?

2. The 'nature of the task' or 'content' (what?)

If you find you can usually perform in a given environment, but that you don't seem able to learn a particular subject or perform a specific task there, the difficulty would appear to lie with the content of what you are learning or the nature of the task rather than at the environmental level. If so, this is likely to be evident in comments such as:

'I can't learn *that*'; 'what's *this* supposed to be about?'; '*this* is what I call nonsense'.

Managing performance at the 'task' level

If you aren't able to change the overall task or subject, look for ways to change the way it is framed or worded. For example:

- look for a different way of thinking about the task;
- break the task into manageable sections;
- rephrase instructions;
- put things into your own words;
- imagine you are explaining the issue to someone much younger;
- look for real-life examples that are similar;
- sketch the problem as a chart, diagram or picture.

> **Reflection** Task-related motivators and inhibitors
>
> - How relevant do you think the nature of the task is in the way it affects your performance in a particular area, either in motivating you or preventing excellent performance?
> - Is it a motivator or inhibitor for your own performance?
> - In what ways does it affect your performance?
> - How can you better manage any negative impact?

3. Behaviours (what do we do?)

You may feel you want one thing, but behave as if you want something else. For example, students usually want good grades for their work but may not study in ways that develop their knowledge and understanding sufficiently. These behaviours may be the result of peer pressure, unhelpful habits, poor induction into a job or programme, lack of awareness of what is expected, etc. There can be all kinds of reasons for counter-productive behaviours but if you are motivated by behavioural change, that is the focus for action. If, for you, the issue is primarily behavioural, this is likely to be expressed in speech that emphasises verbs ('doing words'):

'I can't *learn* or *do* that'; '*writing* essays is too difficult'; 'it takes me too long *to do* that'.

If you are motivated at this level, you may notice that typical responses from you include phrases such as:

'I'll *do it*'; 'I'll *have a go*'; 'I want *to get on with it*'.

Managing performance at the behavioural level

Managing behaviour at the performance level means that you address the behaviours directly, looking for ways of changing how you act or respond, rather than using an analysis of why the behaviour occurs to find a way forward. It can feel motivating if you feel you have the power to adapt your responses in ways that produce the outcomes you want. Some actions you can take are:

● Become aware of contradictory behaviours – ask a blunt friend, partner or sibling!
● Identify the trigger points – something you do that indicates to you or others that the unwanted behaviour or habit is about to kick in.
● Decide what you will do differently at that trigger point so as to initiate a different set of behaviours.
● Decide on appropriate rewards for particular changes in your actions.
● Ask a friend to prompt you if you don't spot the trigger.
● Make sure you do reward your successes in changing behaviour.

Counter-productive behaviours could indicate a lack of motivation for attaining the end goal. If a behavioural approach doesn't work, it is worth looking for solutions at one of the other levels. For example, it could be that the key inhibitor is at the environment level; tackling that directly might lead to a change in behaviour. Alternatively, the solution might lie in increased attention to one of the higher levels as outlined below.

> ### 📖 *Reflection* Behaviour as a motivator or inhibitor
>
> ● How relevant do you think your behaviour is in the way it affects your performance in a particular area, either in motivating you or preventing excellent performance?
> ● In what ways does if affect your performance?
> ● How could you change your behaviours in order to improve your performance?

4. Capability (how can I?)

If your prime difficulty in accomplishing a task lies at the capability level, you are likely to put the emphasis on words and phrases expressing ability:

'I'm *not able* to learn that'; 'I *don't know how* to learn that'; '*How can I* do that!'

If you are motivated at the capability level, you are likely to place emphasis on your ability to do something- or at least to have a go.

'*I can!*' '*I'm able to do all sorts of things!*' '*Let me!*' '*I've done this before* . . .'

Managing performance at the capability level

If you feel you are having difficulties because of lack of knowledge, ability, skills or experience, consider why you are not able to do what you wish:

● it could be lack of practice;
● it could be because you have not spent long enough building up a good foundation of knowledge and appropriate thinking skills: see Chapter 7 on the way the brain develops to support new learning;
● you may need to improve study skills;
● you may benefit from the section on 'Attitudes' above (p. 81);
● you may be in the 'transitional stage' referred to above (p. 96);
● you may work better at a different pace: many people find university programmes are very rushed;
● you may benefit from additional support and guidance.

Give yourself time to approach each task. Break bigger tasks into smaller, manageable targets. Find or set up a support group or action set (see Chapter 6).

5. Emotional (how do I feel about . . . ?)

If the primary difficulty lies at an emotional level, you may emphasise words that refer to emotions:

'I *feel* I'll never learn this.' 'This *irritates, angers, upsets* me.' 'I *don't feel good* about this situation'; '*I'm getting annoyed* by this essay!'

Alternatively, you may express emotions through tears or your behaviour. The emotion may be related simply to difficulties with current study. However, there is very often a link to earlier learning which was distressing in some way.

On the other hand, positive emotions can have a beneficial effect upon learning. Positive feelings about oneself, the learning context, the course, and potential outcomes can produce much higher motivation and make learning easier.

Managing performance at the level of emotions

Key factors in managing emotions are being able to recognise that your emotions are engaged in a negative way and that you need to address these. Pretending that they don't matter probably won't help much, unless action at other levels results in a change in those feelings. Examining your emotional intelligence as outlined above (pp. 85–9) can help.

If you do feel your feelings are getting in the way of you performing at your best, some basic steps you can take are:

- Don't push the emotions away; notice them, sit with them for a while; see if they change if you give them some attention.
- Consider whether there are some ways of approaching the task that would make you feel better.

- Query whether your emotions are in proportion: is this something that you can just 'shake off'?
- Consider whether you are displacing emotions (see p. 90). If so, what might the real emotional issue be?
- Consider using the ABC model to address these (p. 91).
- If the emotions persist, talk to someone about them.

6. Beliefs and values (why?)

Our belief systems exercise a strong hold over our learning. We use beliefs as a basis for action. Beliefs about self-worth and individual potential are especially powerful: some students have a deeply held belief that they 'not supposed to be' at university. Have you ever felt that you are 'not good enough', or 'people like me cannot do well at university level study'? Do you believe the subject you are studying is really worthwhile? If your primary difficulty lies at the belief level, this may be apparent in speech such as:

- 'I'm not likely to star at this subject';
- 'This is a soft option: I need to focus my attention on the other modules';
- 'It's only a discussion group so I don't need to turn up.'

There may also be a conflict between values and behaviours: 'Music is what is important to me, that's what I'd like to study, but I need a job at the end of this so, here I am, taking Business Studies.'

Managing performance at the level of beliefs and values

- Check whether you can reconnect with any

initial belief in the value of the task that might then help you through;

- Identify a source of motivation that makes sense in terms of your values and motivation (pp. 16–20; p. 24);
- Check whether there is consistency between your values, beliefs and actions (See *Congruence* p. 31);
- Challenge negative thinking (p. 82);
- Speak to someone who can give you useful and constructive advice about how to achieve your aims;
- Bear in mind that it can take time to change something as fundamental as our beliefs.

📖 ***Reflection***   Emotion as a motivator or inhibitor

- How relevant do you think your emotional responses are as key factors in particular areas of your own performance, either in motivating you or in preventing excellent performance?
- In what ways do they affect your performance?
- What could you do in order to manage your emotions better so as to improve your performance?

---

7. Identity (who am I?)

Some students, when they encounter difficulties, experience this at the identity level. They decide that they are 'the kind of person' who can't learn or doesn't perform well. They emphasise the 'I' in descriptions of their difficulties: '*I* can't learn it . . .' or even 'People *like me* can't . . .'.

Our sense of identity is very powerful, so if the primary difficulty is at the identity level, it is a good idea to address this as a priority.

Managing performance at the identity level

- Consider the positive aspects of your identity: what makes you who you are?
- How can you harness those positive aspects of your identity to help you accomplish the particular task or goal? What is it about you, or 'within you', that can make success possible?
- Do you identify with being:
  - a 'bad student';
  - a 'lost cause'

- 'mediocre' or 'average'
- 'the clown in the group'
- 'the one who sits at the back'
- 'not a scientist'
- a similar kind of negative identity?

If so, where did this sense of who you are come from? What can you do now to challenge that way of thinking about yourself?

If you are unsure of what your 'identity' is, it may help to work through selected aspects of Chapters 1 and 2, such as your vision for your life, your values, your life narrative and the kind of 'hero' you are in your own story (see pages 38–40). Don't get too tied down in the philosophical aspects of identity at this point.

📖 ***Reflection***   Identity as a motivator or inhibitor

- How relevant is your sense of your identity as a key factor in motivating you or preventing excellent performance?
- In what ways does if affect your performance?
- How could you make better use of your sense of who you are in order to better manage your performance?

---

8. Higher purpose or mission

'Higher purpose' and 'mission' refer to the overall direction and motivation that drive a person. This might be the good that you hope will stem from completing your degree, such as providing better for your family, being a role model, gaining more independence, entering a profession that matters to you, etc. As the term suggests, higher purpose is typically associated with ambition for something greater than self-centred desire – that is, it is 'higher than ourselves', such as:

- 'doing good'
- helping others
- 'making your life count'
- making a difference to your community, family, institution, country, sport, etc.
- creativity and artistic endeavour
- spirituality and/or religion.

Managing performance through 'higher purpose'

If you can find a relevant and meaningful connection between what you are doing and what really matters to you in terms of 'higher purpose', you are more likely to be well-motivated and to persevere through difficulties. Conversely, if there is never any space in your day to engage with what matters to you – or even to consider what that might be – then you lack an essential source of motivation and may eventually feel that life is frustrating or dull.

- What does 'really matter' to you? What would drive you to accomplish the most difficult of tasks if you really needed to?
- How or when do you provide space for that higher purpose in your life now?
- How or when could you enable more time to be given to what really matters to you?
- For tasks that you are finding problematic now, list some ways that you could change the way you think about these, or the way you perform them, so that they help you to connect with what really matters to you.

📖 **Reflection** 'Higher purpose' as a motivator or inhibitor

- How relevant is a sense of 'higher purpose' or mission in motivating you or preventing excellent performance?
- In what ways does this affect your performance?
- How could connecting to a sense of a higher purpose help to improve your performance?

📖 **Reflection** Identify your primary level for improvement

- Which of the previous levels do you think is most significant in its effects upon your learning and performance?
- Which levels have positive effects upon your studies or performance?
- To which levels do you most need to pay attention?

Closing comments

This chapter covers a great deal of ground. As with any issues that relate to intra-personal matters, it is not a chapter to race through and feel you have 'got it'.

Many of the exercises in this chapter can be repeated with specific issues or questions in mind. You will also find that the responses you give on a day when you wake up feeling confident and happy are very different from those you give on days when you feel more vulnerable. This is to be expected. The issues covered in this chapter provide useful material for further exploration through your reflective journal.

This chapter offered a basic introduction to some of the issues associated with personal self-management. The activities and strategies here may be all you will need for the issues that face you as a student and in your first graduate jobs. The chapter offers tools for analysing a situation quickly, for identifying resources, for managing your time, and for exploring your own mind-set. It offers strategies for developing a solution-focused, positive thinking style that can be applied in any circumstance, and not simply for study. It also offers you tools for beginning to analyse and understand emotional intelligence.

As a student, you are especially likely to experience times of uncertainty. A stimulating, higher-level education should be challenging. You should feel stretched. You should feel that occasionally the ground is moving beneath your feet. Confusion and uncertainty are characteristics of moving from 'novice' to more expert or sophisticated levels of thinking. If you know this, then you should be able to cope with that uncertainty without feeling something is very wrong.

(continued)

Closing comments

(continued)

Your intra-personal life is a rich source of information for you. It is one of the most important and valuable subjects you can ever study: you cannot know enough about the 'inner life' of your mind. The knowledge you gain about yourself and how you can best manage your own attitudes and thought processes will enable you to optimise your performance in any walk of life.

Further reading

Cottrell, S. M. (2008) *The Study Skills Handbook*, 3rd edn (Basingstoke: Palgrave Macmillan).

Cottrell, S. M. (2010; new edition annually) *The Palgrave Student Planner* (Basingstoke: Palgrave Macmillan).

Covey, S. R. (2004) *The Seven Habits of Highly Effective People: Powerful Lessons in Personal Change*, 15th Anniversary edn (London: Free Press).

Fennell, M. (2009) *Overcoming Low Self-esteem: A Self-Help Guide Using Cognitive Behavioural Techniques* (London: Robinson).

Goleman, D. (1995) *Emotional Intelligence* (London: Bloomsbury).

Heron, J. (1992) *Feeling and Personhood* (London: Sage Publications).

Neenan, M. and Dryden, W. (2002) *Life Coaching: A Cognitive–Behavioural Approach* (New York: Brunner-Routledge).

Chapter 5

Successful problem-solving and task management

A problem well stated is a problem half solved.

Charles F. Kettering

Learning outcomes

This chapter offers you opportunities to:

understand what is meant by problem-solving
develop techniques and approaches associated with successful problem-solving
develop the confidence to take on tasks, problems and projects
become a 'good self-starter'
understand the processes involved in basic project management
audit your own 'competitiveness'.

Introduction

Problem-solving is highly valued by employers. They want graduates to 'hit the ground running', able to apply skills to new situations and deal with new tasks with minimum supervision. Almost every activity, task or problem will draw on the following set of processes and skills:

1. Strategy: tactics and an overall plan.
2. Techniques: methods to use.
3. People skills: working with others in appropriate ways to achieve the goal.
4. Self-management: managing your time, personal issues, feelings and performance.
5. Creativity: finding ideas that contribute towards a solution.

People who are very good at problem-solving usually bring people skills, self-management and creativity to the task. These three factors are so important that they each have chapters dedicated to them. This chapter introduces some basic problem-solving and task-management techniques.

Tasks and problems

'Task' covers a wide range of circumstances. In this chapter, 'task' is used flexibly to refer to any activity or part of a larger project. The term 'problem' is also used flexibly. It can be:

● any question that calls for an answer;
● a puzzle waiting to be solved;
● a situation requiring a response;
● a challenge to be met.

It is important to separate the idea of 'problem-solving' from that of 'difficulty' or 'trouble'. Problem-solving is not necessarily difficult, although it can be applied to difficult situations. Any situation that presents a challenge or an opportunity for a new approach can be treated as a formal 'problem' that requires a solution.

Activity: Selecting a focus

In order to provide a focus for this chapter, identify one problem, task, assignment or personal goal that is relevant to you. Refer to this as you work through each of the sections below.

Trial and error

You may prefer to jump in at the deep end, trying out various ideas until you hit the right one. This works well for some people, but is a very labour-intensive way of working unless there really are no options. You may find you are good at 'trial and error' for some areas (such as cooking) and less so in others (gardening). This is sometimes regarded as intuition, but may be the result of expertise built up over time.

Visualising

You may have pictured the problem in your 'mind's eye', checking off the places where you might go on such a holiday or what the meal might be like. You may have visualised yourself performing each of the activities. Successful sportspeople tend to use visualising techniques to see the exact details of how they will achieve victory. It can be applied to most areas of life.

Charting

You may have used a chart, flow diagram or other graphic device to draw out the problem, so that you could work it out visually.

Calling upon a similar experience

You may have thought about recent meals that you have cooked and whether you could adapt these to suit a child or the person with the allergy. If you have already completed an essay, you may have run through the processes involved, working out the time needed for each, based on your experience. You might even have been able to work out some ways of saving time in order to meet the deadlines.

Many problems are relatively simple like these. We can use different problem-solving strategies at once, moving back and forward between them as necessary. For example, to organise yourself to meet essay deadlines, you might:

- ask an academic adviser or tutor for advice;
- negotiate with other people to arrange for cover for your work shift or cooking rota;
- draw on a similar essay you completed for a previous programme;
- calculate the time available for what you need to do;
- chart in your diary the time available to you;
- visualise where you left your notes;
- draw a network or outline pattern of all the ideas you have on the essay;
- research further information;
- go for a walk to clear your mind.

Seven key tips for task management

1. Clarify the task: know exactly what you need to do and why.

2. Start where the energy is . . . all other things being equal.

3. Start much earlier than you think is necessary. This gives you more room for manoeuvre.

4. Think several steps ahead: plan out all the steps required to take you to the end point.

5. Always look for several solutions . . . it is easier than looking for THE one answer.

6. Give yourself tight time limits with early deadlines . . . otherwise tasks tend to expand to fill *all* the time available.

7. Find out the background to the project. Not only are you more likely to meet the project aims, things are also more interesting from the position of an 'expert'.

Problem-solving on the back of an envelope

Simplify

If you feel daunted by all the things there are to consider in working with a problem, begin by simplifying the problem down to essential features. See if you can summarise your strategy in ten steps on the back of an envelope.

Basic problem-solving

1. Define the problem — What is the real issue?
2. Desired outcome — What do I want?
3. Options — What outcomes are possible?
4. Feasibility — What is the best option I am likely to achieve?
5. Feelings — If I follow through on this option: how will I feel?
6. Decision — What is my decision?
7. Steps — What must I do, when, with whom, where?
8. Obstacles — What might get in the way? How will I deal with these?
9. Action — Do it!
10. Evaluation — Did it work?

Find the natural sequence

You may need to address stages of a task in a particular order, which may mean dealing with subsidiary issues before addressing the core problem.

When using a problem-solving model or framework, it is likely that you will move back and forth between stages, or between the kinds of questions identified on the envelope above, until you reach the decision-making and action stages. It is worth noticing how many of the ten stages above refer to thinking about the problem before any action is taken.

Problem elaboration

Research shows that people who spend more time at the beginning working out what a task really involves, perform much better. For example, successful mathematics students spend much longer reflecting on what category of mathematical problems they have been set. They look for similarities with problems they have worked on before. They consider various approaches and weigh these up before beginning calculations to solve the problem. Less successful students tend to launch into an assignment too quickly without defining clearly what the problem entails and what needs to be done.

The early planning stage is sometimes referred to as 'problem elaboration'. Elaboration involves analysing a task from all perspectives and defining what the task really involves. The similarity approach outlines one way of doing this.

The 'similarity approach' to problem-solving

Butterworth (1992) argues that we are more likely to succeed at new tasks if we can find similarities with ones we have accomplished already. If we cannot see those parallels, then we may believe ourselves incapable of tasks well within our actual competence. This suggests that it is worth giving time and thought to what we have achieved in any one context and its applicability to other contexts.

1. Clarify the core questions
State the core questions as simply as possible. Remove unnecessary wording so as to pare the problem down to the essential features. This makes it easier to see whether it is similar to one with which you are already familiar.

2. Identify an analogous problem
- What are the core features or components of the problem? What skills, methods or techniques are needed?
- What similarities are there between problems or activities have you undertaken before and the current task?
- How can previous problems help you to think through what is needed for this problem?
- How can you make use of previous skills and experience to solve this problem?

3. Identify the limitations of the analogy
List the differences between the current problem and previous tasks. The situations will not be identical so the same strategy may not work for the current problem. Identifying the difference is as important as identifying the similarity.

4. Establish significance
- Weigh up the significance of the similarities and differences.
- How will you adapt your strategy to take account of these differences?
- What else do you need to know or to do?

ⓒ The OPAL strategy applied to task management

The OPAL strategy (Cottrell, 2010), shown in the diagram below, offers a set format to help analyse a problem and manage the tasks that lead to its solution. This is a cycle that can be applied both to project management and to tasks that form part of a project. Reflection is at the core of the cycle, undertaken as you work through a task (reflection in action); it is also a process taken outside of the cycle, standing back from it to gain a vantage point (reflection on action). OPAL stands for:

- Orientation
- Planning
- Action
- Learning

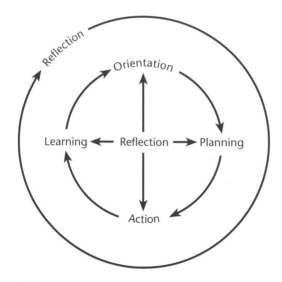

The OPAL strategy

Orientation

The cycle begins with orientation, which includes problem elaboration and good advance planning. The orientation stage is rather like starting a journey. Before setting out, you would define your task and elaborate what needs to be done by considering such questions as the purpose of the journey, the starting point, the route, your mode of transport, and how you will know when you have arrived. Similarly, to solve a problem or manage a task, you need to consider the following:

- Define the task and identify the purpose of the task: what are you hoping to achieve? You may find it helpful to describe the problem in different words so that it is clear to you what needs to be done.
- What is the desired endpoint – what will indicate that you have accomplished what you set out to do?
- Where are you now – and what is the distance to that desired endpoint?
- Broadly speaking, how are you going to get from where you are to where you need to be?
- Is there another way of thinking about this? What might be an alternative way of achieving the desired endpoint? How many possible solutions can you generate in order to give yourself options on the way forward?
- What do you need to get the job done? Are these resources going to be available?
- What expertise can you bring to bear? You may find it helpful to use the activity on p. 49 to identify your expertise and consider its application to this problem.

Time spent productively in elaborating the problem in this way pays dividends later in the process.

Planning

Before launching into action, devise a strategy to achieve your goal and then plan out the various stages of what you need to do.

Strategy

What is the broad approach you will take to achieve your goal? Some of the following might be applicable in working out your strategy:

- Are you going to apply an approach you have used before, or try something new?
- Will you have a trial run, pilot or draft version first?
- Will you do this all at once or over a longer term?
- On your own or with others?
- Within current resources or do you need further resources? If so, will this involve fund-raising of some kind or securing a grant?
- Will you apply a particular model or theoretical framework?

- Are there key features to your strategy, such as a particular focus or emphasis?

Actions, targets, deadlines
Plan out what you will do, in what order, and by when:

- What are the main steps or stages?
- Set targets and time-scales for each stage?
- Set SMART-F targets (see p. 118)?
- How will you meet these targets?
- Draw these up into an action plan (see p. 119).

Draw up an action plan, identifying your mini-goals or targets as well as deadlines for these. Your action plan might be elaborate, or it may just be a list. It depends on how complex the problem is – and what suits you. (An outline is provided on p. 119.)

Priorities
- Identify priorities: what are all the things you need to do?
- What is essential? What can be left out?

Monitoring points
- Set specific times for monitoring your progress as you go along. Write these into your action plan.

At the end of the planning stage, you should feel that you have planned effectively, having thought through all possible angles. You should be clear about what action now needs to be taken.

Action

This is the 'doing' stage. Work through your action plan, observing your targets. This is the first real test of your planning and strategy.

Monitor and review your progress
Use your action plan to check that you are on target towards your goals.

- Do you need to amend your plan in any way so that it is more realistic?
- Are you meeting targets and deadlines? If not, do you need to revise these?
- Are you maintaining your motivation? If not, what can you do to improve this?

- Are you working within your budget and resources? If not, what action must you take?
- Do you need to revise your overall strategy?

Keep records
- Consider how you can demonstrate that you have worked to a strategy, reflected on your progress and revised your plan to increase your effectiveness. Gathering evidence as you go along will help you to do this.
- Keep a record of what you do and the outcome.

Learning

At the end of the task or project, before rushing on to your next project, or drawing a line under this one, pause to see what you can can learn from the experience. This stage consists of:

- Reflection (see Chapter 8);
- Evaluation;
- Drawing out lessons for the future.

Reflection
Once you have completed the task overall, or specific actions that went either especially well or badly, stand back from it and take stock. You will find material and models for reflection in Chapter 8 that can be applied usefully here.

Evaluation
Evaluation is easier if clear targets have been set and, usually, is measured in terms of how well you have achieved those targets. However, it is useful to evaluate the overall strategy as well.

Achievement
Did you:

- Achieve your targets?
- Meet the deadlines for the overall project?
- Achieve the overall goal?
- Keep to budget?
- Maintain good working relationships?

Strategy effectiveness
- What worked well?
- What could be improved?
- What evidence is there of your performance, reflection and achievement?

Problem-solving techniques

This section introduces some common problem-solving techniques. These include:

- setting goals;
- setting criteria to evaluate a solution;
- identifying priorities;
- setting targets and drawing up an action plan;
- planning project time;
- getting down to it;
- becoming a good 'self-starter';
- sticking with a task;
- completing a task.

Setting goals

Setting goals is an important part of the orientation stage of your strategy. When considering your goal:

- Visualise what it would be like to achieve it (see p. 20, Chapter 1).
- Identify how you will know when you have achieved it: what will be different?
- Evaluate whether it is realistic.
- Identify what you will have to sacrifice in order to achieve it. Is it worth it?
- Think about your beliefs and values. Is it 'you'?

Setting criteria to evaluate a solution

Although evaluation takes place at the end of a task or project, you need to consider, at the beginning, the criteria by which you will evaluate success. Develop criteria that give you what you want but which are achievable.

Dream solution
Begin with the ideal. As Chapter 1 emphasises, it is important to work towards a 'vision'. However, use the vision to inform what you want, using it as a guide rather than a strait-jacket.

Realistic option
What would you accept as a reasonably good outcome that is both motivating and achievable? What are the main features of this option?

Identify relevant criteria for a solution
For each problem, consider the relative importance of issues such as those listed on the 'Evaluating Multiple Solutions' sheet on pages 114–15. Jot down details for each of those criteria that are most relevant for the task or problem on which you are working. Use these details to help you decide between solutions or to identify the best aspects to take on board from each of your potential solutions.

Identify priorities amongst the criteria
When you have a complete list, write these down in the order that is most important.

- Which criteria are essential and must be met?
- Which criteria are relatively flexible?
- Which criteria are very flexible?

Select only a few essential criteria and be prepared to be flexible on the others. The more essential criteria you set, the more difficult it will be to find a solution.

Identifying priorities

One common reason for not getting under way with a problem or project is that there are too many things competing for your attention. Emotions such as fear of not getting everything done, or guilt at letting someone down, make it hard to separate out what can be left and what must be addressed straight away.

To help set priorities, Neenan and Dryden (2002) suggest dividing tasks into one of four categories:

1. Urgent and important
2. Not urgent but important
3. Urgent but not important
4. Not urgent and not important

You may find it helpful to colour-code these using the resource sheet on p. 118 so that you can see urgent items most easily. For example:

1. **Red – Category 1: urgent and important**
   Deadlines, crises, tasks timed for today, tasks which must come first in a sequence.

2. **Yellow – Category 2: not urgent but important**

Category 2 activities enable you to plan ahead. These should be addressed before they become urgent. Prioritise between these according to when they must take place in a sequence, or the consequences of leaving them for too long.

3. **Orange – Category 3: Urgent but not important**
   If possible, leave these until category 1 tasks are completed. Category 3 items may not need to be undertaken at all, but can attract our attention unduly because they are 'urgent'. Emails are a good example of this. What other examples are typical of your own week?

4. **Blue – Category 4: not urgent and not important**
   These are often good time-wasting activities. They can make us feel like we are busy, so that we do not get down to what is really needed. Reading junk mail, sorting out old papers, cleaning out cupboards may fall into this category.

Activity: Identify priorities

For the problem you are addressing at present:

● Brainstorm a list of all the things you need to do.
● Divide the items on your list into the four categories on the priority sheet on p. 118. Write the things that are most important and urgent in the top left-hand box. Use the top left of that box for the most urgent items.
● Use the bottom right of the page for the least important items.

When you have completed the priority sheet, use it to guide you in organising tasks into a logical order:

● Reorganise your original list of priorities into the order in which you will now complete tasks.
● Set targets for each priority (see 'SMART-F targets' below).

SMART-F target setting

Most tasks benefit from clear, achievable targets. SMART targets make it easier to see what must be done and then to evaluate success. SMART-F targets build in reasonable flexibility, so you can plan for unexpected contingencies. SMART-F stands for:

● *Specific*: 'I will complete the first section of my essay by this evening.'
● *Measurable*: 'I will produce the first three draft pages of my essay by this evening.'
● *Achievable*: 'This should be achievable because I have completed the research, organised my notes, and already produced the outline plan.'
● *Realistic*: 'I should be able to write three pages as I have written up to ten pages in a day before, and have done the preparatory work.'
● *Time-bound*: ' I will finish by 8:30 p.m.'
● *Flexible*: 'I could continue until 10:30 p.m. if necessary. If I find I have additional research to do for those pages, I can slot that in tomorrow between 9:00 and 11:00 a.m.'

Targets should provide clear guidelines for action and be built into an action plan (see p. 119). However, they are not written in stone: they should be monitored and reviewed as the project proceeds so that it can be completed on time.

Evaluating targets

Activity: Evaluating Targets (p. 120)

An example of a set of targets is provided for you to evaluate against SMART-F criteria and to check your responses. This will give you some insights into your own understanding of setting SMART-F targets.

Evaluate your own targets
Before launching out on a project, stand back for a moment and evaluate whether your targets are really helpful. An evaluation is provided on page 121 as a ready-made structure for your evaluations. You can copy this sheet for future use, or use it in the Electronic Resource Bank.

Priority Sheet

Divide your list of tasks into the four categories below. Then set targets for each priority (see 'Identifying priorities' on pp. 116–117).

---

1. **RED**
Urgent and important

2. **YELLOW**
Not urgent but important

3. **ORANGE**
Urgent but not important

4. **BLUE**
Not urgent and not important

Action Plan

Goal:

Completion date:

Target	Milestones (steps to be taken)	By date	By whom	Evidence that milestone is completed	Done (✓)
	1				
	2				
	3				
	4				
	1				
	2				
	3				
	4				
	5				
	1				
	2				
	3				
	4				
	5				
	1				
	2				
	3				

Successful problem-solving and task management

Activity: Evaluating targets

Evaluate each of the following targets and tick (✔) where appropriate. Which of these are well-formed targets? How far is each a SMART-F target? Look for key weaknesses in each.

Target	Specific	Measurable	Achievable	Realistic	Time-bound	Flexible
1. Everyone will like me.						
2. No mistakes in this essay.						
3. Give up smoking.						
4. Accomplish something by 6:00 p.m. tonight.						
5. Write a 250–300-word introduction by 3:00 p.m. today. (Essay to be handed in at 6:00 p.m. in two days' time.)						
6. Write a 1000-word report within the next 24 hours.						
7. Attend more lectures from October onwards.						
8. Increase my marks by 5% for all assignments during this semester.						
9. Find a 3-month work placement in a retail industry before the start of next semester.						
10. Gain a work placement in the BBC by September.						

In your journal, jot down any weaknesses you can identify in these targets. When you have completed your evaluation, check your responses with those on p. 132.

Planning project time

Project schedules

Good time management may require you to use several time-management tools simultaneously:

- Action plans: set targets and deadlines for each step. Action plans are organised according to theme.
- Schedules: organise all tasks and steps in the order they must be completed. For large projects, there is software available to organise the work schedule.
- Diaries: organise tasks more closely within a week or day.

Activity: Evaluate your own targets

Evaluate how far your own targets are well-formed, SMART-F targets by using the table below. Use one row per target. Consider whether each is specific, measurable, achievable, realistic, clearly time-bound, and flexible. Write 'yes' or 'no' in the boxes as appropriate. The final column provides space for some reflection.

Target (write below)	Specific	Measurable	Achievable	Realistic	Time-bound	Flexible	Comments
1.							
2.							
3.							
4.							
5.							

Example of a work schedule

Item	Jan 1	Jan 2	Jan 3	Jan 4	Jan 5	Jan 6	Jan 7	Jan 8	Jan 9	Jan 10	Jan 11	Jan 12	Jan 13	Jan 14
Group meetings	X			X	X		X		X	X		X	X	X
Elaborate the problem	X	X	X	X										
Allocate group tasks and roles	X													
Allocate research tasks		X		X	X				X	X				
Finalise strategy				X										
Research			X	X	X	X	X	X	X	X				
Discuss research progress				X			X		X					
Analyse and discuss data									X	X	X			
Allocate writing tasks				X					X					
First draft to group											X			
Responses to first draft												X		
Etc.														

Work schedule and project diary

The time slots on the project schedule are very broad. Several days are allocated for some aspects of the project. So that every project team member knows what they are doing, the project diary organises time in detail on a daily basis. For your projects, you may find it helpful to map out in diary form more specific aspects of each task, indicating when each task will finish. An example of a project diary entry is given below.

Projects often go wrong because there is no flexibility to the time schedule, or no 'slack' time, built in. Final deadlines are usually strict, leaving little scope for changes at the last minute. It is useful, therefore, to schedule the early stages of a project very closely, in order to increase the incentive to work efficiently. Set interim deadlines so that there are early achievements and so you can check if the project is running to schedule. This will make it easier to meet the final deadlines.

Example of a project diary

Tuesday 2nd January

9:00–10:00	Jane buys coach tickets.
11:00–12:00	Jane and Miko attend the primary school to discuss project with headteacher.
10:00–12:00	Paul undertakes literature search.
12:00	Jane and Miko catch the coach back to college.
12:00–2:00	Paul and Raphaela look for articles on similar projects.
2:30	Whole team meets to discuss findings.
4:00–6:00	Elaborate the problem and define the area of research.

Getting down to it!

Do you delay beginning an activity because:

- you get easily distracted into irrelevant activities?
- the time isn't right?
- you need more experience?
- you work better at the last moment?
- tomorrow is better?
- you worry that the outcome won't be right?
- you think something will go wrong?
- everything else is more important?

If so, procrastination prevents you from following through on an action plan.

As the project deadline looms, Michael finds it ever more essential to ensure that his pencils are lined up parallel to the Greenwich Meridian.

Procrastination can be a chronic condition (Sapadin, 1997). If you always struggle to start a task, you may need professional help. However, if the problem is less serious, some of the following steps can help.

Identify the core issue
- Acknowledge that you are procrastinating.
- What sort of things are you better at getting down to?

- What kinds of activity do you keep putting off?
- Identify what characterises the things you put off: are there any themes?
- Do you procrastinate more over some tasks than others? Are some times worse than others?

Check your motivation, vision and targets
- Check your motivation. Give yourself more rewards for each stage you complete.
- Check your 'vision' (see Chapter 1). It may not be motivating you sufficiently. Link tasks more closely to your long-term vision.
- Break goals and targets into small chunks that could be completed in a short burst.

Identify the hindrance zone
- Identify what feelings (boredom, fear, irritation, anger, frustration) you associate with the activity. Can you commit yourself to putting up with the discomfort of these feelings until the task is done? What would help you tolerate these until the task is completed?
- Give yourself more encouraging messages about the task.
- Find a different way of describing the activity so that it becomes more interesting for you.
- Combine the task with something you enjoy, such as listening to music.
- Stay away from anyone who encourages your procrastination.
- Identify the 'level of inhibition' (p. 98).

Commandeer support
- Arrange to do tasks in pairs or a group. It is harder to avoid a task if others are involved.
- Ask a friend to check on you. Give them permission to tell you to get started.
- Join an action set (see p. 144).

Create unavoidable reminders
- Write yourself 20 'Post-its' ™ giving yourself instructions to get started on a particular task today. Put these on surfaces where you cannot avoid them.
- Write 20 'Post-its' ™ detailing what you will gain by completing the project.
- Write more precise details of what you have to do into your diary.

Becoming a good 'self-starter'

Many job specifications ask for 'good self-starters'. Some people are naturally motivated to launch into a project with minimum assistance. However, the characteristics of a good self-starter can be acquired by most people. Self-starters tend to be:

- highly motivated; they create a clear vision of the task and set themselves specific goals;
- able to use strategies for 'getting going';
- open to the possibility of success;
- solution-focused: they will search out information that will bring about a solution;
- organised: they develop a strategy and they use their time well;
- self-confident: they trust they can manage the task reasonably well;
- good at finding support and asking for help when they need it;
- good at people skills (this is necessary as, when starting a new task, they usually need information and assistance);
- aware of their own limitations: this is essential – a good self-starter will be open about what they do not know and what they cannot do. They either develop the skills themselves or find someone who can help.

Such characteristics are usually acquired in the process of other tasks, such as team working, leading groups, managing smaller projects, and working up to larger projects. However, each time you undertake any assignment, you can practise techniques that are relevant to being a good self-starter.

Sticking with a task

The characteristics of successful people, noted in Chapter 1, included a willingness to 'do what it takes', even if this means working very long hours, and developing patience. Thomas Edison, who is quoted in the activity below, is remembered today for inventions that contributed to the development of film and the light bulb. Edison is also famous for his adage that genius owes only 5 per cent to inspiration and 95 per cent to perspiration!

Completing a task

The following characteristics are usually needed to take tasks through to completion on a consistent basis:

- enthusiasm;
- ability to see or conceptualise the 'end product';
- perseverance ;
- patience;
- self-belief: belief that you can do it;
- being willing to give the task sufficient time;
- being prepared to practise;
- being prepared to keep thinking of different solutions;
- accepting constructive criticism;
- searching out a point of interest;
- keeping the goal and benefits in mind;
- pride in a job well done.

📖 **Reflection** Finishing off

- Which of the above characteristics are your strongest?
- What examples can you give of where you used those characteristics?
- Which do you need to develop further?
- Do you have other qualities that help you to take a task through to completion?
- Think of five things you could do to develop your 'finishing' skills.
- How and when will you apply these to meet your current goals?

If you find it very difficult to develop these characteristics, you may find it helpful to speak to a student counsellor.

Projects

What is a project?

A project is:

'A temporary endeavour undertaken to create a unique product or service.'

Project management is:

'The application of knowledge, skills, tools and techniques to project activities to meet project requirements.'

(Project Management Institute, 2000)

Characteristics of a project

Projects are characterised by:

- *A goal*   There is a purpose, a desired outcome.
- *A discrete focus*   The activity is 'set apart' in some way. It is not part of the usual course of day-to-day events.
- *Magnitude*   Projects are associated with setting aside time to focus on something special, important or that needs to be completed. It suggests a mustering of effort and resources.
- *Time limits*   Projects must be completed within a set time-frame. It should be clear when a project is complete. As the definition above indicates, a project is a temporary event.
- *Management*   Projects are managed, organised and planned events, leading to an outcome within a time-frame.
- *Individuality*   The nature of a project is that it is a one-off event, leading to something unique.

Scale of the project

The characteristics of a project could apply to activities of any scale. An essay, for example, has:

- *A goal*   To address the essay title; to gain a good grade.
- *Discrete focus*   Each essay is a separate assignment.
- *Magnitude*   Essay writing requires a 'mustering' of time and resources.
- *Time limits*   Deadlines are set for assignments.
- *Management*   Essay writing involves multiple processes of elaborating the question, research, information management, selection, organising ideas, drafting, editing, fine-tuning, proof-reading. These have to be orchestrated to achieve the final goal.
- *Individuality*   Although all students on a programme may be given the same assignment title, each student is expected to provide an individual answer.

Writing essays can develop some of the skills needed for project work.

Student projects

However, essays are usually distinguished from student 'projects'. For example:

- *Goal:* the purpose of a student project is to develop a more in-depth study than would be expected in an essay. The desired outcomes are usually both the results of the project itself and the development of the competences necessary to manage a project.
- *Discrete focus:* projects are usually one-off pieces of work, related to the overall programme but covering ground decided by the student.
- *Magnitude:* projects usually have greater word limits, but the magnitude is in the level of personal responsibility involved.
- *Individuality:* as you have more control over the content and processes, it is typical for student projects to be more individual and varied than student essays.
- *Time limits:* the time allocations for projects tend to be greater than for essays.
- *Management:* projects are usually more complex than essays, requiring more management of the various processes.

Employers' interests in student project skills

Employers are interested in:

- skills and qualities associated with project management;
- experience of undertaking projects;
- the scale of the largest project that you have taken part in;
- the scale of the largest problem you have managed alone.

The scale of projects can be differentiated by such factors as:

- how many people were involved;
- the time scale – how long it was planned to last and how long it did last;
- who 'commissioned it' – whether it was yourself, a tutor, an employer, an agency;
- the size of the budget;
- how many beneficiaries there were (who benefited?);
- the significance of the outcomes. What was the impact of the project?

Student projects do not always give opportunities to develop all these skills or to work on a grand scale, but some work placements do. The student union and voluntary work are also good sources for gaining such experience.

Successful project management

The skills identified on p. 106 are applicable to most projects as well as to general task management. The following items also contribute to project success.

Problem-solving

Problem-solving techniques can be applied successfully to projects.

Elaboration

Problem-elaboration is especially important to project work as the wrong strategy wastes time and other resources. Heerkens (2002) warns against 'solution jumping': 'the tendency of people to talk about what to do before analysing the situation adequately, trying to develop a solution before thoroughly understanding a problem'.

Piloting the methods

Have a trial run or 'pilot' to test out your methods and materials on a small scale before embarking on the full-scale project. Identify what needs to be changed. This is easier to do after a pilot rather than when the project is well under way.

'Doing what it takes'

Make a commitment to achieve specific goals. You can decide that you will give 'whatever it takes' to make a relationship work, to get good grades for your course-work, to get to grips with a subject you do not understand, to get a job in a specific field, or to launch a business.

'Doing what it takes' may mean that the majority of your time, energies, thinking and even finances go towards the achievement of the goal. This is not necessarily a healthy approach. However, that might be the difference between fully achieving a goal and accepting a compromise. It is a personal decision how far you want to accept a reasonable compromise.

Because projects work to set deadlines and focus on new areas, they tend to demand more time and thought than is usually anticipated. The project leader, in particular, is likely to spend every waking moment on the project if it falls behind deadlines, or if new solutions are required.

'Doing what it takes' is difficult to apply to more than one goal at a time.

Reflection   Commitment

- How far do you think you are generally someone who is willing to 'do what it takes' to gets something done?
- What kinds of activity are more likely to prompt you to put in the most effort and commitment?
- What conditions encourage you to increase your level of commitment?
- What are your limits?

Clarity

Good problem elaboration and planning should mean that it is clear what needs to be done, by whom, where and when. When the plan is clear, the team can work more effectively. Confusion leads to additional work, puts deadlines at risk, puts the team under stress, and can put up the costs.

Decision making

When projects are under way, you may have to make decisions at speed. This is easier if you have already considered different solutions and planned for contingencies. Keep the main goal in sight and know which compromises are possible.

You will also have to weigh up the relative importance of key criteria such as:

- costs;
- deadlines;
- effects on other people;
- the availability of expertise;
- aspects of quality;
- which changes will be acceptable to the client or commissioning agent (or tutor).

Know the project 'inside out'

To make decisions under pressure, you need to know the project 'inside out'. You need a keen sense of what the 'client' (maybe the tutor in your case) will consider acceptable. Spend time finding out the background to the project. For example, why is it considered important? Are there ethical or political considerations which should be taken into account? What are the most similar projects that have been initiated in the past – and what were the outcomes of these? This information can help you with your own planning and decision making.

Keep the vision in mind

Whilst it is important to keep to deadlines and budgets, it is easy to lose sight of the main purpose of a project. A good leader will keep the team focused on the end-point as well as on interim targets.

The leader is the one who climbs the tallest tree, surveys the entire situation and yells "Wrong jungle!" But how do the busy, efficient producers and managers often respond? "Shut up! We're making progress." (Covey, 1999).

The whole team must be clear about the background to the project and understand the vision of the person who commissioned it (you, your tutor, a client). This makes each team member feel more involved. It also means that each person is better informed to make interim decisions in line with the overall 'vision'. All project decisions should be guided by the overall goal, not by the requirements of short-term targets.

Team work

Most projects in the workplace are team efforts. If the team does not pull together, the project becomes a 'sick' project: people are unhappy and less willing to put in the extra effort needed to bring the project to completion. Successful managers ascribe their achievements to good team work and to trusting their team.

Team work requires the ability both to be a good team member, and to be able to take the lead where relevant. This calls for a range of people skills. Hallows (1997), argues: 'Hard though it may be to admit, the people side of projects is more important than the technical side.' Because of the importance of people skills, a specific chapter has been dedicated to this (Chapter 6).

Performance indicators (PI)

How do you know whether what you are doing is successful? 'Performance indicators' are one way of monitoring and evaluating your performance. They 'indicate' where you are doing well or need to improve. Performance indicators should be 'measurable' so that you can compare performance either over time or against the performance of other people. Some examples are:

- 95 per cent of targets to be achieved by the deadline.
- The project to be completed within 5 per cent of the project budget.
- 75 per cent of the participants to indicate in a feedback questionnaire that they are 'very content' with the outcome.
- A mark of 60 per cent or more to be achieved for every assignment.

- Attendance levels to achieve at least 95 per cent.
- Punctuality to be at least 95 per cent.

Meeting the criteria

Performance indicators should be closely linked to the criteria for success identified earlier in the project (see p. 114). They are unlikely to be exactly the same because some criteria may not be measurable. You may meet the criteria of a project without feeling that you performed well in all respects. Your individual or team performance may be different from the criteria for individual projects.

> ### Activity: Meeting the criteria
>
> When you have completed a current project, return to the criteria you set near the beginning of the project (see p. 114). Consider:
>
> - Did you meet the essential criteria (the 'bottom line') that you set?
> - Were these criteria realistic?
> - What criteria do you think could have been better, if any?

Work with performance indicators

Performance indicators you could use for study or project work include:

- how often you meet deadlines for assignments;
- the number and percentage of the times that you complete a particular action successfully;
- how long it takes to perform a specific activity;
- how often you reach your targets;
- feedback received from others;
- how many of the milestones you set for yourself were achieved;
- how much it cost compared to budget;
- percentage improvement over previous performance;
- grades and marks.

Soft criteria

Some project criteria cannot easily include a number or 'measurable' component. For example, it is hard to quantify:

- creativity;
- innovation;
- ethical approaches;
- sensitivity;
- flexibility;
- emotional intelligence;
- how well you manage a difficult situation;
- responsiveness;
- assertiveness.

Soft criteria require you to develop skills in being an objective evaluator of your own performance. You have to develop a 'feel' for whether something is going well or not. Wherever possible, this should still be evaluated against specific criteria and performance indicators to get a rounded picture of how you are doing. Compare your personal evaluations with feedback from others.

Benchmarks

A benchmark is a point of comparison. For example, a sportsperson might benchmark their speed or accuracy against the records of people at the top of their own sport. A programme on TV might benchmark itself against audience ratings for other programmes. Organisations and projects use benchmarks to measure their performance against other companies or projects.

Good benchmarks compare like with like. For example, if your project involves writing an information leaflet for the public, the benchmarks would need to relate to another project that aimed at producing a similar number of leaflets in a similar time-scale on a similar kind of issue. The performance indicators for such a project might include some of the following:

- how much it costs to produce each leaflet;
- how many readers, when asked, rated the leaflet as useful;
- the percentage of readers who, when asked, rated the leaflet as useful;
- an independent mark (by an independent assessor or tutor);
- a measure of how far the leaflet changed opinion or behaviour.

A good benchmark enables you to evaluate your own outcomes against those of a comparable project or set of benchmarks.

For example, you may find that you wanted to achieve a 90 per cent return for a questionnaire and yet received only 35 per cent. This might feel like failure as it is far short of the target. If you compare this with similar questionnaires in comparable circumstances, you may find that a typical (or benchmark) response is only 20 per cent. This would mean that your target was unrealistic but your performance for the questionnaire was good.

Further reading

Davidson, J. (2000) *The Ten-Minute Guide to Project Management* (Indianapolis: Alpha Books). (A basic introduction to project management.)

Heerkens, G. R. (2002) *Project Management* (New York: McGraw-Hill). (A readable introduction that also covers the 'softer' aspects of project management, such as personal qualities.)

Mingus, N. (2002) *Alpha Teach Yourself Project Management in 24 Hours* (Indianapolis: Alpha Books). (An advanced text.)

Feedback on activity: 'Evaluating targets' on p. 120

- Target 1: This is too vague, has no time limits and is unlikely to be achievable or measurable. It isn't realistic.
- Target 2: This is unlikely to be achievable or measurable as it is hard to define a 'mistake' with respect to an essay. Very few essays are perfect. This is not a realistic target.
- Target 3: This may be realistic and achievable for the person. Success could be measured. No time-scales have been set so the target is not SMART.
- Target 4: This has a clear time-scale and is likely to be achievable and realistic. However, it is so vague that it is meaningless.
- Target 5: This is specific, measurable, and time-bound. It is likely to be realistic and achievable, and if not, there is sufficient time before the hand-in date to adjust the deadline.
- Target 6: This is specific, measurable and time-bound. You would need to know more about the writer and the circumstances to see if the target was achievable and realistic and sufficiently flexible.
- Target 7: 'More' is too vague. 'From October' sets an initial time-scale but does not indicate how long this will continue.
- Target 8: This is specific and measurable. A 5 per cent improvement is likely to be achievable and reasonable, unless the mark was already very high. Setting a target for *all* assignments is challenging: it does not contain much flexibility. This target would need to be accompanied by other targets which specify more clearly how the improved mark will be achieved.
- Target 9: This target is likely to be a SMART-F target.
- Target 10: This is too precise and allows for little flexibility in choice of work placement. It is not likely to be realistic or achievable.

Chapter 6

People skills

The most important single ingredient in the formula of success is knowing how to get along with people.

Theodore Roosevelt

Learning outcomes

This chapter offers you opportunities to develop skills in:

building a good rapport with others
being a better team member
setting up an 'action set'
giving and receiving constructive criticism
assertiveness
dealing with difficult people
negotiation
leadership.

Introduction

'People skills' are a combination of good inter-personal skills (being able to work well with others) and intra-personal skills (being able to manage one's own attitudes and emotions). 'People skills' are now critical to success in a wide range of careers. They are as important to the modern economy as are knowledge, information and technical skills.

This has been a much neglected part of the curriculum in the past, perhaps because there was less demand for subtle understandings of inter-personal relationships. However, changes in the kind of work we do, in technology, in tele-communications, in social structure, and the global economy have altered the way we interact. There are now much higher expectations for good inter-personal and communication skills.

In particular, compared with previous generations, we are more likely to meet and work with an extremely diverse range of people, often in global contexts. In the past, most people grew up and worked within a very confined world, with a

narrow set of social rules. It was clear what behaviour was expected of you down to the finest detail of your personal life. People knew almost from birth what they should say, to whom and when. They tended to meet people from a very small geographical area, often only their own village or part of town. Horizons were very narrow.

Today, most of the old social codes are disappearing. The context is infinitely more varied than in the past, the range of options in any one situation is much greater. This requires much higher levels of sophistication in our attitudes to others, in how we manage our personal beliefs and values in social settings, and how we respond to diversity. We have much more personal responsibility for developing good social relations, making relationships work and forming judgements about the appropriate behaviour in any setting. We all, too, have greater individual legal responsibility for our decisions and actions.

'People skills' is a vast and rapidly developing area. This chapter looks at some key aspects of developing people skills from the perspective of a student or new graduate.

Activity: Self-evaluation – How good are your people skills now?

Make two copies of this table. Complete one now and one later in your programme. Rate each of the following statements as follows:

Rating: *Stongly agree = 3   Agree = 2   Sort of agree = 1   Disagree/don't know/no opportunities = 0*

	Score
1. I have worked with a wide range of people of different ages and backgrounds	
2. I am told that I am very good at working with others	
3. I feel very confident about talking to people I do not know well	
4. I am comfortable about leaving silences whilst other people gather their thoughts	
5. I can start a conversation easily	
6. I find people extremely interesting	
7. I am aware of my body language and its effects upon others	
8. I can be very helpful and polite to people I hate or despise	
9. I can see the good points in most of the people I meet during a week	
10. I can listen well without interrupting somebody who talks a lot	
11. I am very good at developing trust between myself and others	
12. When I am in a group, I can easily tell the strengths of each person	
13. When I am in a team, I can tell easily who will be the best for each job	
14. I work very well as a member of a team	
15. I am clear about the particular strengths I bring to the group or team	
16. I am able to be very supportive of other people	
17. I am very good at resolving difficulties that arise in group or team work	
18. I know what support I need from others	
19. I am able to ask for what I need	
20. I am assertive	
21. I can deal well with difficult people	
22. I am able to accept, publicly, responsibility for my own part in interactions that go wrong	
23. I am skilled at offering constructive criticism to others	
24. I am able to take negative criticism well	
25. I am able to accept praise well	
26. I negotiate well with other people	
27. I know how to arrive at a good compromise	
28. I am clear what direction I need from people in leadership roles	
29. I feel very comfortable about taking the lead in activities	
30. I am very aware of what other people need	
Add up your score **Total**	

Interpreting your score

70–90   This is an excellent score. If your ratings were accurate, you are able to manage very well your relationships with other people. This suggests an invaluable set of people skills. Consider how you could develop these further. How can you use these skills in the career areas that interest you?

40–69   This is a good score. If your ratings were accurate, this suggests your people skills are already well developed. Look for themes in the statements to which you gave lower ratings. Which areas could be further improved?

20–39   If your ratings were accurate, this suggests you have developed some people skills as well as an awareness of where you lack strengths currently. Look for themes in the statements to which you gave lower ratings. Taking your programme needs and career interests into consideration, which is your next priority for development?

0–19   If your ratings were accurate, this suggests that you have identified that people skills are not currently a strength for you. Check with people who know you well whether you have rated yourself too harshly. It is also important that you identify which people skills are most critical for meeting the requirements of your programme and career interests. Consider speaking to the careers service or your tutors to identify areas of priority for future development. This score also suggests that you might have difficulties in relationships generally. That can be stressful. If so, student counselling services can offer useful ideas about how to make your interactions with others run more smoothly.

📖 *Reflection*   People skill needs

Which people skills are needed for:

- the careers areas that interest you;
- meeting the requirements of your programme;
- your personal needs and interests?

- If you are unsure, speak to the Careers Service at the university and to your tutors.

- What are your priorities for developing your people skills?

Developing rapport

Forming a good rapport is the cornerstone of relationships with other people. Rapport requires such behaviours as:

- 'making a connection';
- taking a genuine interest in the other person;
- skilful listening;
- developing mutual trust and cooperation.

Making a connection

Making a connection requires only a little effort. From this, the basis of good trust or even life-long friendships can develop. The minimum required are a few very basic gestures that show good will:

- making eye contact;
- giving a genuine smile;
- being helpful when asked;
- giving a friendly greeting;
- showing basic consideration for the other person;
- using a friendly, polite manner;
- making a comment or asking a question that shows interest without being intrusive;
- being consistent in either friendly or distant behaviour.

These may seem small and obvious. However, think about the contact you have with people you find difficult. Which of the above gestures were missing either at your first encounter or on a regular basis? Which of these gestures do you value? A forced smile, an abrupt response, an unpleasant tone of voice, and such small details can put relationships on a wrong footing – making hard work of any future connections.

Taking a genuine interest

Generally, we appreciate people with similar values and beliefs to our own, who do not challenge our own view of the world or our material interests. 'Difference' can be unsettling. It suggests there might be more than one way of doing or being. Our survival mechanisms do not like this idea: it suggests someone else might be 'right' and our way 'wrong'. We are not usually comfortable with such ideas. Our minds tend to throw us lifelines such as 'that's boring', 'he's a fool', 'that's rubbish!' very early, before we are even aware it is happening, so that we do not have to really consider what we are feeling.

As we develop people skills, we are better able to accept a wider range of differences in other people. We learn to find the point of interest in difference and the value of diversity. We cease to see the world in terms of 'right' and 'wrong', but as a rich spectrum.

The benefits of finding the point of interest in other people are that:

● we find the world around us to be more interesting;
● boredom disappears and our life experience is richer;
● we feel more comfortable, emotionally, when with strangers;
● people are able to feel more comfortable around us;
● we have a better understanding of the world around us and of the motivations of others;
● we are better able to manage any situation that involves other people.

Activity: Balloon game

In your journal or a notebook, give one page to each of the following (ten pages in all).

The characters
First, write the name of one person on the top of each page, so that you have the names of:

● two people that you really know, like and admire;
● two people that you know vaguely and have no strong feelings about;
● two people that you think are just not like you at all and that you do not like much;
● two that you know well and really dislike or despise;
● two people that you do not know at all (you may invent names for them if you do not know them).

The motivation
Now, imagine you are in a television challenge. You are aloft in a balloon with these ten people. You will receive a prize of your choice (up to £5 million) if you can bring all ten people back to earth. Otherwise, you will be fined your income for a year. If you fail, they get a prize instead.

The challenge
However, you are only allowed to transport back any person if you can convince the audience that each person is really worth saving. You will need to show that you know about the person and can say things about them that bring out their best features.

For each person, use their name page to brainstorm responses to the following:

● what I like, value, admire, find interesting already about this person;
● what I dislike about this person at present;
● what this person contributes to the world that is different or valuable;
● questions I could ask, to find out more;
● anything I could do to develop a better understanding of this person.

Skilful listening

Good listening skills are invaluable to forming a rapport with others. Most people react very strongly to feeling they are 'not heard' or that 'someone really listened'. This is especially true where people feel vulnerable (if they are new to a group, distressed, angry, have received bad news, etc.).

'Listening' is something we take for granted. However, skilful listening is about more than 'hearing the words'. It involves understanding the message, the situation and other people.

Good listening skills enable other people to feel at ease, to trust the listener, and to express more easily what they really wish to communicate.

There is an art to being able to discover what another person is trying to communicate, and this can take many years to perfect. However, the following are good starting places.

Body language
Demonstrate clearly that you are listening, using appropriate body language. Usually this means slightly exaggerating what you would normally do anyway. For example, ensure you make eye contact, without staring.

Use body language that shows you are listening: lean forward a little, tilt your head slightly to the side, nod occasionally to show you are taking in what is being said. Many people do this naturally when they are really listening but some do not.

Let them finish
Let people complete the point they are making without interruption. Wait for a pause or an intake of breath before you start to respond. Make any necessary interruptions with consideration for the other person – even if you feel they have not been considering your needs. If you really must interrupt, because of time constraints, for example, apologise for interrupting. State the reason for the interruption politely. Make some reference, however brief, to what has been said, before you change the subject or rush away.

Listen for the underlying message
The 'underlying message' may be different from the actual words used. What does the person really mean? What do they really want you to hear or to know? Are they saying one thing but communicating something different? For example, they may say 'I'm fine!' but look or sound very angry or distressed. Just note these differences. If it feels right to say so, you may point out the message that you are receiving: 'You sound very upset' or 'You look very angry.'

Check for meaning

People may not be skilled at communicating what they want you to hear. Alternatively, you may mishear or misread the situation. The only way to be sure of the message being communicated is to feed it back to the person and check their response. Summarise what you think you have heard. Usually, this is best in brief phrases, prompts or questions when the other person is pausing for breath. Do this in ways that suggest you are trying to understand:

- 'They said you have to fill in the form today?'
- 'And that wasn't what you wanted?'
- 'So you don't want to go ahead any more?'

Clarify details

- Ask questions to clarify points and show your interest.
- If something isn't clear, point out that you haven't quite understood. Ask the other person to explain it again or in a different way.
- Be specific about the exact points you do not understand. Your confusion may arise because the other person is not fully clear about the issue either. Your questions may help them to clarify their thinking.

Leave silences

Some people find silence awkward and it can be tempting to keep talking in order to avoid silences. However, silence fulfils important functions:

- it gives a clear signal that you have finished speaking;
- it gives opportunities for other people to contribute;
- it allows time for reflection;
- it gives people time to develop their ideas;
- it allows people time to manage their feelings and emotions;
- it can enable non-verbal communication to take place, which is often more powerful than speaking.

Reflection   Listening skills

- In your reflective journal, note down which of these listening skills you find easiest.
- Which do you find most difficult?
- Which could you develop further?
- Can you think of recent examples where you used any of these skills?

Developing mutual trust

Reflection   Developing trust

- Who do you really trust with your secrets?
- Who do you really trust with your money?
- Who do you trust to tell you the truth about themselves?
- Who do you trust to tell you the truth about yourself?

In each case, what created that trust?

Your responses to the above activity probably elicited an awareness that trust develops out of acquaintance. It also takes time. It can be easily broken. It can take time to repair once broken. You cannot force trust onto people; the harder you try, the more suspicious people may become. You really do 'earn it' through the proof of your actions.

It is difficult to establish good working relationships if these are not founded on trust. Co-operation with others, sharing ideas, revealing personal information, negotiating compromises, commissioning work, offering contracts, and numerous other everyday activities are all facilitated by the development of mutual trust.

Reflection   Losing trust in others

In your reflective journal, think of an occasion when you lost your trust in somebody.

- What happened?
- What did this feel like?
- What were the consequences?
- How has this affected your behaviour towards that person?
- What would that person have to do to regain your trust?
- Which kinds of behaviour break trust?

In your reflective journal,

- Think of an occasion when you did something to undermine other people's trust in you.
- What happened?
- What did this feel like?
- What were the consequences?
- How has this affected the relationship between you and that person?
- What was (or is) needed to restore that person's trust in you?
- What did you learn about trust from this experience ?
- Which kinds of behaviour break trust?

Brainstorm:

- What kinds of behaviour develop people's trust?
- What kinds of things could you do to develop your abilities in gaining other people's trust in you?

You can build trust if you:

Are clear what you can and cannot do

Do what you say you will do

Avoid making promises you can't keep

Keep confidential information confidential

Are consistent in your behaviour from one day to the next

Are dependable and fulfil your responsibilities; turn up on time

Team work

Learning in groups reaps greater benefits than attending formal lectures or presentations. It gives students more scope to express themselves, to establish effective relationships with tutors and others in the group, and to develop a range of skills such as team working.

Skills and Enterprise Network, 2001

'Finding and keeping a good team' is amongst chief executives' most highly rated ingredients of success (Taylor and Humphrey, 2002). Despite the importance of team work to working life, few people have developed outstanding team skills. Team players are usually well-appreciated by both employers and colleagues. On the other hand, our natural self-interest in our own needs, moods, beliefs, wants and feelings can make it very easy for us to sabotage the teams or groups that we find ourselves in.

Sabotaging the team

You may have come up with a long list of items. Typical responses include:

- not bothering to get to know some of the team members;
- dominating the group;
- not contributing enough;
- leaving one or two people to do all the work;
- speaking badly about some team members;
- trying to split the team into 'goodies' and 'baddies';
- not taking responsibility for tasks that need to be done;
- being late or not turning up at all;
- putting your own needs before those of the team;
- not listening to other people's ideas;
- not using the strengths and qualities of each person to best effect;
- messing about;
- not caring what happens to others on the team;
- not being able to take criticism.

Creating a good team

A good team will show the following characteristics:

Works as one
- It has a shared vision. It knows what it wants to achieve;
- puts the desired team outcome first: individual interests take a secondary place;
- is clear about targets and priorities – and agrees these together;
- shares information;
- can make decisions.

Works to strengths
- It has members with different qualities, who can make different contributions;
- takes time to discover the experience, skills and interests of all and how it can make best use of these;

- shares expertise. A team that is together for some time is strengthened if individuals share their knowledge and skills.

Includes everyone
- It makes efforts to ensure that nobody feels left out or undervalued;
- gives room to individuals. Teamwork does not mean that everybody has to be and think the same. On the contrary, variety and difference can be a source of strength. There are different ways of being a good team player.

Respects its members
- It respects everyone's time by: being punctual for meetings, completing individual targets on time, being aware of how one person's own work affects other people's achievements, monitoring personal contributions to meetings so that time is not wasted in long anecdotes and tangents;
- respects the opinions of the team and uses strategies to enable all team members to give their views: feeding in at the beginning of meetings, giving each member equal time to speak on an issue, inviting people who have not spoken yet to contribute their views.

What I can contribute to the team?

The skills and qualities you contribute to a team will develop through experience. However, if you are not used to teamwork, you will feel more confident at the beginning if you think of what you are already able to contribute. The following activity helps you identify some things you could contribute to team work at present.

Activity: Contributing to a team

For each way of contributing to teams (listed below) tick as many boxes as apply to you.

Contribution	Willing to do	Have experience of	An area of strength	Want to develop
Hearing other people's views, ideas and opinions				
Listening to others				
Weighing up options				
Making decisions, based on the facts				
Finding ways of working effectively				
Looking for solutions				
Administrative skills				
Working out priorities				
Speaking my mind				
Specialist skills that can be useful				
Seeing when the discussion has gone off track, and pulling it back on target				
Working hard				
Keeping going when it gets tough				
Seeing when people are left out				
Drawing in other people				
Logical thinking				
Numbers and statistics				
Charts and drawings				
Researching information				
Writing up findings				
Organising events				
Networking				
Time-keeping				
Other things:				
(1)				
(2)				
(3)				
(4)				

Activity: Weaknesses in team performance

How well do you perform in teams at present? Use the following statements to evaluate your performance and to guide your reflection.

Tick as relevant ✓

- ☐ I talk too much
- ☐ I turn up late
- ☐ I interrupt others
- ☐ I take up too much of the discussion space
- ☐ I let other people carry the team
- ☐ I always think I am in the right
- ☐ I act as if I were the team leader
- ☐ I like everything to stick exactly to the agenda
- ☐ I keep going off at tangents
- ☐ I get caught up in the details and lose the big picture

- ☐ I have lots of ideas, but many of them are not relevant
- ☐ I get too emotional
- ☐ I don't keep to the deadlines

Other things:

- ☐ (1)
- ☐ (2)
- ☐ (3)
- ☐ (4)

Activity: Turn short-comings into strengths

- How realistic is the above view of yourself?
- Would you have the confidence to discuss this with someone else and be able to cope with their responses?
- What targets can you set yourself to improve your performance for one of those areas?
- What, if any, are the positive aspects to your 'short-comings'? What do these suggest about your potential strengths (such as flexibility, caring for others, willingness to accept responsibility, confidence in speaking your mind) that could be adapted to the benefit of the team?
- Take at least one short-coming and look for the way this could be adapted or converted into a strength. For example, if you are poor at attendance, how could you make up for non-attendance in other ways?

Research Unit made a dramatic discovery about teams. In an experiment that was repeated many times with different participants, it was found that teams made up entirely of the best business brains were far less successful than those with very mixed memberships. Belbin (1996) went on to outline different kinds of roles that people could occupy in a team, depending on their personal characteristics. The activity on p. 143 summarises some of the characteristics associated with each Belbin type.

- With which types do you identify?
- With which one type do you identify the most?
- Which three other types would you most appreciate having in your team?

Belbin team types

Belbin and the Cambridge Industrial Training

Activity: Identify your team personality

Belbin type	Positive characteristics	Potential short-comings	Tick all that apply to you. Draw *** by the most typical	The three 'types' I would most want on my team (tick)
Implementer	Steady, reliable, sensible, gets things done. Well-disciplined, organised approach.	May not welcome change and new ideas. Expects too much from others.		
Co-ordinator	Focused, looks for consensus, tries to involve everyone. Delegates work; chairs meetings well. Can accept and reject the ideas of others.	Doesn't shine intellectually; may be seen as manipulative. Passes their own work onto others.		
Shaper	Outgoing, high-energy, no-nonsense, blunt; speaks their mind; ready to overcome obstacles; gets things moving.	Impatient, irritable, insensitive to others' feelings; may say the wrong thing at the wrong time.		
Plant	Creative, lateral thinker, generates ideas, enjoys looking for solutions, inventive. Good at holding the 'big picture'.	Inflated sense of their own 'genius'; ignores targets and details; in their own dream-world; does not communicate ideas well to others.		
Resource investigator	Curious, interested, out-going. Likes exploration, information, meeting new people, challenge, trying out new gadgets.	Short interest or attention span; invests and then moves on to something else; may pilfer other people's ideas.		
Monitor–evaluator	Considers all angles; unemotional; takes on many perspectives; good at weighing up the evidence and making a judgement; good at decision making.	Rigid in ideas and in their love of 'logic'; not open to creative or lateral thinking; over-critical. Not good at generating novel ideas.		
Team-worker	Observant; listens and responds well; smooths over conflict; diplomatic; good social skills; sensitive to others; puts the team first.	Can be swayed by all views; easily influenced; prevaricates; finds it hard to come to a decision.		

Belbin type	Positive characteristics	Potential short-comings	Tick all that apply to you. Draw *** by the most typical	The three 'types' I would most want on my team (tick)
Completer-finisher	Good attention to detail; conscientious; responsible; reliable; delivers to target; fine-tunes their final effort.	Bad at delegating and trusting others; picks fault; over-perfectionist.		
Specialist	Single-minded, dedicated, offers skills that are hard to find; gets on with the task; self-motivating.	Not interested in the big picture; doesn't mix with the team; narrow horizons.		

The best mix?

Belbin found some combinations work well. In particular, a group seems to work well if there is:

● a co-ordinator type – to chair the group;
● a good 'plant' – an imaginative person with the right kind of creative skills for the project;
● a monitor–evaluator who can spot and weigh up good and bad ideas;
● a spread of other types. In particular, an implementer or completer-finisher is useful. A balance of types is valuable: extrovert and introvert, those who generate ideas and those who can assess them, those who bring in change and those who maintain some continuity.

What kind of balance is there in the team of four (including yourself) that you selected in the activity above.

What strengths would a team like that demonstrate? What would its weaknesses be?

If you wish to complete a full Belbin self-perception inventory, ask for a copy at your University Careers Service.

Action sets

'Action sets' (McGill and Beaty, 1992) are a particular kind of team. They are semi-formal groups which offer opportunities to gain input and alternatives from others and receive structured support.

Action sets, as the name suggests, focus on getting things done. Unlike most groups, however, the aim is to help each person to find a solution to a problem or difficulty of their own choice. The group brainstorms ideas and discusses solutions within a tight time-frame, and at the next meeting checks to see what action was undertaken. The group itself does not carry out the action: it merely proposes and monitors action, at the invitation of each member.

Advantages of action sets

The advantages of action sets are:

● the rules are easy to follow;
● all members are equal;
● they provide supportive contexts: usually, you choose to be in an action set;
● you have a place where you can take a difficult issue and work it through;
● they are very focused;
● they offer a range of perspectives on a problem you choose to bring;

- they generate ideas and solutions;
- they require rapid decision making, and so assist decision-making skills for all members;
- they give practice in arriving at a solution in a very short time;
- they offer an additional source of motivation: reporting back to the group at the next meeting encourages you to take action;
- members get to know each other well and know what works for each member.

You may find it useful to select an action set according to Belbin types. If so, bear in mind the aims of the group. What types of person are likely to work best together for the kinds of problems that arise from your programme? Would it help to include someone who is not on the programme?

The limits of action sets

Action sets are not usually:

- emotional support groups;
- discussion groups: talk is very circumscribed;
- social groups;
- project groups: they do not 'do' the work needed to solve an individual's problem outside of the meeting.

Guidelines for the meeting of an action set

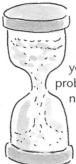

Ideally, leave at least 15 minutes for each member. If you have only an hour a week for such meetings, a set of four people is probably best. If you have 2 hours, a group of six is probably the optimum size. An even number will work best. The timing below assumes six people in a 2-hour slot. With a 15-minute break, that gives each person 17 minutes each.

For each person:

Stage 1 (3 minutes)
- Each person has a set time to discuss the area they wish to improve. Time is limited so each person needs to get to the point quickly.
- While that person is speaking, the group listens without interrupting.

- One person keeps the time.
- Once the time is up, the person must stop speaking immediately.

Stage 2 (2 minutes)
The group may ask one or two questions, briefly, to clarify the situation.

Stage 3 (3 minutes)
The person whose issue is being considered listens without speaking whilst the rest of the group brainstorms possible solutions and ways of thinking about the problem. Again, a limited time is allowed.

Stage 4 (4 minutes)
The person and the group have a set time to clarify and discuss options together briefly.

Stage 5 (2 minutes)
The person whose issue is being discussed has a set time to state which actions they will undertake before the next meeting. All members write down what has been agreed, and monitor this at the next meeting.

Stage 6 (3 minutes)
In the following session, each person reports back on actions they have taken. The group encourages successes and improvements. If the person has not followed through on what was agreed, this may be used as their focus for the session. Feedback must be timetabled into the time allocated to each person.

Running the action set

Ideally, action sets are meetings of peers where everybody takes equal responsibility. Tasks are rotated or allocated to individual strengths:

- organising the room;
- phoning members to remind them of the next meeting and of agreed actions;
- time-keeping in meetings;
- keeping the group strictly to the right stage and item under discussion;

- maintaining a supportive atmosphere;
- ensuring everyone contributes;
- ensuring everybody gets equal time;
- ensuring different people go first or last each time.

Roles

You may find action sets work better if you allocate roles to the team. Useful roles to include are:

- **A Co-ordinator or Implementer**: to ensure the group sticks to task, keeps to time, and that everyone gets equal time. Each stage must be very strictly timed.
- **A Plant or a Shaper or Resource Investigator**: who may bring a different way of looking at things.
- **A Team-worker**: to enhance the social skills of the group.
- **A Monitor–evaluator or Completer–finisher**: to assist the group to move on and to choose between options.

Constructive criticism

> **📖 Reflection**   Constructive criticism
>
> In your reflective journal, jot down some ideas about what you think is meant by 'constructive criticism'.

Criticism does not mean pointing out 'what is wrong'. Technically, criticism draws out what is good, bad and satisfactory. Constructive criticism goes further: it offers a clear and practicable 'next step forward' and is expressed in a positive way. It leads towards improvement. For constructive criticism to be effective, it has to be expressed in a way that is easy to 'hear' and understand.

Making constructive criticism and giving feedback

The aim of feedback is to help other people to see how they could improve their performance or gain a new perspective on their work. The focus of

criticism is the other person, their needs or the requirements of the task. It is not about showing how clever you are at 'picking holes' in what other people do or say.

Constructive criticism is phrased so that it offers truthful but skilful feedback with ideas on how to improve or to progress. It is very easy to hurt people's feelings through unskilful feedback, and nothing is gained by this.

Good feedback involves:

- waiting until invited for your opinion;
- recognising effort;
- being well informed: ensure you know the circumstances, intentions and requirements before offering feedback;
- being clear and truthful but not blunt or hurtful;
- indicating what the other person has got right – so they continue to do this in the future;
- indicating what has already improved;
- indicating a small number of achievable goals for improvement;
- giving concrete examples of what is required: 'I think this would look even better if . . .' 'I like this. Have you thought about . . .' 'The first half was good. The second half would benefit from . . .'

It should:

- be formulated positively – as something which can be done to improve performance, rather than what is wrong;
- take the person forward – it is not simply a vague directive to do something differently;
- be realistic – the suggestion can actually be put into practice by the recipient;
- be selective – it addresses priorities rather than every aspect of performance;
- be offered kindly – delivered in a voice and manner that make it easier to accept.

Poor feedback includes:

- too much comment and criticism. This is off-putting. People stop listening and may get distressed;
- negative feedback. People ignore this if they feel their efforts are not recognised;
- vague feedback such as 'Unclear' or 'More detail needed'. State exactly what is unclear or which details are needed;

- demoralising comments such as 'this is nonsense'; 'gobbledegook!'; 'could do better';
- illegible feedback. People usually do not bother to decipher illegible writing unless they think it says something very positive about them.

> **📖 Reflection**   Offering constructive criticism
>
> Think of a recent occasion when you offered feedback to someone about their work or study. Jot down:
>
> - What were the circumstances?
> - What did you do or say?
> - Which of the above constructive characteristics did you include or omit?
> - What else could you have said or done to improve your feedback?

Constructive questions and responses

Use constructive questions to discover why the person made the choices or took the steps they did – and to explore their next step forward. For example:

- 'What did you think worked well?'
- 'Is there anything you would do differently next time?'
- 'What was your inspiration for this?'
- 'Did you find this worked?'
- 'That is an unusual approach. I am interested in why you did it this way?'
- 'Have you had any ideas about where we could apply this?'

Jane was starting to realise that her helpful advice was not universally appreciated.

Receiving criticism

Accept criticism gracefully, however it is given. Not everybody is skilled at giving criticism.

- Consider all criticism carefully, even if it sounds unacceptable.
- Look for the elements of truth in what is said. This is sometimes easier after you have had some time to reflect.
- Hear both the positive and the negative aspects. Many people hear only negative feedback.
- Check you have understood what is being said. It is easy to mishear, especially if it didn't sound positive.
- Acknowledge the feedback. It was probably not easy for the other person to give it.
- Say thank-you.
- Reflect upon the meaning of what you have heard. What steps could you take to improve your performance?

> **📖 Reflection**   Receiving criticism
>
> Think of a recent occasion when somebody offered you feedback or criticism about your work or performance.
> In your reflective journal, jot down:
>
> - What were the circumstances?
> - What did they do or say?
> - How did you respond? What else could you have done to make best use of the criticism?
> - What does this experience tell you about giving and receiving criticism well?

Being assertive

What is assertiveness?

Assertiveness means standing up for yourself without demonstrating anger. Assertive people look for solutions that suit both parties, respecting the rights of both.

> **📖 Reflection**   Characteristics of assertive people
>
> What picture comes to mind when you think of an assertive person? Jot down your thoughts in your reflective journal.

Assertiveness is about:

- respecting your own and other people's rights;
- respecting your own and others' needs;
- being clear and straightforward with other people;
- taking more control over your own life and taking responsibility for changing what you do not like.

Rights

Palmer and Dryden (1995) offer a list of rights associated with assertiveness. These include the right to:

- say 'no';
- make mistakes;
- consider your needs important;
- express your feelings in an appropriate way without violating anybody else's rights;
- take responsibility for your actions;
- respect yourself;
- set your own priorities;
- be assertive without feeling guilty.

You could include others, such as the right to:

- do well in life;
- ask for what you need to know;
- be taken into consideration in decisions that affect you;
- fairness and justice;
- personal safety;
- love;
- think;
- be free of insult and discriminatory behaviour on the grounds of race, colour, nationality, sex, sexual orientation, disability, parentage, work history or personal beliefs;
- your opinions.

Respecting your own and others' rights and needs

'Rights' are not universal nor equally applied. They are not all 'human rights' by international agreement and may not apply in all countries or conditions. People in prison cannot set all their own priorities, for example. Some rights are protected by law; others are commonly held beliefs about human rights. You may have to decide what

> **Activity: Your rights**
>
> What other rights are important to you that you would like to add to the above list?
>
> 1.
>
>
> 2.
>
>
> 3.
>
>
> - Which rights are most important to you?
> - Do you know what your rights are in the circumstances which you usually encounter?
> - Which of your rights do you find you need to defend the most often?
> - Which do you find hardest to claim?

rights are reasonable or legal for your own circumstances.

An individual's interests have to be weighed against the rights of other people and the nature of the circumstances. We are not generally comfortable with the idea that a surgeon might have 'the right to make mistakes' on a regular basis. Having the right to an opinion means you have the right to hold the opinion, but not necessarily to subject other people to insult or harm as a result.

Assertiveness is not about insisting on your own interests, irrespective of the consequences to yourself and others or without consideration of the circumstances. When you are assertive, you ensure that:

- you look at the whole picture, but you put yourself in that picture;
- you know your own opinions;
- you are able to identify your own needs and interests;
- you weigh up, realistically, whether it is appropriate to stand up for your rights and interests in the situation. Sometimes it is too dangerous or risky to assert our rights unless we can ensure safety and support.

Being clear and straightforward with other people

When we state our needs in a calm, clear, straightforward manner, then we are showing respect both to ourselves and to others. When other people know where you stand, they can then choose to respond in an appropriate way. You gain a clearer picture of their position.

Assertiveness is not:

- **Being aggressive** Assertiveness does not include: rage, shouting, forcing other people to do what you want, physical force or threats of force, aggressive body language, intimidating others. You have the right to feel angry, or to shout in private, but not to express these to others in ways that might make them feel coerced into doing what you want.

- **Being manipulative** Assertiveness does not include: using psychological games to manoeuvre people into doing what you want. For example, it does not involve shaming people, trying to make them feel guilty or anxious, reminding them of debts, playing upon people's doubts and fears.

- **Being passive** Assertiveness does not include: being silent about your own needs and interests; being a 'martyr'; letting other people have what they want whilst you go without; staying quiet when you want to speak out; effacing yourself so that you are not seen, heard or considered. This behaviour can be very irritating to others – and means they have to take responsibility for your needs.

- **Being passive aggressive** Assertiveness does not include: appearing to be passive whilst being clear that you are angry. Passive aggressive behaviour is very distressing to other people, and confuses situations so they are harder to resolve. It includes behaviour such as saying 'I don't mind', 'do what you want', 'whatever!' whilst using angry facial expressions, body language or tone of voice. Angry silences, walking out of the room, making a noise to block out what another person is saying, not

turning up to appointments and generally not co-operating, are ways of expressing passive aggression.

> ### Reflection Evaluating personal assertiveness
>
> It is rare for anybody to go through life in an assertive and completely fair, reasonable, manner. Most of us tend to use at least one or two of the above approaches (aggressive, manipulative, passive aggressive, or passive) for some or all of the time in order to get our own way or to avoid an unpleasant situation. In your reflective journal, consider:
>
> - Which approach do you use most often to get your way or to avoid unpleasant situations?
> - Do people who know you well agree that this is the approach you use?

Taking control over your life

When we use assertiveness techniques, we take responsibility for our actions in order to increase our control over an aspect of our life.

> ### Reflection A recurring siuation
>
> Select one situation where you feel you deserve to have your opinions, needs or interests taken into consideration and respected – and where you feel this does not happen at present. Select an event that recurs, which you will have to face soon.
>
> - What usually happens?
> - What do you do?
> - What do you say?
> - What rights are at issue in this situation?
> - What are the rights of others in this situation?
> - What kind of behaviour do you demonstrate when you feel you are unlikely to get your way (aggression, passive aggression, manipulation or passivity)?
> - What do you gain by this behaviour?
> - What are the effects of this upon others?

Assertiveness techniques

> ### Activity: Assertive techniques
>
> Consider the assertiveness techniques below in relation to your 'recurring situation'.

1. Identify blocks to assertiveness

What has been preventing you from using assertive techniques up to now?

- ☐ Not being aware of the differences between aggression, passivity, manipulation and assertiveness
- ☐ It wasn't part of my family or cultural background
- ☐ Fear of other people's responses
- ☐ Fear of failure
- ☐ Blaming myself for the situation
- ☐ Not wanting to hurt other people's feelings
- ☐ I wanted a quiet life
- ☐ My current methods may not be fair but I get what I want

2. Put yourself in the picture

This means that you:

- look at the 'big picture'. Identify all the interests of all the parties, including your own;
- ensure you are in the picture. If you are more likely to respond in a passive way, you may not feel you have a right to be considered;
- consider whether you really should be at the centre, near the centre or on the periphery of the picture. Passive people can believe it is polite or kind or good manners to put themselves on the margins. If this happens all the time, it is likely to be irritating to others, as they will always be put into the position of being the more selfish, greedy, inconsiderate person, which is not pleasant. Aggressive people may always find reasons to be at the centre.

3. Make 'I' statements

People who find it hard to be assertive can find it difficult to make 'I' statements such as:

- 'I want . . .'
- 'I need . . .'
- 'I am responsible for . . .'

Sometimes this is very noticeable because they refer to their own needs in very general terms:

- 'Everybody needs . . .'
- 'We all need . . .'
- 'It is important to . . .'
- 'You have to . . .'
- 'One has to . . .'

Activity: Making 'I' statements

Make 'I' statements for the 'recurring situation' you selected on p. 149.

Aspect	'I' Statement
What do you want?	I want . . .
What do you need?	I need . . .
How do you feel?	I feel . . .
What rights are involved?	I have the right to . . .
What are your responsibilities?	I am responsible for . . .
My behaviours	I will (do). . . .

In your reflective journal, jot down your responses to the following:

- How easy was this activity for you?
- What kind of speech do you use in order to avoid using 'I' statements?
- Which statement was the most difficult to make?
- When will you use these 'I' statements?

---

4. Choose the moment

Ensure that:

- *The time is right.* This does not mean waiting for a perfect moment that may never arrive. It means choosing the best time available. Make an agreed time with the person or ensure that, at a meeting, time is put aside to discuss the matter. Be clear how long you need.
- *You have the person's full attention.* Ask for this if necessary. Choose a moment when they are able to give you attention. Avoid competing with television, radio or loud music.

5. State the issue and the desired change

Take responsibility for letting the person know what you find unacceptable or difficult about their behaviour. Do so in a manner that is calm, and does not sound blaming. Describe behaviours rather than the person. Say what the behaviour is, and acknowledge responsibility for your own part in the event and for your own feelings and responses. Make it clear what you want.

Example 1

'I feel hurt when you do not respond when I speak to you in the mornings. I would like you to say "hello".'

Rather than:

'You are so rude in the mornings. You make me feel ignored and angry and it affects my whole day.'

Example 2

'I need the price lists by 4:00 p.m. If you send them after 4:00, it is difficult to get our updates in the post.'

Rather than:

'You know the post goes out at 4:00. I don't know how you expect us all to get everything done when you can't be bothered to get the lists to us in time. It's your fault I was so upset last night – you really stress us out.'

6. Use positive language structures

When you make 'I' statements, use positive language structures. Positive language structures avoid the use of 'no', or 'not'. They are also clear, to the point and say exactly what you will do. Avoid words such as 'try', which suggests hard work or failure. Avoid modifiers such as 'some', 'maybe', 'sort of', 'quite'.

Positive language structure	Avoid
● I will ask for a lift.	I'll try and see if I can get a lift.
● I am entitled to this money.	I really think I should have what is due to me.
● I want these comments to stop.	I think it would be better if there were a little less of these comments.
● I will complete the race.	I intend to make a good shot at completing the race.
● Can I have help lifting this, please?	I can't lift this on my own! You could help!
● I need to say something.	I'm never given a chance to say what I need.
● I feel angry and upset.	I am trying not to get angry here!

7. Ask the other person's opinion

When you have stated what the issue is for you, check whether there could be a different interpretation. Ask the person how they see the situation and what they think about it. Show that you have a genuine interest in hearing their point of view. Let them give their interpretation without interrupting them.

8. Acknowledge the feelings

It is very common to see people arguing, even hissing through gritted teeth, 'I am not angry! I am not angry!' when it is clear to others that they are. This can make a situation difficult to resolve because the truth isn't being acknowledged.

It isn't always pleasant or easy to talk about feelings, but it is usually useful. Even if you do not voice your feelings, make sure that you at least know what they are. Otherwise, other people will know more about you than you do yourself.

- ● Check what you are feeling.
- ● Acknowledge to yourself how you are feeling.
- ● Make an 'I' statement about this: 'I feel . . .'
- ● Take care not to spill out the emotion on the people around you. You have a right to feel angry, for example, but not to coerce others with your feelings.
- ● Be prepared to hear how other people feel and consider what that means. You might not like hearing what they say, but they have the right to express how they feel too.

9. Suggest and invite solutions

Being assertive means looking for a solution that suits both sides as far as possible. Make constructive suggestions for a way forward. Point out the advantages to both parties. Ask the person for their suggestions and be prepared to negotiate (see p. 156).

10. Clarify what has been agreed

Check you both agree the details of what is agreed. This will avoid disputes later. Writing down the agreement strengthens the commitment. Read what the other person has written and check you agree with the details. Keep a copy.

If you are not used to being assertive, it will take time to change your habits and thinking. You can build your confidence by using some 'practice runs', either with a trusted friend or with a student counsellor. Keep a record of times when you are assertive so that you can monitor your progress.

> 📖 **Reflection**   Assertiveness
>
> In your reflective journal, jot down your responses to the following questions:
>
> - ● What could you gain by being more assertive?
> - ● What difficulties are there for you in putting assertiveness techniques into action?
> - ● How will you address these?
> - ● Which of the above techniques could you use?

Dealing with difficult people

On becoming a monster

Any of us can be a difficult person some of the time. Most of us have 'pet hates': situations and people that we do not manage skilfully and which seem to make us unreasonable. When we are confronted by a 'difficult person', empathy can be a useful starting place. It is worth considering that this person might, like us, be very reasonable if the circumstances were different.

> ### 📖 *Reflection*   Being difficult
>
> In your reflective journal jot down one occasion when you acted unreasonably or 'out of character' – when you found yourself shouting at somebody, complaining unnecessarily, making a difficult situation worse, or blowing something out of proportion.
>
> ● What was it about the circumstances that led you to behave like that?
> ● What can you learn from your own experience that might help you to understand when other people seem to be unnecessarily difficult?
> ● Jot down a list of all the circumstances that can turn you into a 'monster'. Are these things that might be typical of the day of a 'difficult person' you know?

Is it just me?

If you experience the same person as difficult on several occasions, you might conclude that the person is just plain awkward. That may be the case, but there may be ways that you can ease your own relations with that person, so that your day runs more smoothly. Consider:

● Do other people find this person difficult?
● Who seems to manage situations with this person best? What do they do?
● What is it about the difficult person that provokes a response in you?
● What is it about the person that makes you find it difficult to give calm and measured responses?
● What do you do that contributes to making the situation more difficult than it need be? What could you do to improve the situation?

> ### 📖 *Reflection*   Dealing with difficult people
>
> Think of one occasion with a 'difficult person' that you consider had a significant impact upon you. Jot down a brief outline of what happened.
>
> ● How did you feel at the time?
> ● How were you affected afterwards? For example, was it hard to settle down to work, enjoy your evening, sleep, feel calm?
> ● How many times did you narrate the episode to others? How much time did this take up? What would you have done with that time otherwise?
> ● In retrospect, how might you have responded differently, either during the event or afterwards, so the experience affected you less?
> ● What do you have to gain by changing the interaction you have with this person?

The effect on me?

Difficult people can have a profound effect upon the people around them. They can become the source of constant conversation and a good source of gossip. Dealing with them, talking about them, going back over what happened, planning what you will say or do on the next occasion, all take up time and energy. That time could have been spent more fruitfully. Although it may be important to plan how to cope with a difficult person, it is just as important to ensure that the person does not become an excuse for time wasting, and for diverting energies from other problems.

Whatever the difficult person may have done, you have a personal responsibility to yourself to manage the effects upon yourself.

Managing the situation

Identify the behaviour
The golden rule for interacting with people is to separate the behaviour from the person. This is easy to say but much more difficult in practice. When thinking about the person, make a conscious effort to focus on their actions. For example: '*That* irritates me' rather than '*She* irritates me'. This distinction will then come more easily to you when you are with the person.

Isolate the source of irritation
For the 'difficult person' you identified above, jot down all their behaviours that really irritate or concern you. For example, do they:

● interrupt you all the time?
● refuse to let you express your point of view?
● interrupt your study or work?
● arrive late for each seminar or meeting?
● take up all the discussion time with their opinions?
● other things?

Look for positive interpretations of their behaviour
Look for characteristics about the person that you can genuinely appreciate. Look for a positive aspect to their unwanted behaviour, such as a desire to please, a willingness to contribute, a sense of humour.

Consider their needs
Usually behaviour has an intention – even if it is inappropriate to the context. Sometimes people simply go about getting what they need in a misguided way. The people you find difficult will be acting the way they do in order to achieve something. This might be to:

● gain attention;
● be noticed;
● be respected;
● feel that people think they are clever;
● be heard;
● draw attention away from something else;
● make friends.

Consider how you (or the group) could give that person some of what they need. This may make them less demanding, and easier to cope with.

Acknowledge the other person
People behave unreasonably when their needs are not met. Listen to what they are communicating, and let them know you have heard. For example:

Their situation	Your response
● They are distressed	'I can see/hear that you are upset.'
● They are angry	'I can see/hear you are angry.'
● They want attention	'That is a good idea.' 'That's an interesting point.'

Identify what they want
● Ask the person what they want.
● Repeat this back to them so they know you have listened and heard them correctly.
● Consider whether the request is feasible.
● Let them know what is feasible.
● Stay calm and repeat this if the offer is refused.

Acknowledge your own feelings
● Identify your own feelings. This will give you more control over your own responses. Are you angry? distressed? unhappy? raging? guilty? irritated?
● Check how well you are managing your emotions? Do you need to calm down?
● State your feelings clearly and simply so that the other person knows how you feel.

State indisputable facts
Rather than get into an entangled argument, focus on statements of fact:

- 'They are closing the doors. We have to go now.'
- 'This is a seminar. The issue cannot be resolved now.'
- 'We haven't got the receipts here. We can look at this again once we have them.'

Keep it clear and simple

- Keep it simple. Unless it is really necessary, avoid arguing about points of detail.
- State what needs to be done.
- Keep to the present situation: avoid going over past events.

State what you want

Consider what would be a reasonable outcome for you from the situation. State this calmly, simply and clearly. Avoid unnecessary details or commentary. You may need to repeat what you want several times if the person is shouting or in full flow.

- 'I want to leave this until we all feel calmer.'
- 'I want you to stop ringing me after 9 p.m.'
- 'I want to have more time for group discussion.'
- 'I want to hear what other people have to say.'
- 'I want a refund.'

Offer positive solutions

- Maintain a positive focus. Look for an acceptable solution.
- Offer a way out of a stalemate.
- State the advantages of the proposed solution.
- Be prepared to negotiate a reasonable compromise or to find a 'bridge' – even if you feel the other person should be taking the initiative.
- Invite all parties to write down the agreed solution so that it is clear and on record.

Clarify tasks

If people are difficult team members, they may not be clear or happy about what is expected of them.

- Involve them in key decisions.
- Negotiate and clarify targets.
- Ensure their role offers sufficient challenge and interest.

Look for the 'bottled up' emotions

Even if somebody is being difficult, they probably think they are very reasonable. At that stage, there is probably very little you can say to change their mind. When we are emotional, we are not open to logical reasoning. Be prepared to let your perspective wait until the person is calmer.

The probability is that the person has built up emotions such as anger, frustration, rage or fear over a very long time. If this has not been acknowledged, they may be 'dumping' this emotion on other people without realising it. This will be evident in disproportionate responses to small things.

If the emotions are dumped on you: this is not fair, and you should not put up with it.

The angry person probably cannot see what they are doing. It is unlikely to be helpful to discuss this at the time unless:

- you know the person very well;
- you have a relationship which permits discussing personal matters (as the source of the emotion may be very personal);
- you have agreed to set time aside for this;
- you are both very calm.

Don't 'pass the parcel'

It is very tempting to respond to emotional 'dumping' by unloading all your own emotions. This may even feel good at the time. However, it is not a skilful way of dealing with the person or the situation, and makes it even harder to resolve differences over the longer term. To avoid unloading your emotions on others:

- Check which emotions you are most likely to unload onto others.
- What are the triggers for this response?

- What kinds of 'emotional dumping' do you seem to invite most from other people (their anger? guilt? shame? anxiety? fear?)?
- Plan a coping strategy so that you are not drawn into this sort of interaction.

Negotiating

Negotiation covers a wide spectrum. It can cover everyday situations, such as how much of the food budget goes on beer, chocolate or vegetables. It is an important part of group work, and most types of work include at least an element of negotiation with customers, clients or third parties.

Good negotiators exercise a broad and very subtle set of skills and qualities. These include:

- decision making;
- reading the situation and the 'opposition';
- persuasiveness and communication skills;
- assertiveness;
- dealing with difficult people.

Decision making

When negotiating, you may have to make decisions very quickly. It is important to be well prepared before you arrive, and to have thought through the issues and the questions you will face so that you are clear about your own position.

The stakes

What is really at stake? What is the ultimate aim? This should inform the negotiation process. The ultimate aim may not be achievable now: world peace, a harmonious group atmosphere, or a successful group project will not be established by solving a single argument or making a single deal. However, the negotiation should aim to take you closer to the ultimate aim. If it takes you a small way forward, then something has been achieved. If it takes you a long way forward, then you have less to do in future negotiations.

The ideal outcome

Consider the ideal outcome for you. What would this look like? What would be the benefits? Form a clear picture of this so that it motivates you to negotiate strongly.

The bottom line

Consider your 'bottom line': what is the minimum you will accept? This is usually less than we really want. Negotiation usually involves two sides with competing interests. Each side will have to concede something if an agreement is to be reached. Be clear what you want from the situation. Consider:

The ideal solution What would be your ideal solution? A clear vision can strengthen your bargaining position.

A good acceptable outcome What would this look like? What would be the benefits of this for you? What parts of your 'ideal outcome' are you prepared to relinquish?

The next best option This may mean giving up more of the 'dream option'.

The likely outcome Be realistic. What is likely to happen? Is this acceptable? You may gain a better deal, but if you do not, how will you come to terms with the likely outcome?

The minimum offer What is your bottom line? What aspects are you prepared to negotiate, and what are your upper or lower limits for these? Practise saying these in a calm, clear way so that you sound firm and convincing when you come to argue your case. Write these down and take them with you so you do not concede on essentials.

Know when to concede

It is not always easy to strike the perfect balance between holding out for the best possible option, and knowing when to concede in order to gain something from the negotiation. You will need to weigh up:

- *Deadlines*   How much time you have in order to hold out for the best option.
- *Costs*   What might you lose if you take a long time to come to an agreement? How long can you hold out for what you want?
- *Risks*   What will happen if you hold out and do not get what you want? Will you still be able to manage the situation (or your life)?
- *Competition*   Is anybody else likely to make a better offer and put you out of the bargaining?
- *The history*   In similar situations, or with this person or team, what usually tends to happen? What is likely to be agreed? What are the points that they are unlikely to concede?

All too late, George realised he hadn't included negotiation skills in his personal development plan.

Flexibility

From what has been described above, it should be evident that negotiation requires you to weigh up many possibilities, to assess the situation, and be able to accept one of a number of outcomes, depending upon the circumstances. One option is to be inflexible, and to insist on the best possible option. You may be successful, but you are more likely to leave with nothing. This usually means you have to start again on a new set of negotiations, so you need to weigh up the costs of a 'Nothing' option very carefully.

Reading the situation and the 'opposition'

Investigate the background

Find out as much as you can about the other person or team and their needs, interests and motivations. This puts you in a stronger position to negotiate.

Clarify mutual positions

Invite both sides to discuss their objectives and the possible options. This will enable you to see where there is room for manoeuvre. There will be a range of items that are not negotiable. It can take a lot of energy to try to alter the 'non-negotiables'. Ensure you are clear what the other side will or will not accept. If you can live with these requirements, then leave them out of the discussion, and focus on what can be negotiated.

Body language

The Institute of Management draws attention to the significance of body language as a means of communication – and the importance of understanding its impact in the workplace. Ribbens and Thompson (2001) argue that up to 90 per cent of communication may be non-verbal. Look for signs that suggest the other party is feeling defensive. People are less likely to negotiate to your advantage if they feel they need to 'defend' their own position. Look for:

- signs of distress (fidgeting; agitated movements; rocking; eyes looking downwards; moving hands over the face; pacing);
- a closed stance (arms and legs crossed; pursed lips; hands tightly clasped, the body leaning forward in a defensive position);
- obstructiveness (avoiding eye contact; shaking the head; refusal to engage in communication);
- anxiety about speaking (moving hands across the mouth; biting the lips);
- unwillingness to listen (sitting forward with hands moving over the ears; moving to interrupt; drumming fingers on the table).

Persuasiveness and good communication skills

Create an open relaxed atmosphere

If people look, sound or feel defensive, as described above, it helps to put them more at their ease so that they open up to your ideas. You can improve the situation if you:

- avoid 'hard sell' approaches;
- focus on their agenda for a while, as this is familiar terrain for them;
- ask for a break so you can interact more informally for a few minutes;

- mirror their body language for a few minutes and gradually introduce more relaxed postures (arms in relaxed positions, legs uncrossed, sitting back in the chair, using calm movements of the head or hands);
- smile;
- think through the situation from their point of view: you are more likely to act in a way they can accept if you are genuinely thinking about their position.

Speak to their vision

Let them know you have been listening to what they said. Keep referring to their objectives and interests, identifying how your proposal goes some way towards achieving these. Spell out the advantages. It is important that the other parties see that their goals can be met through the solution you propose. If not, they are unlikely to agree.

Show willingness to compromise

Let the other party know that you are willing to make concessions. Do not identify your own 'bottom line' straight away, as you will have no room to negotiate. Be clear about your 'ideal' scenario, so they can see clearly where you are prepared to negotiate: people do not like to feel that they are the only ones making concessions. Watch their response to your offer to see whether it is one they look comfortable with, or whether more persuasion is needed.

Keep the lines of communication open

Stay calm, even if you are not getting what you want. Do not 'burn your bridges' by walking out or giving ultimatums. Leave possibilities for further dialogue. If necessary, brainstorm more options together, take breaks and reconsider your options, start again from the beginning, or look for different combinations of options.

---

[e] Activity: Changing a recurring situation

For this activity, identify a recurring situation where you could apply skills in assertiveness and negotiation. This may be the same situation that you used for other activities in the chapter. Write your responses in the boxes.

The situation. Give brief details of the context and what usually happens.	
What do you do? What kind of behaviour do you use?	
What are the effects of this behaviour?	
How do you feel about the situation? 'I feel . . .'	
A constructive way of thinking about this situation is . . .	

Identify your goal. 'The change I want to bring about is . . .'	
What are your rights? 'I am entitled to . . .'	
What are the rights of the other party or other people in this situation? 'They are entitled to . . .'	
What are your responsibilities in this situation? 'It is my responsibility to . . .'	
What are the responsibilities of other people? 'They are responsible for . . .'	
What will be the right time and place? How will you ensure you have their full attention?	
What other 'I' statements could you make?	
Your recommendations for a solution are . . .	
The minimum you will accept is . . .	
What support can you get from others (such as practice runs, somebody to encourage you)?	
Other comments	

Activity: Monitoring effectiveness in negotiating skills and assertiveness

	Situation	What I did (include details of how you applied an assertiveness technique)	Positive outcomes for myself	The effect upon other people	Further action needed
1					
2					
3					
4					
5					

Leadership

The role of leader

Leaders provide the vision. They motivate others. Leaders need to have a clear internal model of their role. This is likely to be strongly influenced by other roles that they fill in life, by their values, and by the sources of inspiration that they call upon. You will have an internal model in your head, now, of what you think a leader is or should be. For example, some people might describe a leader by using one or more of the following metaphors. A leader is:

- an architect, designing and constructing a project;
- a sales-manager, selling a vision;
- a social worker, intervening to improve the lot of others;
- a general, commanding an army;
- an actor, playing to an audience;
- a diplomat, pouring oil on troubled waters;
- an artist, with a particular vision.

Leadership from the position of the led

> 📖 **Reflection**   Leadership
>
> - What metaphor of your own best describes your view of a good leader? What does this metaphor tell you about your feelings towards leaders and leadership?
> - Does your view of leaders and leadership encourage you to be a leader or to avoid this? What metaphor would inspire and encourage you more to be a leader? Does that metaphor apply to any roles that you already fill?
> - How do you feel a team would respond to a leader who fitted the metaphor you have selected?
> - Which metaphors for leadership would best encourage active, motivated, self-reliant team members?

Characteristics of an effective leader

Inspire others

A good leader will ensure that the vision is kept in view, and does not become lost amongst a forest of targets, deadlines, and problems.

Heerkens, 2002

A leader develops the vision and exudes a realistic confidence in that vision. They must also communicate it well to others, ensuring that everybody else can see what the benefits of achieving that vision would be.

A good leader can see ways that the overall goal can contribute to individual and personal goals. Typically, the vision of successful leaders is for the project or the team, rather than for their personal goals (Taylor and Humphrey, 2002).

Activity: Your advice to the leaders?

- If you want some ideas on how to motivate and lead others, give consideration to what it is like to be 'led'. What kind of behaviour, communication or strategy would motivate you to 'go the extra mile' that is often needed for successful project completion?
- Jot down a list of behaviours that you would associate with an effective team leader.
- Use your insights to formulate a list of 'Advice' points for team leaders.

When you have completed your list, compare it with the 'characteristics of an effective leader' given above.

Create a sense of commitment

Team members are more likely to contribute if they feel committed to the project. An effective team leader:

● offers a clear and motivating 'vision';
● ensures that the whole team is clear about the purpose and aims of the project;
● identifies the significance or relevance of a successful outcome to the project;
● clarifies how the work of each member is significant to the overall project;
● leads by example.

Develop the strategy

One of the main tasks of the team or project leader is to develop the strategy. This will orchestrate the efforts and resources of the team towards the goal. A strategy may be simple or complex.

Encourage contributions from others

Team members are more likely to contribute if they feel valued. An effective team leader:

● notices people's contributions;
● thanks people for their contributions;
● makes it clear to the whole team where everyone fits in – and draws attention to achievements that are less visible;
● clarifies how the achievements of individuals contribute to the benefit of the overall project;
● treats all of the team with fairness, courtesy and consideration.

Demonstrate the value of all team members

Team members are more likely to contribute if they feel their opinions are valued. An effective team leader:

● creates opportunities to ask the team for their opinions and encourages them to help evolve a solution;
● creates opportunities for the team to contribute to the planning and setting of targets;
● demonstrates how suggestions and comments from the team have been considered and adopted;
● allows individuals opportunities to develop their own plans for achieving targets.

Clarify expectations

Team members are more likely to contribute if they know what is expected of them. An effective team leader:

● negotiates clear targets for each person;
● clarifies how each person's work connects to the work of others;
● negotiates clear ground rules for group behaviours;
● makes it clear what a successful outcome would be for each person;
● ensures that feelings of uncertainty are kept to a minimum.

Ensure the team works

Leaders ensure that the team works well, knowing what different people can contribute. Good leaders ensure their team is functioning smoothly, and intervene when it is not. They act as full members of their teams, and are readily available if things become difficult. (See 'Team work', above.)

● For what aspect of team work would you find it easiest to take a lead?
● When or where do you do that now?
● If you lack experience in leading groups or sessions, what opportunities could you create to gain that experience?

Take responsibility

Leaders are the most prominent members of the team. They take the lion's share of the glory when things go well. They must also be prepared to take responsibility if things do not go well. This can be quite a daunting thought. However, taking responsibility for our actions is important in most contexts.

Demonstrate excellent 'people' skills

Leaders need to communicate well. Without good inter-personal skills, it would be almost impossible to bring a set of people to share a vision, pull together, commit to a project, meet deadlines and resolve their differences. Leaders may also have an ambassadorial function, speaking and negotiating on behalf of the team.

Consider a situation where you had responsibility for the outcomes. If possible, select an occasion when it was difficult to take responsibility but where you did so.

● What happened?
● What was your role?
● What did it feel like to take responsibility then?
● What have you learnt from the experience that will be useful to you in other circumstances?

Activity: Updated self-evaluation

Complete a new self-evaluation of your people skills (see p. 134).

Compare this with the initial self-evaluation you undertook. What differences do you notice?

● What are your current priorities for developing your people skills?
● What opportunities could you create to develop your people skills further?

Closing comments

Increasing numbers of graduate and non-graduate jobs will include a managerial function, with responsibility for managing other people and their relationships with each other. There are much higher expectations of most employees now for managing other people, whether colleagues, customers or clients.

On the other hand, academic work is often organised to emphasise individual effort and achievement. There are a number of reasons for this, including the need to secure academic standards and to ensure every student is performing well on an individual basis. However, many programmes now include group work, team work and work placements to ensure students have real opportunities to develop their people skills.

Whether inter-personal skills are provided through the curriculum or not, it is a good idea to search out opportunities to develop them. Careers Services, the Students' Union, Schools Liaison Offices at the university, and voluntary agencies can provide such opportunities.

(continued)

(continued)

Inter-personal skills require, above all, good self-management. This chapter should be read alongside Chapter 4. Emotional intelligence is a key factor in being able to manage oneself in interactions with others and to understand the needs and requirements of other people. Some universities run additional programmes such as basic counselling skills and assertiveness to develop people skills.

Effective people skills are invaluable in all aspects of life, study and work. They provide the oil that enables your interactions with others to run smoothly. When you develop good people skills, you can see ahead to where difficulties may emerge, take steps to minimise these, and increase the harmony in everyday social interactions. This reduces stress, saves time and improves conditions for everybody. Everybody is happier – which is why people skills are becoming so valued.

Further reading

Belbin, M. R. (2010) *Team Roles at Work*, 2nd edn (London: Butterworth-Heinemann). (For more about using Belbin types for team work.)

Benson, J. F. (2009) *Working More Creatively with Groups*, 3rd edn (London: Tavistock). (Useful for dipping into; contains many ideas about making groups work effectively.)

Cottrell, S. M. (2008) *The Study Skills Handbook*, 3rd edn (Basingstoke: Palgrave Macmillan), Chapter 5. (An introduction to the skills of working with others, specifically in university contexts.)

Kozubska, J. (1997) *The 7 Keys of Charisma: The Secrets of Those Who Have It* (London: Kogan Page). (Particularly useful for those considering management, media and high-profile jobs.)

Luft, J. (1984) *Group Processes: An Introduction to Group Dynamics*, 3rd edn (Mayfield, CA: Mountain View). (For more advanced reading about group dynamics.)

McGill, I. and Beaty, L. (2001) *Action Learning: A Practitioner's Guide*, 2nd revised edn (London: Routledge), Chapters 2, 5 and 9. (For more detail specifically about action sets.)

Ribbens, G. and Thompson, R. (2002) *Understanding Body Language* (Abingdon: Gower). (Looks at body language in a range of everyday work settings.)

Taylor, R. and Humphrey, J. (2002) *Fast Track to the Top: Skills for Career Success* (London: Kogan Page). (The skills associated with successful chief executives, including inter-personal skills.)

Chapter 7

Thinking outside the box

All acts performed in the world begin in the imagination.

Barbara Grizzuti Harrison

Learning outcomes

This chapter offers opportunities to:

understand how your brain works so you can use it more effectively
develop your natural ability to learn new things
develop confidence in your creativity
use strategies to generate ideas
use creative approaches to thinking.

Introduction

Born to learn

Learning is a natural process. Our brains are set up to learn – they consist of approximately a hundred billion neurons, which are linked in elaborate networks. These neural networks enable us to:

- transmit information from one part of the brain to another;
- form associations between new information and what we already know;
- make sense of what we experience;
- encode information for memory.

We can envisage our brains as billions of trees laid out in all directions, and whose roots and branches are all in contact. For any one activity, several billion contacts may be made between those branches and roots – and this happens in milliseconds. A thought is like a bolt of lightning illuminating a vast forest of connections.

Our brains are also very flexible. They allow us to learn in innumerable ways, through:

- listening
- imitation
- taking small steps
- practice
- watching others
- day-dreaming
- taking an inspired leap
- linking different problems

and so on.

Learning can be easy. The most complex things our brains will ever have to learn were accomplished when we did not even know what 'learning' was, before the age of five. This chapter will look at how you can make best use of your brain's amazing capacities. The earlier part of the chapter looks at some characteristics of your brain, so that you can use its natural tendencies to best effect.

Inspiration is most difficult when we think in rigid, logical ways. This chapter looks at ways of stimulating the idea-generating capacities of the brain – which may mean thinking and acting in ways that are not typical of your usual study or work habits. To begin, do the activity below.

Activity: The 'box'

In your reflective journal, jot down your response to the following question:

- What is the use of a shoebox?

We will return to this later in the chapter.

Limiting intelligence

Are cleverness and creativity the same thing? If you did well at school, does that mean you are automatically a creative thinker? De Bono (1994) argues that clever people are often hampered by their apparent intelligence in two keys ways:

1. They are very good at arguing and are usually better at defending their position. As they are more likely to win the argument, they are more likely to think they have the best solution. You may know people like this. If you think you are 'right', there is no reason to listen to other people or to look for a better solution.

   As a result, many intelligent people are trapped in poor ideas because they can defend them so well.

   (De Bono, 1994)

2. It is easier, quicker, and more dramatic to prove somebody else wrong than to devise constructive solutions. Negative criticism adds to your visible 'superiority'. Being constructive can take longer and can make other people look good rather than yourself. However, negative criticism doesn't promote creative thinking.

Our views of what is 'intelligent' can prevent us from developing our minds to their full potential. If we hold negative thoughts about our own intelligence, for example, those thoughts can also limit our ability to perform well (Cottrell, 2008). People who feel they are 'not very bright' or 'not very creative' probably will fulfil that estimation of themselves. On the other hand, positive thinking and constructive mental activity develop the mind. Creativity is like a muscle: it gets stronger the more you exercise it.

📖 *Reflection*   Limiting creativity

Note in your reflective journal:

- any ways that you currently put limits on your capacity to think;
- any ways you prevent yourself from achieving your full potential as a creative, imaginative person.

Activity: Self-evaluation of creative thinking skills

Make two copies of this table. Complete one now and one when you have completed the chapter or later in your programme. Rate each statement as follows:

Rating: *Very often = 4*   *Often = 3*   *Sometimes/it depends = 2*   *Hardly ever = 1*   *Never/don't know = 0*

	Score
1. I experiment with many ideas before I make a decision	
2. When I am working on a project, I discuss 'work in progress' with others	
3. I like to find out a lot about things I do not understand	
4. I have a wide range of interests	
5. I enjoy talking to a wide range of people	
6. I take a different route home at least once a week	
7. I set myself new challenges, regularly, so I feel 'stretched'	
8. I like the challenge of difficult problems	
9. I actively look for patterns and trends	
10. I actively look for similarities between things	
11. I actively look for connections between things	
12. I enjoy looking for the reasons that underlie patterns and trends	
13. I like to think up new ways of doing things	
14. I try to break my routine	
15. I actively look for new sources of inspiration	
16. I try things out even if I am no good at them	
17. If I get something wrong, I look to see what I could have done better	
18. I like to imagine different ways of doing things	
19. I take calculated risks	
20. Even if I am good at something, I look for better ways of doing it	
21. I have strategies for generating ideas when I need to	
22. I look for solutions even when it looks as if something is impossible	
23. I look for more than one perspective on an issue	
24. I like to play about with different ideas	
25. I spend time thinking about how I think	

Add up your score   Total _____

Interpreting your creative thinking score

You now have an approximate score for creative thinking. This is not an exact science, but it gives you an idea of how confident you are about your own creativity. It also gives you an insight into how you could develop your creative thinking skills further.

75–100   This is an excellent score. If your ratings were accurate, you already use the kinds of strategies that contribute to creative thinking. This suggests an invaluable approach to problem-solving and to life in general. Consider how you could develop these further, especially in relation to your programme and to the career areas that interest you. It is also worth checking whether your logical, analytical skills are as well developed as your creative thinking skills. It is important to develop both kinds of thinking.

50–74   This is a good score. If your ratings were accurate, this suggests your creative thinking skills are already well developed. Look for themes in the statements to which you gave lower ratings. What else could you do to develop your thinking skills? This chapter may give you some ideas.

25–49   If your ratings were accurate, this suggests that you have started to develop creative thinking skills. There is probably a lot more you could do to build these further. It is worth spending time considering what prevents you from developing your creativity at present. It is important not to try too hard at creative thinking: it may be that you worry too much about doing things the right way. Experiment with a more relaxed approach and make sure you leave plenty of time to try out new approaches as well as your usual methods. It can take time to build confidence in new approaches.

0–24   If your ratings were accurate, this suggests that you have identified that creative thinking skills are not currently a major area of strength for you. Check with people who know you well whether you have rated yourself too harshly. Identify what kinds of thinking skills are most critical for meeting the requirements of your programme and career interests. Read through the comments for the score 25–49 above. These may also apply to you. Most importantly, do not be discouraged. This is not a scientific test – and creative thinking skills can be developed.

A dozen really useful things to know about your brain

- The brain loves complexity and change;
- the more you learn, the easier it is to learn;
- it uses short cuts;
- it loves organisation and patterns;
- it is naturally playful;
- it works when you are not looking;
- you can send it on errands;
- it likes to be fed;
- you can take it for a walk;
- it won't work well when it is upset or does not feel safe;
- it works well when it is excited;
- it likes to be refreshed.

The brain likes complexity and change

The mind loves complexity. Even babies get bored with simple patterns; they look at complex images for much longer. Choirs prefer more difficult tunes:

these are harder to learn but retain their interest when rehearsed and delivered many times. Throughout history, people have been fascinated by riddles, puzzles, codes, mazes and labyrinths. In many ages, art has been heavily allegorical or symbolic, so that an apparently simple picture could be decoded or interpreted, item by item, to read out a hidden message.

📖 ***Reflection*** Complexity

- What kinds of complex, skilled, multi-layered or multi-sequenced activities do you enjoy?
- What kinds of complicated tasks do you avoid?
- What makes you seek out and enjoy one kind of complexity and avoid others?

Our brain can cope with very complex problems. It sets up connections between our new experiences and what we already know. It develops increasingly elaborate networks as we become more expert in an area. However, it can't do this all at once.

What we are *able* to learn is partly the result of what we have *already* learnt.

The more you learn, the easier the next thing is to learn

When we encounter new situations, we draw upon and develop our existing knowledge. We then organise this into internal models called 'schema'.

If we have been on one picnic, for example, we do not know how typical that is of any other picnic. When we have been on ten picnics, we have an elaborated idea of a picnic. We know the variations that are possible, we can anticipate what to expect at future picnics, plan for such occasions, and develop criteria to evaluate whether they are 'good' or 'bad' picnics depending on our experience. At this stage, we have a well-developed schema.

As we go through the day, this process is going on all the time. According to Piaget (1952), our experiences reinforce or alter what we already know.

If we expose the brain to varied and complex problems at a reasonable pace, it will usually develop the neural networks we need. It isn't how many neurons or brain cells we have that makes us capable of tasks, but the number of connections between them. We develop these connections through engagement with the environment, with activity, with stimulation.

If we try to be experts when we are still novices at a task, the brain may not have developed the right connections to solve the problems we encounter. It can leave us feeling that we are incapable of the task. This can seem like failure and encourage us to give up when we may simply need more practice. The longer we perform or practice an activity, the more we build up the mental connections that we need to do it well. There really is sense in the old saying, 'If at first you don't succeed, try, try, try again.'

We often find that the things we found hardest to do, and had to practise the most, are those for which we develop the best overall and long-term understanding.

📖 ***Reflection*** Stimulating your brain

- What kinds of new challenges do you give your brain to keep it 'stretched' and stimulated?
- For what kinds of activity do you tend to stick with the task, increasing your chances of succeeding in the long run?
- What kinds of activities do you 'give up on' early?

The brain uses short cuts

The brain likes short cuts. Professional magicians know this and trick the eye by encouraging such 'short cuts'.

If the brain thinks it knows what it is seeing, it stops looking for explanations. It matches what it thinks it is experiencing with the 'schema' or mental models it has already built up. If it finds a good enough match, it uses the stored information to make sense of the new experience. If not, it uses the new experience to adapt the mental models.

Most of the time the brain's short cuts are useful. We often refer to these as 'generalisations'. Generalisations help us to make sense of what is going on from one moment to the next, without having to start from scratch each time. We are able to tell what are 'typical' experiences, what are variations and what is new. If we can see a connection between something we are good at and the problem in hand, then we may offer the brain a short cut to solving the problem (see Chapter 2).

We can also feed messages to the brain that encourage it to take short cuts. 'I have tried and cannot do this' is one such message. Alternatively, we could choose to feed it encouraging messages such as: 'There is a way to solve this', or 'Let's look at this again' or 'This is interesting', and the brain will respond differently.

📖 **Reflection**   Spotting the short cuts

- Which short cuts does your brain take? In other words what kinds of things are you less likely to notice that other people seem better at spotting?
- Which messages do you give your brain that may encourage it to think it can't do things?
- How could you change those messages?

The brain likes organisation and patterns

The brain organises information in many different ways. A colour, a scent or a few bars of music can evoke very detailed memories. Similarly, we can generate information quickly on the basis of the first letter of a word, the end of the word, words that mean the same thing, or any number of other similarities or differences. It is easier to remember information if we:

- organise it into groups, clusters or categories;
- organise it into hierarchies;
- make links between pieces of information.

If we find links between one kind of activity and another, we are better able to perform the second activity. Looking for patterns or similarities enables us to transfer 'expertise' from one area to solve new problems (see Chapter 2).

Expert chess players

Experts are experts because of the power of the brain in recognising patterns. Expert chess players can recall how all the pieces were arranged on a chessboard even if given only five seconds to view it. This is not because they have superior memories. Expert chess players see the whole configuration as one meaningful whole. They see it as one 'chunk'. They can only do this if they recognise the pattern as one that they have seen and used before. In effect, they are remembering only one pattern, which is easy.

Novice players have to remember the positions of up to 32 items – but the short-term memory struggles with more than 5–7 items. Novices have to work harder in order to remember more items – and are less likely to get the answer right. However, expert chess players are no better at remembering the layout of the pieces than anyone else if they haven't seen the pattern before (Chase and Simon, 1973). The effect of spending time practising, seeing and learning significant patterns over and over again, is very evident here.

Significant patterns

Although the brain can get used to any pattern, it works more effectively if the pattern you look for has an underlying meaning. The brain likes significance and meaning. For example, it is easier to remember a set of names if they all belong to members of your family. Similarly, if expert technicians are asked to reconstruct a circuit board, they will do so on the basis of what each part does – its function or significance to the working of the board. Novices will try to assemble the board according to how it looks (Egan and Schwartz, 1979). This approach is superficial and recall is less effective. You can test this for yourself with the activity below.

Activity: Memory for patterns (1)

- Write down the start time.
- Time how long it takes you to learn the following sequence, in order. You can learn this in any way you like, as long as you end up being able to recite it or write it without looking.

O h n s t d o w t e u o r h

- Put the sequence and all copies where you cannot see them. Now write it down.
- Check for accuracy.
- If you have not got it right, keep going until you do. Then write down the time again.
- Write down how long it took you, altogether, to learn the sequence perfectly.
- When you have finished, time yourself learning the second sequence, found on p. 186.

You probably found it took less time to remember the second sequence, even though you may never have seen this written down before. This is because you are familiar with the chunks of meaning (the words) and a single bigger chunk (the meaning of the sentence). The knowledge of experts for any task is divided into meaningful chunks, similar to words and sentences.

As you become more expert in any subject, you will start to construct the 'meaningful chunks' of the subject, so that you can 'read it off' as quickly as you did the second sequence in the activity on p. 186.

Activity: Subject chunks

Sometimes working from two or three books, seeing how the material is arranged in each, can help to develop a sense of how the information can be organised into different sets of meaningful chunks. You may find some texts organise information in ways that are easier for you to understand.

- Look at three different books for a topic you find difficult.
- Write down the headings and sub-headings used by each.
- Browse the material written under each.
- Which book organises the information in the way that suits you best?

If you work with material in this way, you may also find that seeing the same information from several different angles helps to build up your overall picture of the subject.

The brain is naturally playful

The brain makes odd, unusual and unexpected connections. This enables us to make jokes and puns, to invent, to find solutions. Children use play as their main tool for learning. They act out adult roles. They play with the world around them, and experiment in order to find out more about it. As adults, we may be self-conscious about using 'play' to develop our thinking. When we allow it to be playful, the brain can provide the answers we need.

However, the brain often presents information to us in unexpected ways. It may disguise the answers in riddles or give us clues to decipher. It encourages us to 'play' with information.

Our brain may spot a dinner fork on the table, make a connection with garden tools, and send us a signal about gardens. In the past, we may have associated gardening with hard work, and the brain has spotted the fork as a reminder to us to work on an essay. Sometimes we can catch hold of this odd train of connections, which is meaningful only to the person concerned. More often, the links are hidden. When the brain plays with us in this way, we can, if we play with the 'clues' it sends us, find the solutions to problems that are teasing us.

The brain works when you are not looking

The brain is working on our behalf all of the time. Most of what we do and learn, we do without even realising it. The brain does not respond well to being forced. For example, if a word or idea is 'on the tip of your tongue' you can try for hours to remember but without success. However, a few hours later, when you are focusing on something else, the answer will seem to 'pop into your head' from nowhere.

You can use the brain to work for you by focusing on a problem, analysing it as far as you can, generating as many solutions as possible – and then leaving it for a while. When you stop analysing and labouring over the problem, allowing the mind to relax, the brain will continue to work on the problem for you.

Indeed, if you change environment, and return to a problem, your brain may have drawn your attention to clues from your surroundings without you being aware of it. Experiments with children show that they used the shape of the light bulbs, clouds, even shadows on the ceiling or cracks in the wall to resolve problems they had been discussing before taking a rest break.

You can make use of this capacity of the brain if you:

- spend time elaborating the problem so the brain is absolutely clear what you are looking for. 'Day-dreaming' alone is not enough;
- give the brain some space to work on the problem;

- enter a relaxed state of mind for a while;
- return to the problem after a break.

You can send the brain on errands

As the brain will work on a problem when you are not consciously thinking about it, you can give it directions about what you want it to do. You need to be precise about what you want, and be prepared to wait. For example, if you know where the Buddha was born but can't remember and want to know, the brain will often deliver the answer a few minutes or hours later. Sometimes, it sends the message in code: you may find yourself thinking about an Indian film or Indian music or food, even though the only link with the Buddha is India. Be aware of this so you are ready to spot the clues.

Sleep on it

Work on a problem before you sleep. Identify the core questions as far as you can. List the things that are puzzling you. Write these as questions. Focus on one or two questions that are really key.

Whilst you sleep, your brain may continue to work on the problem. It may not. However, you increase the chances of your relaxed, unconscious mind working on the problem whilst you sleep. Keep paper and a pen by the bed as you may wake up with lots of ideas.

The brain likes to be fed and watered

Greenfield (2001) describes the brain as the greediest organ in the body. Although it is less than 2.5 per cent of our body weight, when the body is at rest the brain uses up 20 per cent of the body's fuel input. It consumes oxygen from the air we breathe and glucose from the carbohydrates we eat, burning these off at ten times the rate of any other body tissue. A good diet assists the brain. Over time, starving the body of carbohydrates will reduce the fuel that the brain needs in order to function.

Our bodies are mostly water. Water conducts electricity – and the messages our brain sends and co-ordinates are ultimately electrical impulses. These are affected by dehydration. When we are dehydrated, we reduce the efficiency of our brain as well as the general functioning of the body. Drinking water increases brain efficiency; other drinks do not have the same effect. We need about eight glasses of clear water a day, taken in gradually over the day.

The brain uses energy to process food and drink. After a large meal, you can become drowsy as the brain diverts its resources to deal with digestion. A big meal or drink is best avoided just before an exam or interview.

'The brain is fundamentally a chemical system' (Greenfield, 2001). The chemicals ultimately come from what we feed the body. Nicotine, for example, puts the body into survival mode, raising heart rate and blood pressure, whereas creative thinking is associated with more relaxed states. Various oils have also been associated with the way the brain functions (Stordy, 2000).

For most people, a varied diet provides the small amounts of a very wide range of chemicals that the body needs.

> 📖 **Reflection**   Nourishing your brain
>
> - How well do you feed and water your brain?
> - How much water do you drink each day?
> - Does your diet help or hinder your brain? If you are unsure, speak to somebody at your student health centre.

You can take your brain for a walk – physical exercise

Our brains first developed to manage movement and to respond to the environment whilst moving. The brain is stimulated by movement. It has been shown that mice learn better after a period of brisk exercise, as the supply of endorphins and other chemicals to the brain is increased.

In humans, a very large part of the motor cortex in the brain is devoted to the fine motor movements of the fingers and mouth (for using tools, writing, playing an instrument, speaking). If you want to stimulate your thinking, take a walk, play an instrument, draw, *do* something.

> **Activity: Exercising the problem**
>
> When working on a problem, take a brisk walk for about 20 minutes before returning to study. What is the effect? Do you come up with any ideas about your study whilst walking?

If you are required to sit and listen, find ways of increasing your personal engagement. For example, in long presentations or lectures, it is natural for the mind to wander after a few minutes. You can manage this process by;

- deliberately diverting yourself from listening for a few seconds at regular intervals. You can time this to coincide with when the speaker pauses or changes a slide. Otherwise, the brain will automatically 'switch off' but at less well timed occasions, and without you noticing.

- Listening actively, in a questioning way, jotting down your questions and opinions.
- Making notes: this can be an act of 'translation' of ideas from someone else's speech into your own words and ideas. Your listening is more active if you are choosing what to note, considering how to summarise, turning the talk into a diagram, and looking at how different aspects link up.

The brain won't work well when it is upset

When we are anxious, our body releases chemicals, such as adrenalin, which put us on the alert for danger. It is a very ancient bodily response, to help us survive. Our eyes look for movement at the periphery of our vision, so that we can detect danger, and we become more alert to noise, ready to react. We are easily distracted by our environment. Resources are diverted to large muscles in the arms and legs so that we can fight or run.

If we are anxious about an essay or exam, we can have the same adrenalin and survival response. As the body is then ready for large movements, we confuse it if we simply sit still. When we read or write or use the computer, we focus our attention on a small central space whilst our eyes want to look around for danger. We give mixed messages to the brain.

When we are stressed, the brain is not interested in 'thinking' tasks: it wants us to move, to escape, to survive. The more distressed we become at not understanding something, the more the brain diverts energy away from the thinking brain to the survival brain. Some strenuous activity, such as exercise, a brisk walk, housework – anything which uses the arms and legs – uses up the excess adrenalin, leaving us more relaxed and able to concentrate.

Strategies for managing stress and thinking positively can 'trick' the survival brain into believing that everything is OK, even if we do not fully feel or believe that at first. This allows us to use the parts of the brain needed to work out a complex solution. If we get too stressed, it becomes necessary to get help from somebody who isn't – and who can think more clearly.

The brain works well when it is excited and engaged

The brain likes to be stimulated and engaged. When tasks are not challenging enough, the brain finds it hard to stay focused. If tasks are too difficult for its current level of experience, the brain may become stressed. To work well, the brain needs to find a task that is stimulating but not a threat at its current level of competence.

If you look for the interest in a task, you are more likely to find it manageable than if you dismiss the task as too difficult. When we are excited or frightened, similar sets of chemicals are released in the body. We can direct the brain on how to interpret those chemicals. If we approach complex thinking problems as 'difficult', we may feel ourselves 'freeze up'. On the other hand, if we choose to look for the interest and excitement in them, we are less likely to 'go blank' and more likely to use the expertise we already have.

The brain likes to be refreshed

Although the brain enjoys being stimulated, the mind can become too busy. It becomes cluttered with thought and benefits from being 'stilled' occasionally. This is one of the most difficult things to achieve. One way of practising this is outlined above.

📖 *Reflection*   Creative potential

● What do you think creativity is?
● Where did you gain that understanding of what creativity is?
● How many marks out of ten would you give yourself for your current level of creativity?
● What marks out of ten do you think you are capable of achieving? On what do you base that estimation?

Creativity

Most people equate creativity with a particular kind of person. You may have associated creativity with being an artist, designer, performer or inventor.

Most of us underestimate our capacity for creativity. We may compare ourselves with great artists, for example, ignoring all the occasions when we have used our minds and resources creatively to deal with the situation we are in. We all have our own spheres where our natural creativity shines. This might be, for example:

● knowing the right things to say;
● seeing the funny side when things go wrong;
● finding ways of avoiding work and inventing unusual but convincing excuses;
● co-ordinating the activities of several children so that they are all entertained, occupied and safe;

- making patients feel at ease before an operation;
- cooking a special meal on a budget;
- soothing the waters when people are arguing;
- finding the perfect present for other people.

📖 *Reflection*   Personal creativity

- If you think of creativity in the ways suggested in the list above, what kinds of creativity do you show in your life? For example, what things do you do that seem easier for you than for some other people that you know? Do you have your 'own ways of doing things' for certain tasks?
- In which areas of your life would you like to be more creative?
- Do you feel comfortable with the idea of yourself as a potentially creative person?

Creative problem-solving

Previous chapters looked at problem-solving when managing tasks, yourself and other people. The magic element in all these situations is coming up with something new when it is needed – the 'creative spark'. This is often the hardest part of problem-solving. It is easy to sit waiting for inspiration, expecting an answer to fall from the sky. This chapter looks at strategies you can employ to oil the brain and assist it in generating ideas when needed.

The 'many quickly' approach

If you have one solution, look for five, ten, twenty more

Those who feel they know the answer to a question rarely look for a better one. Also, looking for one solution can take longer than ten possible solutions. We can be so concerned about finding the one 'right' answer that we block our thinking. If we look for ten solutions, our thinking can be more relaxed: we will not use nine of the ideas so it is safer to have some bad ones. Even if we then only find six ideas, we still have lots to work from.

The chances of finding the best idea first time round are quite remote. The more alternatives we consider, the more likelihood of finding the best solution.

Phrase brain-stimulating questions

In the first activity, you were asked to consider the use of a shoebox. This usually prompts one response, as the wording of the question suggests there is only one use. However, if asked, 'How many uses can you think of?' people usually generate many more responses. The way we phrase the question influences the way we approach a problem.

📖 *Reflection*   Multiple solutions

Jot down your responses to the following:

- How many uses for a shoebox can you think of in three minutes?
- For one problem that faces you on a regular basis, how many possible approaches to solving this can you generate in five minutes?

You probably found many more uses for a shoebox this time round. Answers people give include: carrying shoes; storage; for making a doll's house or garage; a door stop; carrying things; hiding things; a sandwich box; stepping on when the floor is wet; cardboard; rattling things as a musical instrument; protection from the rain; holding CDs; a small bench or seat; for babies to tear up; holding pencils; a treasure box for children; to decorate as a gift box; sending something in the post; papier mâché; food for goats, etc.

📖 *Reflection*   Multiple solutions

- How typical is it for you to push yourself to keep looking for more answers?
- For which activities would it be most useful for you to adopt this kind of approach?

Just a minute

It may seem paradoxical, but it is often more productive to give yourself a short time limit to generate ideas. The brain can leap into action better if it knows it has a time limit. This does not usually work well if you leave things to the last minute, as you need to be relaxed. Approach the task in a 'playful' way.

Try it. Give yourself just *one* minute to jot down everything you can think of to solve a problem you are working on. If you do not generate any useful ideas in that time, you have lost only a minute.

Play with time

If an activity is likely to take three hours, leave at least four hours to complete it, but aim to complete it in two. If you plan to allow more time than you need, you reduce the need to 'get it right' first time. Less stress can mean more creative thinking. You will also have more time to fine-tune your answer and deal with emergencies. The time challenge creates just enough excitement to generate adrenalin to help with the task and reduce 'sluggishness'. If you have too much time, it is easy to start too slowly or work at a slower pace. Set off at a good pace, aiming to finish at an earlier target time rather than your absolute deadline.

'What if questions . . .'

'What if . . .', Why not?' or 'Supposing . . . ?' questions stimulate the imagination. The wording suggests an imaginary state that is safe to explore (it isn't real so it can't do any damage) but which might provide real answers. If you reach a point where your ideas feel stuck, use 'what if . . .' questions. For example:

- 'What if . . . we designed a model that worked on its side/upside down/in reverse . . .'?
- 'Why not . . . ask those residents what they want their town to be like?'

- 'Supposing . . . we ate ten small meals a day rather than any big ones?'
- 'Supposing . . . we drew our reasoning rather than using words and numbers?'
- 'What if . . . witnesses were never visible to the accused?'

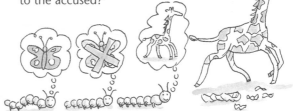

'What if' questions open up an area for exploration.

Activity: What if . . .

Take one problem or issue that you are working on at present.

- How many 'what if...' questions can you generate in three minutes?
- Select three of these.
- How many responses can you brainstorm for each question in three minutes (each)?
- Jot down any leads that arise from this activity. If there were none, take a walk or a break and then repeat the activity.

Generative thinking

There are many techniques that can be used to generate ideas and they are not difficult. An attitude of mind is the most important factor. Many people censor ideas at a very early stage if the ideas do not immediately seem sensible or useful.

Suspend judgement

Negative attitudes strangle creativity. We often dismiss the embryo of a good idea because we will not risk appearing foolish. Creativity, however, involves risks, mistakes, and 'bad' ideas as well as good. Only one in ten or twenty ideas will lead anywhere. To be creative requires the capacity to suggest ideas without immediately worrying about whether they are 'right' or what other people will say.

Nolan (2000) cites research which shows that when people's ideas are judged or dismissed, the number of ideas that are put forward drops dramatically. We tend to become more cautious and anxious if our suggestions are not welcomed, adopting a 'survival' response to avoid being discounted again.

Suspending judgement means:

● encouraging others to suggest ideas;
● avoiding negative self-judgements such as 'I am not a creative person';
● giving all ideas a chance to flow;
● being willing to express 'bad' or 'silly' ideas;
● noting all ideas in the early stages, without immediately evaluating them;
● being willing to look at all ideas for hidden potential;
● not assuming that a good idea holds all the answers;
● avoiding self-criticism if good ideas do not emerge quickly.

📖 *Reflection*   Self-censoring

● How far do you censor your ideas to avoid appearing foolish?
● What allows you to let your imagination work more freely?

Thinking with a 'light touch'

Usually, when we work on problems, we use logical, sequential, ordered thinking. Sometimes this is referred to as 'left brain' thinking, although thinking is not strictly compartmentalised in that way. Logical thinking is a necessary part of arriving at a solution to most tasks. However, such thinking tends to run along tramlines, following predictable routes. If you do not already know the answer, the tramlines may not lead anywhere.

Creative thinking takes a ligher touch. It does not respond well to being forced. It works well with direction and a clear goal, but not if the mind is too rigidly focused on a particular outcome. It works when you 'hover' over an idea, or play with it, teasing out possibilities. It is rather like holding a small bird in the palm of your hand: if you hold

Creative thinking requires a light touch

the intention or goal or idea too tightly, you crush or suffocate it.

You can see this when you know the answer to a question but cannot remember it. The harder you try to capture it, the more the answer seems to elude you. Sometimes, playing with the idea or letting it rest works better than forcing it.

Other generative thinking techniques

Chapter 8 describes a range of other generative thinking strategies. These are useful for developing open reflection, but can be used more generally. These include:

● Brainstorming;
● Free association;
● Day-dreaming;
● Free-writing;
● Drawing and doodling.

Synthesis

Synthesis is an important aspect of creativity. At a simple level, combining any two items creates a new entity.

Activity: Creating from two

Imagine . . .

Take any item from the Animal list below; and any item from the Machine list and imagine them combined into one new object. Choose as much or as little of each item as you like, as long as you 'borrow' at least one characteristic or feature from each side.

Animal	Machine
Giraffe	Car
Penguin	CD player
Dolphin	Radiator
Octopus	Motor bike
Monkey	Book shelves
Snake	Oven
Dragon	Garden hose
Ant-eater	Fridge
Zebra	Speed boat

Experiment
● Do this at least three more times with two different objects each time.

Draw it
● Make a diagram or sketch of one of your creations (even if you 'cannot draw'). What further ideas or details does this generate?

Describe it
● Describe your creation in words. What further ideas or details does this generate?

Apply it
● If you haven't done so already, think of at least three ways your creation could be of use in everyday life (these do not have to be sensible or 'real' applications).

How many ways can you apply this strategy to your academic work or job? Give yourself three minutes to generate a list.

Activity: Synthesis of life experience

Think of two activities where you use very different skills and personal characteristics (such as in seminars, at work, sport, dancing, music, travelling, being with a difficult family member, etc.).

Write a list of the skills and qualities for each in the columns below:

List 1: activity:	List 2: activity:
1.	
2.	
3.	
4.	
5.	
6.	
7.	
8.	
9.	
10.	

● Take any item from list 1 and consider a way that it could be of use in managing your second activity.
● Take any item from list 2 and consider a way that it could be of use in managing your first activity.
● Repeat this at least once more.

📖 In your reflective journal, jot down:

● Which of these are the most practical to put into operation?
● What would be the benefits of transferring these skills and qualities to new situations?

Synthesis as play

The 'Creating from two' activity invites you to play with ideas. Most of the time, ideas do not lead to earth-shattering discoveries. However, even apparently strange and silly ideas can lay down connections in the brain that one day might help you find the solution to a problem you do not yet know exists.

When you have a problem to solve, you can organise your ideas in lists, chunks or diagrams and then chop these up and rearrange them in new combinations. You can write or draw each on a separate piece of paper and shuffle these around until you find the best combination.

Play is about:

- having a go;
- finding out new things;
- stimulating the mind;
- suspending worry about getting it right;
- allowing the mind to relax;
- experimenting;
- 'letting go';
- informality.

Play is unpredictable. You may be playing with one idea, looking for a solution, and find that you are suddenly struck by the answer to something completely different that has been puzzling you for a long time.

📖 **Reflection**   On being playful

- How comfortable do you feel about the idea of 'playing' with solutions to academic work?
- Where do you allow yourself to be most playful?

Making connections

Expertise connections

In the synthesis activities above, you were, in effect, looking for and making connections. As you saw in earlier chapters, whenever you are working on a problem, the early stages are best spent in looking for connections and patterns between the current problem and:

- any similar problems or situations you have encountered before;
- other problems you are working on or subjects you are studying;
- the skills needed and those you have already used elsewhere;
- your areas of personal expertise, even if these seem far removed.

Unlikely connections

It is logical to look for expertise connections. However, creative thinking can benefit from almost any set of connections. As the brain likes to be entertained, it will pay particular attention to what it finds curious or unfamiliar. It can use any change in your surroundings or experience to find unexpected connections with a problem you have been grappling with.

You can assist the brain by searching out new perspectives in an active and interested way. Be prepared to let what you see, hear or experience change your views or inspire you. Some ways of doing this are listed below. Tick those that appeal to you most:

- [ ] walk a different way round the campus or town so that you are exposed to new patterns and layouts;
- [ ] go into shops that you do not normally visit;
- [ ] browse books that do not normally interest you;
- [ ] speak to students from different subjects about themes in their study;
- [ ] talk to people about their work and life experience;
- [ ] make friends with people from different walks of life;
- [ ] find opportunities to talk to or work with people of different ages;
- [ ] take a bus journey; visit a new place;
- [ ] do something you do not usually do: draw, dance, sing, act, run, yoga, learn a language;
- [ ] look at an object from a new perspective: draw it upside down or with both hands at once;
- [ ] listen to different music;
- [ ] draw or write with the hand you do not usually use;

☐ use a different medium to describe a problem (paint, model clay, use graphics, sing it, dance it).

> 📖 **Reflection**   Change perspective
>
> Which of these will you try out? Which could you do today?

Activity: Change perspective

Add at least five other items to the 'Unlikely connections' list on p. 180.

Choose at least three suggestions from that list above and apply these to a problem you are working on at present.

● Jot down your observations of any changes in your thinking.
● If there was no effect, choose three more suggestions and repeat the exercise.
● How can you build some of these opportunities for making alternative connections into your daily life?

Search for 'the missing links'

When breaking your routine with a new activity, act 'as if' the answers or the clues that you are looking for are in that book, object, music, conversation, journey, etc. Search out connections between the problem you are addressing and the new activity. Use language structures such as:

● 'This is similar to my problem because . . .' or
● 'My problem is like this journey/statue/house because they both . . .'

Do this 10 or 20 times. The least likely connection may prompt a useful solution. For example, doing a degree is like going for a walk because:

● you can plan a specific route;
● you can select alternative routes;
● they can both take you to unexpected places;
● the end of both can seem a long way off;
● they both require some effort;
● they both stimulate the mind; etc.

Activity: Connections

Complete the following phrase as in the example above. Compare personal planning to one or more of the items from the list below.

'Personal planning is like . . . because . . .'

Football
Climbing a mountain
Dancing
Painting a picture
Watching a film

Networks

Networks follow the natural habit of the brain to look for patterns. Making notes in patterns to explore a problem is usually much quicker than writing in full sentences and paragraphs. You can use single words, phrases, images, symbols, or colour to indicate an idea. If you prefer, you can create 'webs' of links using images rather than words. Networks can be very liberating as there are few rules to follow. You can:

● start anywhere on the paper;
● move from that focus point to anywhere else on the paper;
● generate other focus points where one set of ideas meets another set;
● write as much or as little as you like at each point (a word or short phrase usually works best. However, if your creative flow is stimulated by the process, go with the energy. You can return to the rest of the pattern once you have captured your idea);
● take the ideas anywhere you like, developing new connections: it is not a 'map' of what already exists but a new structure that you are creating;
● let your mind take you for a walk;
● be focused and logical or 'day-dream' and 'play', depending on what suits.

Information contained in networks is easier to remember if you:

● write in 'joined-up writing' (cursive script). It is easier for the brain to recall a continuous movement. Avoid capitals as these are harder for the brain to process;

- write so that you can read the writing without turning the page around;
- avoid using words such as *no, never, isn't, won't,* etc. as these are harder for the brain to process;
- use colour, symbols and shapes that make sections of the pattern stand out as interesting in their own right;
- take pauses to look for connections you might have missed;
- ask 'what if . . .?' questions about links that initially look unhelpful;
- work on the same problem more than once, designing a different network for each. On the second or third time, you may make very different sets of connections;
- for your last or working model, develop the pattern into an overall image or shape that you find easier to remember, such as a real object. Use a different shape for each topic. You then have only one 'item' for your short-term memory to recall (see the 'Expert chess players' section, p. 170).

There is an example of a network on p. 183.

Activity: Networks

- Do something relaxing, such as going for a walk.
- Then take a large piece of paper and as many coloured pencils, pens, paints as you like.
- Make a network for a problem or issue that you are working on at present. (See p. 183 for an example.) Hold the idea quite lightly at first and let your pen play with ideas.
- Follow the networks guidelines above.
- When you are finished, look at the overall shape that your map makes. Look for a real object or recognisable shape (flower, house, wheelbarrow, table, castle, etc.) that you haven't used before for this exercise. Draw in a few lines to outline the shape.
- Alternatively, use a distinctive image or style within the network to help you remember it.
- Consider how else you could make this pattern more memorable so that you can recall the different sections easily.

Lateral thinking

Much of the ground-breaking work on 'thinking about thinking' was developed by Dr Edward de Bono, who created the term 'lateral thinking'. Dr de Bono encourages unconventional ways of looking at a problem, playing with the most unlikely solutions and then looking for an aspect that might actually work. Lateral thinking values humour, looking for opportunity in the 'accidental', a willingness to do things in new ways, and exploring all ideas.

For example, a de Bono statement might be that aeroplanes should land upside down, or that a car should have square wheels (de Bono, 1994). By working 'as if . . .' this were a serious proposition, this creates an opportunity for really examining all the taken-for-granted processes such as the tyre pressure, tyre threads, braking devices, puncture problems and so forth. In practice, real-life advances have been made through such forms of thinking.

Activity: Crazy questions

- Generate as many apparently 'crazy' 'what if . . .' questions as you can for a problem or issue you are working with at present.
- Select one of these and work through what would need to be changed in order to make this work. If possible, do this in a group.
- What light were you able to throw upon your problem by looking at it in a different way?

As if . . . it were them

You can also brainstorm solutions to a problem from the perspective of different people. This can generate a different set of responses from those you make 'in your own voice'. Imagine yourself 'in the shoes' of somebody who you think would have sensible things to say about the problem.

Network: creative thinking

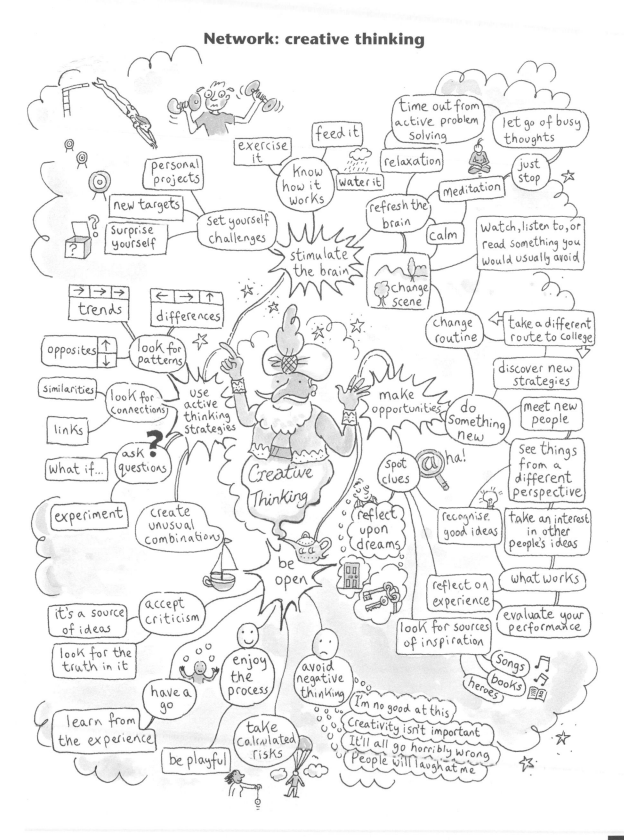

Wear different hats

Dr de Bono (1996) devised a system of imaginary hats, each a different colour and representing a different approach to thinking. When you 'wear' each of these hats, you address an issue in a completely different way. In effect, you give your mind permission to let go of one way of thinking for a while, and explore a different approach.

Although de Bono has a specific series of hats, you could devise whatever set of hats works for you: a

practical hat, a dreamer's hat, a philosopher's hat, a mechanic's hat, a chef's hat, a poet's hat. Alternatively, you could devise a set of coats or shoes that suggest different ways of working and thinking.

Thinking upside down: sabotage

It is usually easy to think catastrophically. Most of us are quite good at imagining all the things that could go wrong. Use this ability to good effect by playing with the idea of deliberately doing everything wrong. The more the wording is exaggerated, the more inviting this task can be.

For example:

- What 20 things could I do, deliberately, to waste my time at college and have zero to show after three or four years of effort?
- What can I do so I feel more pressurised, irritated, thoroughly miserable, and miss all deadlines?
- What are all the things I could do and say in the seminar group to really inflame the situation and make everything thoroughly explosive?
- How can I really work myself up into a stressful state so that I make the job interview as difficult as possible?

It is usually easy to generate a long list of items to answer such questions, attesting to our native wit in knowing what we should and should not do in most situations. Once the list is generated, create a second list alongside it, writing the positive solution to each potentially 'catastrophic' action. It can be remarkably easy to generate ground rules or an action plan using this technique.

Working with raw material

Most of the strategies discussed above are 'early-stage' techniques. They emphasise letting ideas flow. Structure, selection, criticism, censoring, and evaluation are not helpful to the process of generating early ideas.

However, creative thinking does not stop here. The first stage develops a mass of material, which is like undifferentiated dough or clay. The next stage is to shape this into something that works. This means playing and working with your ideas:

- *Analyse*:   What are the interesting aspects of each idea or suggestion?
- *Evaluate*:   What could each suggestion contribute to an understanding of the issue or to finding a solution?
- *Synthesise*:   Which aspects of each idea would work well together?
- *Spot gaps*:   What is missing? For what else do you need to generate ideas and solutions?
- *Elaborate*:   Add details to fill gaps and clarify ideas.
- *Select*:   Which ideas do you want to take forward, and which do you want to leave to one side for now?
- *Organise*:   Structure your ideas into a relevant pattern. This may be a diagram, flow-chart, model or piece of writing.
- *Plan*:   Draw up an action plan to put your ideas into effect.

Develop the narrative

Write down how the whole solution or plan will work from start to finish, in order to provide your initial narrative. If you prefer, record yourself talking through your ideas. Producing the narrative can, itself, allow a different set of ideas to flow. Focus on the aim (to develop a solution) rather than on the quality of the writing at this stage.

Creating the narrative may be a stop–start process. The halts are also part of the creative process. They usually indicate precisely where you need to dig deeper to ensure something will work well. Geologists, for example, look at the surface of the ground for signs of a break or a change or something that doesn't 'fit' or match. This 'glitch' or 'bump' is a sign that something is worth investigating below the surface. The same is true for the creative process. It is the bits that seem to be getting in the way of finding a solution, the tricky bits, that lead to creative and sound solutions.

When you hit a 'bump' or the narrative stops, it is important to return to the early-stage techniques again, brainstorming, free writing, discussing, developing networks of ideas. Focus on the area of difficulty. Then return to the narrative until you hit the next 'bump'.

Creativity and risk taking

Behold the turtle. He makes progress only when he sticks his neck out.

James Bryant Conant

Creative thinking requires risk taking. Most of us have been trained from a very early age to be logical, sensible, not to act the fool. It can be hard to work against that training and to remain confident in what we are doing. It is easy to feel embarrassed or anxious about what others will think.

Creativity and emotional self-management

Nolan (2000) argues that an education aimed at developing innovative, creative thinkers must begin at the emotional level. If we do not have the emotional stamina to deal with other people's opinions, then we divert our creative energies into protecting ourselves from being judged. We won't be able to risk other people's opinions of us.

Creativity carries an element of anxiety and stress. Goleman (1995) has described the physiological reasons for this. It is a natural part of our biology to resist negative feedback. However, we can develop our mental attitudes so that we are less affected by fear of criticism. Goleman's work suggests that the better we are able to manage our anxiety, the more we can think freely and creatively (see Chapter 4).

Calculated risks

The creative risks we take may not pay off. In the early stages of generating ideas, it is a good idea to take risks. At this point, ideas are only on paper.

As you move towards developing an idea, costs come into play. There may be costs in terms of time, money, resources, the environment, or personal prestige. It is then important to limit the risks, without necessarily dismissing the possibility of taking a risk. This means considering such issues as:

● The consequences of a course of action: who will be affected; what are the costs to all parties?
● What are the possible benefits? Who will gain? How significant are the advantages compared with the disadvantages?
● What are the chances of success?
● Can you really afford the solution?
● Is the risk worth it?
● Can you deal with the consequences if it does not work?

Not all risks are worth it. Some will pay off; others will not. You need to be sure that you and all the affected parties can cope emotionally and financially with the consequences if things do not work out as hoped.

Taking responsibility

Because creativity involves risk taking, it also involves taking responsibility for one's own actions. This means:

● thinking through the needs and interests of all parties, including yourself;
● being able to accept the consequences of your own actions;
● planning safety nets where necessary, so that other people do not get hurt;
● being aware of legal and ethical responsibilities.

If you are being creative in the way you approach an essay or experiment, this may simply mean being prepared to accept a low mark if the tutor does not agree that your novel ideas meet the requirements of the assignment. Check what possibilities are open to you, especially if you really need to get a high mark. On the other hand, you may wish to push the boundaries, no matter what the cost. That is your decision.

If, on the other hand, you are designing products for the public or making decisions that affect people's livelihoods, you need to consider a wider range of issues that will become your responsibility, such as:

● health and safety requirements;
● legal requirements;
● financial issues;
● ethical considerations.

Activity B: Memory for patterns (2)

This activity is the second part of the activity on p. 171. Time how long it takes you to memorise the following set of letters, so that you are able to reproduce them without looking.

S h u t   t h e   d o o r   n o w

Compare this result with the time it took you to do the original exercise above. Then return to that page.

Closing comments

This chapter emphasises that creativity is both a state of mind and a way of developing the mind. Creativity is accessible to everybody. Strategies which develop creativity require relaxation, playfulness, a light touch, and enjoyment in order to be most effective. Our level of creativity, and hence our ability to be a creative problem-solver, will be affected by our attitudes and beliefs, our sense of humour, our emotional self-management, our health and well-being. Creativity does remind us that mind and body function as an integrated whole.

Creative thinking strategies are unpredictable. They can be time-consuming. It is hard to say how long 'thinking' or creativity will take. When work is left until the day before a deadline, there is not time for the brain to tease out the connections between things, and for you to mull over possibilities. It is also harder to stay relaxed and open to creative possibilities when a deadline is looming.

On the other hand, creative thinking may lead to answers in a small fraction of the time taken by logical, analytical thinking. Time spent in play, musing, synthesis and making connections can lead to innovatory ways of seeing and thinking.

Further reading

De Bono, E. (1996) *Teach Yourself to Think* (London: Penguin).

De Bono, E. (2006) *De Bono's Thinking Course*, revised and updated (London: BBC Active).

Greenfield, S. (2001) *The Human Brain: A Guided Tour* (London: Phoenix).

McCormick, R. and Paechter, C. (1999) *Learning and Knowledge* (London: The Open University).

Van Oech, R. (2008) *A Whack on the Side of the Head: How to be More Creative*, revised and updated edn (New York: Grand Central Publishing).

Chapter 8

The art of reflection

A single word even may be a spark of inextinguishable thought.

Percy Bysshe Shelley

Learning outcomes

This chapter offers opportunities to:

understand what is meant by 'reflection'
understand the importance of reflection to evaluating and improving personal performance
identify different kinds of reflection for different purposes
develop methods for improving your reflective skills
devise your own model for reflection
consider how to communicate the results of your reflection to other people.

Introduction

If you have a fleck of bright green paint between your eyes, or egg on your chin, you cannot see them as they are too close to your eyes to be visible to them. Without a mirror or a comment from other people, you could pretend there was nothing to see. This won't, of course, prevent others from seeing what you cannot.

Similarly, we are usually too close to ourselves to be aware of the things we most need to know. We can easily fail to recognise what may be very evident to other people. Fortunately, we can stand back occasionally and reflect about such things as our aims, responses, feelings and performance. Well-developed skills in reflection can help us to:

● gain a more in-depth and honest picture of ourselves;
● become more aware of our hidden motivations, our thinking styles, and of how we appear to other people;
● develop a better understanding of what affects our own performance and progress;
● develop our insight and judgements;

● gain more control over our own thoughts, emotions, responses and behaviour so that we are in a better position to achieve what we want to achieve.

Reflection in everyday life

Reflection is a natural activity. To a greater or lesser extent, we all spend time going back over what we have said or done, or what we wish we had said and done. Often, reflection accompanies hindsight: we realise long after an event how things might have been different, or how some small event was more significant than we realised. This is reflected in everyday expressions:

● 'If only I had known then what I know now . . .'
● 'With hindsight, I realise . . .'
● 'I could never have imagined that doing X would result in Y . . .'
● 'Now I realise where this leads, I wouldn't do it again . . .'

- 'If I had the chance, I would do it all over again.'
- 'It was worth it/it wasn't worth it/it was worth the risk.'

In other words, we review what was said or done, weighing up the consequences and considering what the alternatives might have been. We evaluate whether we would do things differently if given the chance again or whether we were right first time.

In retrospect, Ulrika wished she had planned her landing location more carefully

Reflection as challenge

The reflective process is challenging. We do not always like to discover the truth about ourselves: it can be embarrassing to find we have walked around for several hours with a dab of egg yolk on our chin. We would rather believe it wasn't there or that nobody could see it. The same is true of the reflective process. When it works well, we discover things that make us feel uncomfortable. Our natural reaction is to pretend they do not really matter, or to look for an excuse, or to blame someone else. The things we most need to know can be the hardest to hear.

It takes time and practice for people to develop good reflective skills. Don't be discouraged if you think reflection does not come naturally to you. This book structures reflection on a wide range of issues. If you have undertaken some of the reflections and activities, then you will already be developing a sense of what is involved.

Is reflection important?

At university level, you need to take responsibility for your own progress. Students are expected to develop into independent thinkers, capable of evaluating their own performance, drawing conclusions about what they did well and how to improve. Your success will depend, to a large extent, on yourself.

You need to be confident in your own judgements of your work. The feedback you receive from tutors and other students gives you a rare opportunity to compare your own evaluations with those of other people.

Your evaluations should be based upon sound criteria rather than a general feeling that you are right and others wrong. Consider the differences between your own evaluations and the feedback you receive from others: these may hold important clues about how to achieve better grades and to improve your performance generally.

Reflection and Personal Development Planning

All British universities are required to provide personal development planning (PDP) for students as a 'structured process of reflection'. By the time you leave university, you are expected to know how to use structured reflection to understand:

- yourself, your motivations, choices and behaviours;
- what you want to achieve;
- how to plan, follow through, review and evaluate a course of action;
- how your responses and performance affect other people;
- how to take action to improve your work or learning to the benefit of yourself and/or others.

The 'reflective practitioner'

Many occupations now require a 'reflective practitioner' approach. This is built into the work cycle in some way, such as through staff reviews or appraisal. Typically, this means taking personal responsibility for:

- your continuing professional development (CPD);
- evaluating your personal experience, strengths, qualities and skills;
- identifying ways of using your strengths well, within your professional area;
- identifying personal limitations and areas that could be improved through training, practice or informal learning;
- recognising the effects of your own responses and behaviour and taking responsibility for these;
- making useful contributions to team discussions;
- improving individual and team performance;
- identifying your own contribution to the results of a task, project or outcome.

Your current programme may include reflective activity. If not, the self-evaluation questionnaire on p. 192 can help you to decide where you need to work next.

What is 'reflection'?

Reflection is a type of thinking. It is associated with deep thought aimed at better understanding. It includes a mixture of elements, such as:

1. Making sense of experience

It is important to note the difference between 'experience' and 'learning'. Experience can be the basis for learning and development. However, just because we have been through an experience it does not mean we have learnt all there is to learn about it – or even that we have learnt anything at all. Reflection is an important part of the learning experience. It is where we analyse experience, actively attempting to 'make sense' or find the meaning in it.

2. 'Standing back'

By 'standing back', we gain a better view or perspective of an experience, issue or action. It is not always easy to reflect when caught up in the midst of activity.

3. Repetition

Reflection involves 'going over' something, perhaps even several times, in order to look at it critically from several points of view or to check nothing has been missed.

4. Deeper honesty

Reflection is associated with a striving after the truth. It is through reflection that we can come to acknowledge things we find difficult to admit in the normal course of events.

5. 'Weighing up'

Reflection involves a sense of even-handed judgement and critical evaluation – it usually involves 'weighing things in the balance', taking all things into account rather than just the most obvious.

6. Clarity

Reflection can bring greater clarity, as though seeing things reflected back in a mirror. This can be useful at any stage in the process of devising, carrying out or reviewing activities.

7. Understanding

Reflection is associated with opening up to learning and understanding at a deeper level, including gaining insight into theories and concepts that are difficult to access by other means.

8. Making judgements

Reflection involves an element of making judgements and drawing conclusions.

Activity: The relevance of reflection to me

Circle as many of the following as are relevant and of benefit to you. Use the empty circles to add in any others of importance to you.

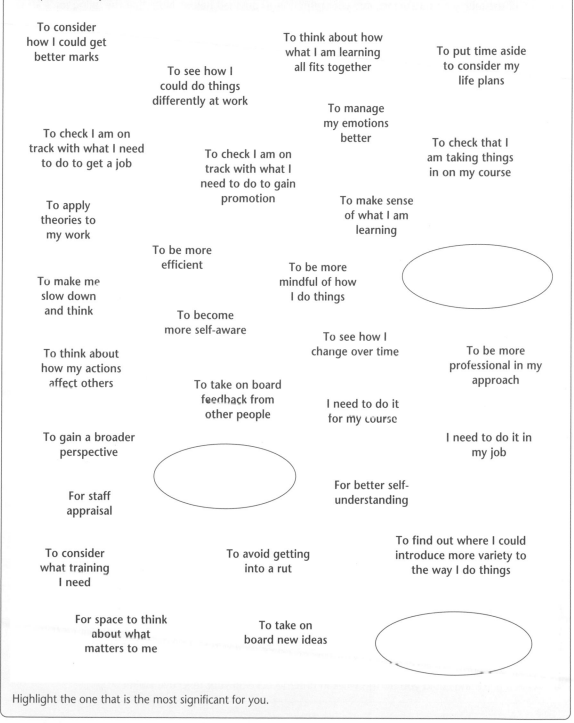

To consider how I could get better marks

To see how I could do things differently at work

To think about how what I am learning all fits together

To put time aside to consider my life plans

To check I am on track with what I need to do to get a job

To check I am on track with what I need to do to gain promotion

To manage my emotions better

To check that I am taking things in on my course

To apply theories to my work

To make sense of what I am learning

To be more efficient

To be more mindful of how I do things

To make me slow down and think

To become more self-aware

To see how I change over time

To be more professional in my approach

To think about how my actions affect others

To take on board feedback from other people

I need to do it for my course

I need to do it in my job

To gain a broader perspective

For better self-understanding

For staff appraisal

To consider what training I need

To avoid getting into a rut

To find out where I could introduce more variety to the way I do things

For space to think about what matters to me

To take on board new ideas

Highlight the one that is the most significant for you.

The art of reflection

Self-evaluation on reflective practice

For each of the following statements, rate your responses as outlined below. Note that the rating for 'strongly disagree' carries no score.

Rating: 4 = *strongly agree*   3 = *agree*   2 = *sort of agree*   1 = *disagree*   0 = *strongly disagree*

'I am very confident that I . . .'	Rating
1. know how to use logs or reflective journals	
2. understand myself very well	
3. challenge my own thinking sufficiently	
4. spend sufficient time looking for relevant links between different things	
5. spend sufficient time 'making sense' of what I learn and experience	
6. spend sufficient time thinking about the significance of what I learn	
7. spend sufficient time thinking about how to improve my academic performance	
8. spend enough time thinking about the effects of my actions and behaviour	
9. make an accurate evaluation of my own strengths	
10. know how to apply my experience and skills to novel situations	
11. am aware of my personal limitations	
12. am aware of my own personal development needs	
13. always consider all options before arriving at a decision	
14. am always aware of all the motivations underlying my behaviour	
15. always take full responsibility for my own part in events	
16. spend enough time thinking about how to improve my skills in dealing with other people	
17. spend enough time thinking about how I could make a better contribution to groups I am in	
18. spend sufficient time thinking about the significance of other people's actions	
19. spend sufficient time thinking about the significance of what other people say	
20. can reflect accurately about my emotional responses to events	
21. could draw upon my reflections well for assessment purposes.	
22. spend sufficient time thinking about how to use the feedback I receive from others	
23. know how to use reflection effectively when applying for jobs	
24. am clear about the different kinds of reflection that are open to me	
25. do not need to develop my skills of reflection any further	
Add up your score **Total**	

Interpreting your score

You have a score out of 100. This is a rough guide to your strengths as a 'reflective practitioner'. If the score is less than 100, then there is more work that you could do to develop your reflective skills.

- What are your priorities for improving reflection?
- Which *one* thing could you do this week in order to develop your reflective abilities?

Basic steps for reflection

If you are new to reflection, the following steps outline some basic features of reflection to help you get started.

- *Small regular bites*   Keep a regular journal, log or blog. Write something in this at regular intervals. Little and often is better at first, so that you develop the habit of reflection. Seven minutes every weekday evening is all that is needed. Alternatively, you may prefer to take half an hour once or twice a week.
- *Be specific*   Choose a particular incident or a feature of your day or week to focus on for each entry. This will develop your critical thinking better than writing on a superficial basis about your whole day.
- *Aim at improvement*   Choose something that was difficult or 'sticky' during your day. Think through what gave rise to the problem. Consider how you might achieve a better outcome next time. Alternatively, spot the things that went unexpectedly well, and consider why that might have beeen the case.
- *Focus on yourself*   Avoid using reflection as a way of blaming and taking out anger on others, even if you feel they deserve it. Focus on your own role, and how you can make a similar situation more manageable next time. This helps to take you forward.

- *Use prompts*   Select an activity from the book and use this to structure your reflection. See pages 206–9 on the 'Core Model for Reflection', for ideas for prompt questions.
- *Critical rather than descriptive writing*   Reflection involves critical, analytical thinking. Weigh up the strengths and weaknesses, costs and benefits, decisions and outcomes. These are thinking skills required for most academic work. Avoid descriptive writing that simply recites what happened, or who said what, unless there are particular reasons for doing this as part of your course. For more about critical thinking, see Cottrell, 2005.
- *Have a purpose*   Reflection should be directed to a purpose. It is better to write a short entry that is meaningful than a long one which is simply pages of description. Find a topic that is useful to you. What do you most need to improve? What do you need to think through?
- *Find the right questions*   Consider the right questions for structuring your reflection. It is easier, when you start out, to answer questions that give shape to your thinking. See p. 194.
- *Review*   After a few weeks, read back over your entries. Look for the main themes in what you have written and consider the significance of these for you. Decide what action to take next.

Example

Brief critical entry aimed at improving performance

How good were my people skills today?

Today was useful as I realised I am still interrupting people when they are talking. I cut right across Mary today during the seminar break. I realise this was not very skilful or considerate. Mary looked annoyed. I just ignored this at the time because I was embarrassed. It would have been better to have apologised as soon as I realised. I will next session. I have to take more care not to burst in when other people are talking. Maybe I could ask Joe and Ali to point it out to me for a while so I notice it more.

Descriptive entry

The following is an example of poor reflection. It simply describes what happens and focuses on other people. The writer doesn't take personal responsibility for actions or plan to improve performance. It doesn't take the writer forward.

In the seminar break today, Mary was talking and I wanted to say something. She had been talking for a few minutes already and I hadn't said anything. I was interested in what she was saying but then just interrupted. It was a simple mistake. I didn't mean to upset her. Mary carried on talking for a moment and then decided to stop. She looked angry. Everybody just looked at me as if I was in the wrong. I didn't even talk for very long. Peter said I had an interesting point. Then we went back in the seminar and Mary avoided looking at me all the way through.

Approaches to structured reflection

There are many ways of approaching reflection and you are unlikely to need them all. Browse through the chapter and see which activities most appeal or are most useful to you at present. The types of reflection introduced below are:

- question-based reflection
- open reflection
- synthetic reflection
- developmental reflection
- evaluative reflection

As you will see, there are overlaps and connections between these different types of reflection. Each type may be useful for a different task or for different stages of a task. As you develop your reflective ability, you will find that you begin to move quite easily between these different methods to suit the task in hand. Your tutors may also be able to guide you about the types of reflective activity that are most suitable for your subject.

Question-based reflection

Question-based reflection is a highly structured form of reflection; it is used extensively throughout this book. The method is relatively simple. Generally, a series of questions is given under a set of headings. Question-based reflection has a number of advantages:

- it prompts and guides you through the reflective process;
- it helps ensure you don't miss out any essential elements;
- it can give shape and direction to the subject of reflection, reducing vague discussion and 'waffle';
- it enables everyone in a group to reflect on the same set of issues in a particular way in order to make direct comparisons on specific issues;
- questions increase motivation to produce a response and can sharpen thinking.

Who does it suit?

Question-based reflection is associated with analytical, serial thinking. It tends to suit people who like or need to work in a logical, ordered or controlled way, and who appreciate some external direction.

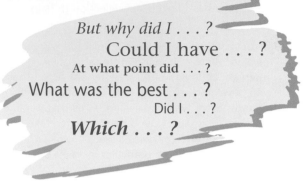

But why did I . . . ?
Could I have . . . ?
At what point did . . . ?
What was the best . . . ?
Did I . . . ?
Which . . . ?

Activity: Setting questions

Select an activity that you engage in regularly or you wish to improve.

- 📖 In your reflective journal, jot down a list of at least ten questions to structure your reflection about your performance.
- Answer your questions.
- What did you find out about your performance by questioning it in this way?

Open reflection

Open reflection methods encourage you to 'let go' of some concentration, and 'go with the flow' rather than trying to control the process too tightly. Open reflection can seem 'unstructured'. However, there is usually a structure of some kind to the method, such as working from prompts, working through several stages in a process or following semi-formal rules.

The benefits of open reflection are:

- it makes it easier to get started on a task as it helps you to generate thoughts and ideas;
- it allows the imagination free rein so that a relatively uncensored set of associations can be formed;
- unexpected ideas may emerge, which can be energising and exciting;
- it can be more personally relevant than working through questions set by somebody else.

Question-based reflection (see page 194)

Question
How did I make use of feedback for my course-work?
Response
I read through it, I accepted most of it, I identified themes that need to be addressed.

Question
Did I make the best use of the feedback I received on my report?
Response
At the time I thought I had made good use of the feedback. I did read it and I set myself priorities for action. However, looking back, I don't think I took it seriously enough. I wondered if the tutor had been too harsh on me, so when I did my essay for the next tutor, I didn't really follow through on the advice I had been given. I then got some of the same feedback again. I realise I ignored my own priorities.

Question
How can I make more effective use of feedback?
Response
I need to set myself a realistic target. I tried to take on too many changes at once last time and then got discouraged. I need to speak to my tutor to work out one or two changes that would make the most impact. Basically, I need to be more focused and accept that I cannot change everything at once.

Open reflection is good for generating ideas, but not always for structuring and making sense of them. It can help to combine open reflection with other methods to structure your thoughts effectively and make meaning from experience.

This method of reflection suits people who like to work in organic ways, and who appreciate things evolving in new or original ways. Open reflection can be conducted in an orchestrated way (a tutor guides the process) or can be personally controlled.

The various methods of open reflection are discussed below.

Brainstorming

Brainstorming is a very simple and quick technique. Take a large piece of paper and a pen. Write the problem or question down somewhere on the paper – the centre is often a useful place but you can choose wherever suits you. Write down every idea or solution that comes into your head. At this

stage, do not evaluate or judge what emerges – just let the ideas flow.

Brainstorming is one of the most widely used techniques for generating ideas quickly. You can use it to start the process of reflection, as well as for writing essays or other assignments.

Reflection
· little and often
· Choose a focus
· Take responsibility
· Not always easy
· Benefits can take time to appear
· Worth doing
· Find a method that suits
· What is needed for my subject
· Avoid waffle
· Keep a journal
· Write a set time for reflection into diary
· Stick with it
· Better self-understanding
· Aim at improving my performance

Discussion

Discussion can be a very valuable form of reflection. It has the advantage of offering multiple perspectives. Paired or group discussions may raise challenging questions that you, as an individual, may wish to avoid. Such questions are often the ones we need most to address – so discussion-based reflection can keep you on your toes.

Discussion, unless strongly steered, can tend to drift in many directions. It is more creative if only a limited number of prompt questions or statements are used. This allows the discussion to wander broadly over the topic. For a more controlled discussion, set more questions and time limits for responses. If the discussion veers away from the agenda, don't dismiss the tangents straight away. The tangents may be giving you important clues about the target subject, or about how well the group is working together, or how you might approach a particular problem.

Day-dreaming

Without forcing the issue, let your mind drift over the target subject. Day-dreaming about the target subject is more likely to occur if we give the subject serious and detailed consideration, and then do something very different for a while. Day-dreaming is not something that can be forced, but it can be encouraged and nurtured. Keep pen and paper, a digital recorder or a lap-top computer nearby to capture ideas as they occur. Reflections that arise in this way are easy to forget.

Sometimes, there is a natural movement from this more relaxed reflection towards more analytical questioning, as you become aware of what you are discovering.

Networks

These are useful for letting your mind develop an idea in a visual way that follows the way the brain works. See p. 183 for details.

Free-writing

Writing as a reflective tool is different from writing intended for an audience or tutors. Its aim is to stimulate thinking, not to communicate a message to others. This means that the writing may look, sound and flow differently from other writing that you do. Your method will be quite different from any other person's. You may just pick up the pen and write; you may write words and phrases rather than sentences; you may scribble and draw as you write; you may write in verse. In other words, you assess the value of this writing for yourself, in terms of whether it helps you to reflect and achieve your own aims.

Reflective free-writing, like other free-writing, will probably take more than one draft:

- a draft that generates ideas;
- a draft that explores some issues in more detail, going off at tangents and with more details;
- later drafts with more structure, as you begin to draw conclusions from your reflection and write them for others to read.

Example

Reflective free-writing

A good day. Enjoyed the session. Made contributions. Really liked it when we saw video and discussed the video. I got very involved in the debate, which surprised me. I hadn't thought I felt so strongly. Not sure why I do. Why do I? I don't like the design of the bridge. Ugly. Not that though. More . . . Reminds me of history lessons more than engineering. Hated history at school. Maybe not a good reason for me to respond to a design now. Or maybe it is. Maybe other people will feel the same way. What else influences my responses apart from history lessons? I like sculptured surfaces . . .

The above example may not make much sense to you, but it did to the person who wrote it. He knew the issue he was trying to explore and this was just his first step. Try for yourself the free-writing activity on page 196.

Drawing and doodling

Drawing and doodling can be used to distract you from controlling your thought processes too closely, allowing your mind to take you where it wishes. You may find that the drawing and the reflection have little in common. On the other hand, you may wish to analyse your drawings for clues about how your mind is working. You could need to check whether your interpretation made sense when weighed against other evidence.

Caricatures, cartoons, paintings or other graphic means may be your preferred methods for reflection, for exploring past actions or events and for getting a feel for their meaning.

Activity: Doodle

- Select a new topic for reflection.
- Take a piece of paper and scribble in the middle.
- Either doodle as you think about the subject or draw a picture or diagram of it. The image does not have to be of good quality: it is simply a tool to distract you from concentrating too hard on the topic.
- If ideas emerge that you want to jot down or develop, then let yourself do so.
- After you have finished, consider how far you find this method suits your learning style.

Generative thinking

The strategies suggested above are associated with generative thinking styles. The strategies and approaches developed in Chapter 7, 'Thinking outside the box', can support the development of this way of working.

Synthetic reflection

Synthetic reflection involves a 'bringing together' or a 'synthesising' of different aspects and perspectives. It is useful for giving shape to a series of reflections or making sense of earlier stages of reflection. It helps you find the meaning behind your reflections, thoughts and actions. It also stimulates creative thinking.

Advantages of synthetic reflection

Synthetic reflection is useful for:

- seeing links and connections;
- gaining a sense of the 'bigger picture';
- gaining a concrete overview from where to begin more detailed analysis;

- giving shape or structure to the reflective process;
- drawing reflections together into a coherent whole.

Synthetic reflection is associated with *gestalt*, holistic, or 'right-brain' thinking. It suits people who like to spot clues, solve puzzles or put things together into new forms. Artistic endeavour and synthetic processes are closely associated. Linking can be made in logical or creative ways, so synthetic reflection can suit those who like order and those who like to work organically. The importance of developing these modes of thinking is highlighted in Chapter 7, 'Thinking outside the box'.

As synthetic reflection helps to draw things together, it can be used to follow up reflection based on free writing or discussion.

Look for links and themes

Synthetic reflection is an active type of reflection. You are looking for links, connections and leads in material you have already produced. Use it to search out hidden themes that are there on the page but which you may not yet have noticed. Going over the material, re-writing it, colouring it, highlighting it, organising it, illustrating it, will help you to focus on each theme.

Activity: Synthesis

- Select one theme that you began to explore in a previous activity.
- Identify themes and links in your earlier reflections.
- Organise your thoughts so that the themes and links stand out clearly.

Developmental reflection

Whilst any method of reflection can assist the process of personal development, the following methods focus specifically on understanding and improving your performance and achievement.

Activity: Developmental reflection

- If you have not done so already, complete the activities on p. 192 to identify your developmental priorities.

📖 In your reflective journal, note down your thoughts about one of your priorities. For example, you may find it useful to consider some of the following questions:

- What made you select this as a priority? What is really the key issue for you?
- What is the goal? What do you hope to gain by developing this area?
- How does this contribute to achieving your long-term or short-term goals?
- What is the problem?
- What have you tried already? How successful was this?
- What will you do next?
- What would be a realistic time-scale to address this successfully?
- Who else would benefit if you addressed this priority?
- What might you do to sabotage your success in achieving this?
- What are your feelings about this priority? What emotions, if any, does it bring up for you?

Monitoring performance

You may be asked to keep a log, blog or journal as part of your course. Even if this is not a requirement, it is a useful practice. Many employers require logs to be kept of actions taken, along with the rationale and outcomes. These may be used in team meetings or staff reviews.

Example

Monitoring performance

Project Group: reflection

20th February
I chaired the project group meeting again today. This went better than last time. I was able to keep the group to the agenda. Unlike last time, this time I did not let people just bring up new topics as they felt like it. I was quite tough, for me. I summarised points well and the feedback on this was good.

Unfortunately, the meeting still ran over time. I did find it difficult to break in to interrupt the flow when Carla and Ian started arguing. I am not sure whether I should speak to them before the meeting, or whether I should just cut across them, which might seem rude. I am worried because they speak loudly and it would look bad if nobody could hear me when I try to interrupt. Because I didn't keep these two in check, we ran over time. Timekeeping looks like my big challenge, but really the issue is about knowing how to interrupt people. This is my next priority. I have arranged to speak about this to my tutor.

Transferable skills

Chapter 2 demonstrated that expertise can be used in diverse contexts. However, skills do not transfer automatically. Skills are likely to be 'transferable' only if we:

- identify the range of skills involved in an activity. It is easy to overlook the wide range of sub-skills that are integrated even into everyday experience;
- make specific attempts to draw parallels between one activity and another, searching out the comparisons;
- are able to see how one situation is similar to the other. If we cannot see those parallels, then we may believe ourselves incapable of dealing with situations that are well within our actual competence. (Butterworth, 1992)

Example

Transferring skills 1

I have been working with children in a local school, helping them with their mathematics. The main developmental points for me were in taking responsibility for others and in using 'plain English'. However, I am also much better now at organising information so other people can use it.

The teacher pointed out that when I first started at the school, I launched straight in and tried to finish as much of the worksheet as I could. Now, I structure the work much better, so the children know what they are learning. This is partly good communication. However, I am also developing skills in structuring information. I look much more closely at how to break down instructions into small chunks that the children can take

in at once. They don't like it if I have to repeat instructions.

I have found that this is useful when talking to adults too. In my part time job, I now do this when giving guidance on technical problems. I find I don't have to go over information so many times. This way of thinking seems to be helping me to plan and structure my written assignments. My tutor says I write more clearly.

It is worth giving time and thought to what we have achieved in any one situation and considering its applicability to other situations. The self-knowledge gained may help us later in new situations.

Example

Transferring skills 2

I was very anxious about writing an essay as I hadn't written one before. My programme mainly uses report writing. Reports are very structured whereas I couldn't see how essays fitted together.

I spoke to a third-year student who talked me through the process. He pointed out that the discussion part of my reports is quite like an essay. If I take out the different sections of the report, such as the method and results sections, and remove all headings and tables, I have the core of an essay already.

I find it easier to write the main part of an essay as if I was writing a report. I use headings and write a paragraph under each of these. This helps me see the structure of my writing. I have noticed I need to check my paragraphs are linked because sections of essays flow into each other more than sections of reports. I then remove the headings when I am ready to hand in the essay.

> 📖 **Reflection**   Spotting your skills
>
> In your reflective journal, write for a few minutes about any one *new* activity that you have undertaken recently. Consider things such as:
>
> - What skills did you already have that you used for the new activity?
> - Were there any ways you adapted your usual ways of thinking or doing to help you with the new task?
> - Did you discover anything about yourself by doing something new?

Reflecting on your academic development

Take time to stand back and look at the big picture regarding your academic development. Consider:

- Are you sufficiently motivated to achieve well academically? How could you increase your motivation?
- How coherent are the choices you are making for options or electives? How will these choices help you achieve your longer-term ambitions?
- Are your choices giving you a strong enough specialist base?
- Will your choices make you stand out as distinctive with interests and capabilities beyond your subject specialism?
- What are the most stimulating aspects of your current learning?
- What is blocking your progress in any area? Are your study strategies still relevant or do they need to be revised?

Example

Academic choices

I wanted to study nothing but chemistry as that interested me most but I am concerned that this will look boring when I go for jobs. I am also interested in travelling abroad. I couldn't see how the two could fit together as I imagined myself in a large British factory near where I grew up.

The Careers Service showed me some case studies of career paths that people from my programme had taken, and I was struck by the opportunities that are available through some big companies for working in international branches. I am not sure yet whether to take a language, which I could start from scratch. This would make it easier to get picked for a placement abroad in the future. However, a specialist IT option might be more useful.

I also need to look at the opportunities open to me if I take a subsidiary in a subject such as health science or nutrition. I have put some time aside next Thursday to look through materials in the Careers Service library.

You could reflect on differences in your performance from one topic or option to another. For example, you may experience a sudden drop or increase in your marks, or find you are more successful in some areas than others. You can begin to investigate this by techniques such as:

- listing how you approach each subject differently;
- free writing about your attitudes or approaches to each subject;
- brainstorming differences between the topics and how you will manage these.

Example

Reflection on assignments

I spent a long time on my last assignment and was disappointed with the marks. This time I spent less time and yet my mark was better. It seems to me the main difference is that I really thought a lot about what the question meant this time. All of my work was very focused on addressing the title. It felt like I really knew what I was doing – so it took less time. I spent more time, though, just working out my initial plans. I think I have made a breakthrough in the way I go about my assignments.

What I need now is to know how to work out what is needed for my land-surveying option. I can't really see how to work out the problems in the same way. I suppose I haven't actually tried applying my 'breakthrough' method to surveying yet, so I don't know if it will work or not.

Reflecting on your professional development

Take time occasionally to consider your short- and long-term professional development. For example:

- What skills are you developing? Are there obvious gaps in your profile of skills and experience? Will these matter when you apply for jobs?
- Are your programme choices the right ones for the type of career you have in mind?
- Are you focusing too much on study at the expense of other experience which would help your career?
- Are you making the best use of all that university has to offer to develop your skills, experience and CV?

- Is there some kind of work experience you could undertake to develop your people skills in the workplace?
- Are you making good (and early) use of the Careers Service and its resources?
- Would it be useful to have a mentor from the area you are considering for a career?

Example

Professional development

I have noticed that many job adverts require good team-building skills. There is not much opportunity on this programme to work in teams. I am worried that this will be a weak point when I come to apply for jobs. I have heard that there are volunteer activities being co-ordinated on campus and I will follow this up this week. Some of that might involve team work.

Another alternative might be to study an elective that includes team work in its skills profile. Unfortunately, I haven't found one that interests me. I might have to choose one that is not especially interesting. I would rather work in a team that was involved in real-life activities rather than study, as I think employers would prefer that . . .

Reflecting on your personal development

Reflection isn't useful only for academic or work-related contexts. You can use it to look hard at any area of your personal development. For example:

- Are your life ambitions changing in any way?
- Are your values and beliefs undergoing any changes? What is influencing such change?
- Are you giving sufficient time to friends and family?
- How are you taking care of your health?
- What are you doing to manage stress?
- What are you doing to ensure a good 'work/life balance'? Do you get time to enjoy yourself without undermining your work and study?

Example

Personal development

I have been working very long hours at college and at work recently. I added this up to 65 hours last week. I was supposed to go to my brother's birthday party but in the end had to work an extra shift as it was double pay. This was good from the money angle, but my family was really disappointed. I am not getting the right balance.

I need clear breaks with no work or study. I have to start planning out my time so I get time to rest and enjoy myself occasionally. Just stop. I have noticed that I am not sleeping well. It would be better for me to start earlier and then finish off earlier in the evening. Studying late just keeps me awake at night, rattling it all round in my head.

I am also neglecting my interest in music. I would really like to spend more time listening to recent releases. I could do this by . . .

Evaluative reflection

Questionnaires and checklists

Self-evaluation questionnaires are useful starting points for self-evaluation:

- the questions help to define the field, indicating the areas that are important to consider further;
- the questionnaire can be used in a 'before' and 'after' way, enabling more precise comparisons between answers given at different times;
- it is often difficult to answer a questionnaire with a straight 'yes' or 'no'. Those questions that resist easy answers prompt longer answers, indicating what the real issues might be for you;
- questionnaires are usually good starting points. They are not particularly useful if used in isolation from other reflective methods.

Critical event

One good way of finding out more about yourself is through an in-depth analysis of a single event. To begin with, select an occasion that was of some importance to you such as:

- the first time you . . . ;
- the last time you . . . ;
- a very difficult occasion;
- a test of your values;
- a test of your abilities;
- a test of your will-power;
- a test of character;

Personal model for reflection

See page 209 for guidance on devising your model for reflection and using this pro-forma.

Stage number	Name of this stage	Prompt questions

Submitting reflections to tutors

You may be asked to submit your reflections to tutors either as part of assessment, or for more informal monitoring. If so, you may be asked to submit either raw or worked reflections, or both. For example, you may be asked to submit a journal, log or extracts from a blog as part of a portfolio of materials.

Alternatively you might be asked to draw on your reflections as the basis of work undertaken in class or to provide material within an assessment such as an essay, case study, position paper or observation, without there being a requirement to submit your journal.

Confidentiality

NB   If anyone else will see these reflections, check first that you have not included names or other information that identify people, departments or organisations without their express permission. The details you provide should not enable people to make a good guess at who is being referred to in your reflections or any other assignment.

Submitting selective portfolios

If your tutors are going to mark your portfolio, they will look for such factors as:

How well it meets the required learning outcomes. How well the portfolio overall meets the learning outcomes of the unit, module or course; make sure you know what these are before you start to put your portfolio together. These are usually provided in a handbook or on a website for the course.

How well you summarise your insights into your learning (or the subject of the portfolio). Most marks are likely to be given for the reflective essay, position paper or similar document, which draws together the main points, rather than for raw reflection and supporting documents, important though these are too.

How well you select and edit relevant information for inclusion in the portfolio. Large, unedited portfolios that contain all the information you could possibly gather on a subject are unlikely to impress. Bulk does not usually gain marks. The tutor is likely to give marks specifically for

skills in selecting, drawing out clearly what is relevant, good editing and cross-referencing.

How well the evidence and examples you refer to in the portfolio really do support the point you are making. If you say the evidence demonstrates a particular skill or insight, it must be a very clear example. You need to specify how skills or the application of theory were demonstrated, rather than assuming these are obvious to the tutor.

How well the portfolio is constructed. Clear contents; all documents labelled; the summary writing makes exact cross-references to the page where the evidence can be found. Use a highlighter pen or number the lines to indicate exactly where the tutor should look to find the evidence if these are submitted in paper form. If you are submitting this electronically, you can use editing and reviewing functions such as those for inserting comments, to provide a commentary on your text. If you make vague references to long free-ranging reflections, leaving the tutor to find what you are referring to, this is unlikley to be accepted.

How well you select one or two good pieces of evidence for each main point you make. More than one piece of evidence is usually not needed or wanted.

How well you draw on relevant theory as part of your reflections. If you are submitting work as part of an academic assessment, then it is generally assumed that you will demonstrate that you are aware of which theories are relevant and how these provide insights on the issue under consideration.

In other words, good guidance for portfolios is:

● include a contents page and a strong summary document (e.g. position paper or essay);
● label and signpost clearly;
● back up your main points with good evidence;
● cross-reference your argument clearly to evidence in the portfolio;
● include only essential evidence;
● keep it as succinct as possible.

A reflective essay

Purpose

Some programmes set reflective essays as marked assignments. The contents of the essay will vary depending on the focus of the programme and the purpose of the essay. For example, some programmes ask for a reflective piece of writing at the beginning of the programme in order to encourage students to focus on their goals and learning needs. Others set an essay at the end of a module for students to draw together their learning and identify next steps. Usually, you will be given specific guidance on what is required.

Structure

Like any other essay, a reflective essay will have:

- a specific title: you must structure your essay to respond to the question contained within the title;
- an introduction that identifies your overall position and prepares the reader for what to expect from the essay;
- a main body divided into paragraphs: this does not usually contain any headings or bullet points;
- a conclusion that sums up the main points: this does not introduce any new material;
- references to source materials within the text;
- a list of all references at the end of the text.

Contents of a reflective PDP essay

Typically, a reflective essay will contain a selection of the following elements.

Personal aims and goals
- Why did you choose your programme: what were your aims and objectives?
- Have these changed since starting the programme? In what ways and for what reasons?

Expectations
- What were you expecting from the programme?
- What did you expect from yourself?
- What led you to form these expectations?

Programme learning outcomes
- What are the learning outcomes for modules you have taken so far?
- What skills development is linked to the modules you have taken?
- How do these outcomes and skills correspond to your own aims and goals?

Other activity
- What else do you do outside of your programme in order to achieve your personal goals or to supplement your learning for the programme?

Learning goals and targets
- What are your current areas of strength in relation to your programme, career or life ambitions?
- Which areas do you need to improve?
- What are the priority areas for improvement as 'learning goals'?
- What are your targets, milestones and time-scales for meeting these learning goals?

Personal reflection
- What methods have you used for reflection?
- How do you use reflection?
- A detailed example of how you developed and evaluated your performance in one area.

Use of feedback
- What kinds of feedback have you received from tutors, students, employers or other people?
- How do you feel about this feedback?
- How have you made use of this feedback?

Evaluation of personal choices
- In practice, how far does the programme meet personal goals and interests?
- Would any other programme or set of modules be more suitable for you?
- What other subject choices, additional modules or supplementary programmes would help you to meet your personal goals?

Evaluation of learning
- How well are you achieving the learning outcomes of your programme?
- What else have you learnt through the programme?
- What are you gaining, additionally, from your programme or from university that was not part of your original goals?

Evaluation of the programme
- How does each module or aspect of your programme contribute to your professional and personal development?

Evaluation of personal performance

- How well are you achieving your personal goals?
- How well have you engaged with your programme? (Attendance? Punctuality? Level of interest? Contributions made in class? Efforts to make personal meaning of the course material? Additional reading or work undertaken?)
- How far do you consider you have taken responsibility for improving your own learning?

Personal development

- How have your opinions, attitudes, beliefs or values changed since starting at university?
- In what ways have you changed as a person since starting at university?

Critical incident

- Identify an incident that illustrates your approach to your learning.
- What does this incident demonstrate about you?

- How does this incident relate to any theories of learning you have covered on your programme?
- What did you learn from this incident?
- See the Reflection on p. 202 above and the Critical Incident Sheet in the Resource Bank, page 281.

Personal statement

Personal statements are important tools for making real use of on-going observation, reflection and evaluation. They are characterised by:

- being written in a more formal manner than reflection for personal purposes;
- drawing together learning that has taken place;
- identifying themes (from a portfolio or journal) and summarising these;
- identifying the overall path that developmental work has taken over a period of time;

Example

Personal statement

This semester, I took three modules in Business Studies. These covered project management, business communication and entrepreneurship. I was able to draw out several themes that ran across the three modules.

First of all, the communication skills were important in identifying ways of varying a message so that it comes across to very different audiences: client groups, bank managers, the buying public, products aimed at different age groups and at people who purchase for those client groups. We also focused on communication within teams.

Communication skills
Communication skills were important to my entrepreneurship project as I was part of a team that took a product (light-weight collapsible bikes) through from idea to design to market. We drew up a business plan that we presented to a funding panel. There was an accountant on the panel who gave us feedback on our presentations. Although our group did not win the funding, we were given valuable advice on what a business plan should look like and how to communicate its strengths when asking for funding.

The entrepreneurship students were not all from a business background: some were from product design, fine art, engineering, marketing and multi-media. One important lesson was in discovering that students from each discipline use very different ways of describing their work process and the product than we expect from a business perspective. Although we learnt that we have to find a common vocabulary, a shared way of communicating, we could have approached this is in a more organised way and avoided some misunderstandings. Communication for team work across disciplines is an area that I would like to investigate further.

Team work
The product designers and engineers, in particular, approached their work in ways that the business students found challenging. This meant that we had to establish ground rules for working together as a team. This took several attempts because our starting points were so different. We had not anticipated this and did not realise at first that this was the case. In the beginning, each of us was unwilling to compromise on methods we had been trained in.

However, as the deadlines drew closer, we made a choice to develop a hybrid way of working that met the needs of the project rather than what we thought we should do as 'business students' or 'design students'. This felt like a risky strategy but we were encouraged by our tutors, who gave us some useful tips on how to negotiate a strategy . . .

Further reading

Boud, D., Keogh, R. and Walker, D. (1985) *Reflection: Turning Experience into Learning* (London: Routledge).

Buzan, T. (2006) *The Mind Map Book* (London: BBC Active).

Cottrell, S. M. (2005) *Critical Thinking Skills: Developing Effective Analysis and Argument* (Basingstoke: Palgrave Macmillan).

Cottrell, S. M. (2008) *The Study Skills Handbook*, 3rd edn (Basingstoke: Palgrave Macmillan).

Mezirow, J. (ed.) (1990) *Fostering Critical Reflection in Adulthood: A Guide to Transformative and Emancipatory Learning* (San Francisco: Jossey-Bass).

Moon, J. (2004) *A Handbook of Reflective and Experiential Learning: Theory and Practice* (London: RoutledgeFalmer).

Thompson, S. and Thompson, N. (2008) *The Critically Reflective Practitioner* (Basingstoke: Palgrave Macmillan).

Chapter 9

Personal records
Recording reflection and achievement

The reward of a thing well done is to have done it.

Ralph Waldo Emerson

Learning outcomes

This chapter offers opportunities to:

create and build your personal records

undertake a profile of current skills and qualities

map your personal competencies in relation to the 'person specifications' frequently required for jobs, and to questions typically asked at job interviews

record your education, training and other examples of professional development

develop personal resources that you can draw upon to write a CV and personal statement when applying for work.

Introduction

It's never too early to start planning for life after university and you can save yourself a lot of time and effort if you record your achievements as you progress through your course. Chapters 1 and 2 focused on an analysis of yourself, and the vision and goals that should be informing and inspiring such advance planning, in order to assist your career development.

When you apply for a job or attend an interview, you will be required to identify, at speed, the best examples for a wide range of questions. Most of us have the information we need to make good responses – but accessing it at speed is not always easy.

This chapter provides resources for collating information about your experience and reflecting upon that experience so that you can identify your achievements easily.

It is important to bear in mind that employers will be looking to see not only what experience you have but also what you made of the opportunity:

your successes, what you learned from the experience, its significance in your life, and how you can use the experience to benefit their company. They will want to see how you make use of experience and opportunity generally – so that they feel comfortable that you will make good use of opportunities on their behalf as well as your own. They will use the information you give them to form judgements about your coping strategies, your work ethic, your attitude to work and life, your character, and even the way you relate to others.

Paper or electronic personal records?

You are likely to need both paper-based and electronic personal records for different purposes. Many certificates, licences and similar records will be provided to you in paper format. It is useful to develop a system of records that holds these together. Moreover, you will be asked to send photocopies or faxes of these to employers, so keeping these together with your personal records will save you time. In addition, you may wish to include reflective notes, examples of your work, photographs, images, and hand-drawn records for your own personal use. These will usually be best in paper form.

On the other hand, some records (such as your CV, education and training history, personal statement, and competence sheets) will need to be updated regularly. This is accomplished most easily if you keep electronic copies. Hard copies of these can be useful for reminding you of things you need to do when browsing through your records.

Developing your personal records

The Introduction to this book (p. 2) referred to the progress file initiative required of all British universities. Progress files should contain records for personal development and career planning, and records that you can call upon to make strong job applications.

Organising your personal records

The contents of your personal records will be particular to you. Whatever you include, it is useful to:

- include a contents page or folder so that you can find records and evidence easily;
- make electronic copies of data that need to be updated, such as records of your employment history, skills and competences;
- number the items in each folder or section rather than from the front of the file. This will enable you to update sections with minimum effort;
- for paper folders, invest in a large folder (as your records will grow as your work history develops) and section dividers.

An example of a *Contents* sheet is offered below (p. 223), as a guide to what you could include in your records.

Records for personal planning

The nature of these records will vary depending on the requirements of your programme. They will also vary according to the importance you place upon your own personal development and the role of reflection in your life.

The various chapters of this book have structured reflection along thematic lines and through a variety of activities and questionnaires. If you completed any of those activities, you will already have compiled a record of yourself, your thinking, your attitudes and your goals. You may find it useful to draw together some of those resources into a single electronic folder and supporting paper-based portfolio. In particular, you may wish to make a photocopy of responses you complete on paper to some of the following activities. If so, include copies of the blank pro-formas so that you can update your responses.

Include your responses to any of the following activities you choose to include: it is what is important to you that really counts.

Introduction
- Do I need personal development?
- What are my PDP priorities?

Chapter 1: The vision: what is success?
- Spectrums of success – or knowing what you want
- A personal definition of success
- Personal values
- The long-term vision
- What do I want to gain from my time at university?
- Short-term goals
- Sources of motivation
- Self-evaluation of personal qualities associated with success
- Extending experience

Chapter 2: Start with yourself
- Top forty strong points
- Seven areas for improvement
- Identifying personal expertise
- The best failure
- Make setbacks work for you

Records for job applications

Chapter 10 looks at the process of applying for a job, and making best use of information about yourself. A good application will be tailored to the particular job and person specification, which takes time to put together well. Good interview answers may require you to reflect upon your experience from quite different angles.

It is extremely common for people to emerge from an interview saying. 'Why didn't I say that?' 'Why didn't I use this example rather than that?' Similarly, it is easy, once the envelope is in the post, to remember information that could have been included to strengthen the application.

The answer is usually in the preparation. Good preparation means that you have much more control over your responses, whether at the application or interview stage. Your memory is primed to call upon the examples you really want to use. Moreover, knowing that you are well prepared will increase your overall confidence, so that you come across as a much stronger candidate.

Records of reflection

Recording reflection

Keeping personal records of some kind is integral to personal development work. Your university may require you to keep a log, blog journal or portfolio and give you very precise directions about what to include and how to present it. Alternatively, you may be asked to devise your own records and presentation. Most of the resources associated with this chapter are provided in the Resource Bank for easy use, at the end of the book and electronically.

Logs, blogs and journals

In this section, the term 'reflective journal' is used to refer to all kinds of reflective logs, blogs, diaries, journals and notes. There are different ways of keeping reflective journals. You can:

1. Note down all aspects of a particular experience, such as the fine details of an observation or experiment or how you designed a product. Some subjects require you to note this objectively (without comment); others require you to reflect upon what you observe.
2. Keep a daily or weekly diary on a particular theme.
3. Keep together all the influences, inspirations, sketches and thought processes that led to a final product or outcome. This is particularly true of art, design and other creative programmes.
4. Share your thoughts with others through a blog.
5. Record all the information you consider significant about your learning. This could include items such as:

   - the general topics covered;
   - exhibitions, placements, visits, field trips, etc.;
   - your feelings about the programme, teaching methods, students, and your responses to these;
   - contributions you make in class;
   - things you find difficult – and how you address those difficulties;
   - thoughts about your learning styles and habits, and the appropriateness of these for you and your learning goals;
   - ideas that arise from your study;
   - what you find most stimulating in your current study;
   - how your studies relate to real life;
   - how theory covered in class is relevant to practical or case work you are undertaking;
   - what you are learning about yourself through your interactions with others;
   - tips and strategies you are gathering;
   - what you are learning about how you manage your emotions;
   - sources of inspiration.

Maintaining a reflective journal

Keeping a reflective journal can be very challenging, especially staying motivated to make regular entries. It takes determination, good planning and a far-sighted approach. It also means having a strong sense of responsibility for your own development over time. Keeping a journal requires the 'stick-with-it-ness' Edison referred to above (p. 124). The benefits tend to arrive very gently and may not be noticeable for a long time. Even if you cannot detect them easily, the benefits are likely to be there.

Using your reflective journal

Reflective journals should be easy to use. This means:

- easy to carry around;
- a notebook you like or electronic variant you enjoy using;
- numbered or labelled so you can find previous entries easily and quickly. Use headings and dates for each entry.

A loose-leaf folder or electronic journal has the advantage that you can enter your responses to events out of sequence, when the idea strikes you. However, you may prefer to keep a notebook, diary or portfolio, depending on what is needed for your course and what suits your own style.

Format for a journal entry

As well as impromptu entries, such as those listed above, you may find it helpful to work to a format to explore your progress on current goals. One format is given on p. 272. Ideally, this should be used in conjunction with an action plan (see p. 119).

Progress files and portfolios

What is a progress file or portfolio?

Progress files were described in the Introduction (p. 2). A progress file or portfolio of personal records is simply a file where you keep together relevant information about yourself. These assist the process of reflection. It is useful to keep and update a portfolio of information that you can call upon to:

- go over your reflections;
- monitor your progress;
- keep important documentation together;
- keep feedback in one place;
- use for sessions with tutors, careers advisers and support staff;
- help staff write your references;
- write your CV and job applications.

Contents of a portfolio

You may find it useful to include some or all of the following in your full portfolio.

A contents page

Divide the material in your portfolio into sections. Number and label these so that you can find material and update it easily: see p. 223. Use a detailed contents page to direct you to materials.

Summary

Include a personal statement or position paper. Aim to be selective and specific, identifying key themes and bringing out what you have learnt. The position paper should refer precisely, but very briefly, to evidence contained within the portfolio.

Formal documents

- Certificates of any qualifications;
- your academic transcript;
- references and testimonials you have received;
- an example of a recent piece of marked work is also useful when seeing support tutors.

Developmental documents

- Completed, dated, self-evaluation questionnaires;
- responses to any activities in this book or similar activities;
- feedback from tutors and peers for past assignments and your commentary on these.

Planning documents

- Documents you completed about your current goals and aspirations, such as what you want to achieve from the course, where you see yourself in five to ten years' time, who or what inspires

you, what motivates you, and what you need to do to achieve your goals;
- your updated action plan to achieve academic or other goals;
- details of priorities you have set, including milestones, targets and deadlines, and how far you kept to these.

Documents relevant to future job applications

- A profile of vocational, technical, academic and other skills you have developed;
- an updated summary of your education and training, including school, college, training courses and relevant short courses;
- an updated list of all work experience, with the dates, addresses of employers, a brief job description, main responsibilities, skills or qualities demonstrated, and what you learned from doing that work which is of value to your current aspirations;
- a curriculum vitae (CV) – a Careers Adviser can help with this;
- examples of experiences that demonstrate typical job competences.

Personal papers

You may like to include personal material that you think relevant to your personal development, such as photographs, letters, school reports, poems, quotations, job descriptions or articles. These may relate to:

- sources of inspiration;
- things that motivate you;
- charts of your progress to date;
- things that remind you of what you wish to achieve;
- things that you find reassuring when stressed.

Maintaining records for job applications

Almost every job application will call for very basic information:

- education and training history;
- employment history.

Although this should be a straightforward matter, information is usually scattered over many different pieces of paper from employers or across several CVs, depending on the nature of the job. It is useful to draw all of that information together in one place, so that you can access it at a moment's notice if the right job appears. Use one file or box to keep all such materials together. Keep a disk/memory stick of electronic records with your paper records.

Education and training history

At some point you could be asked for all or any of the following:

- Schools you attended (usually the schools where you took qualifications after the age of 15 will be all that is required). You will need the name and address of the school, the date you started and the date you left.
- Qualifications you took, the date, and the result. If you are asked for the awarding authority, that is usually printed on the certificate. If you are offered the job, you will be asked to bring in the original certificates, so it is important to be accurate when you give these details.
- If you took your qualifications in a different country from the one where you are now studying, or where you intend to work, ensure that you gather details of the local equivalent for all your qualifications. Provide that information with your application, as well as details of where employers can check this equivalence for themselves.
- Training you undertook as part of a job. Give brief details of short courses and the dates of these.
- Much learning is informal – a colleague may have shown you how to use a piece of software, for example, or you may have trained yourself in using a piece of equipment. Include brief details of the outcomes of such informal learning (what you can actually do as a result).

You will find it useful to draw all your certificates together into one section of your progress file.

Employment history

Employers will look at your employment history to see:

- whether your work history suggests you have the type and level of experience necessary for the job they are advertising. It is important to check that you use similar wording to that in the job description. Slight differences in the wording of a job title may mean that your experience or response is not relevant;
- if there are any gaps in your employment record. Employers are likely to ask you about any periods of a year or more where no work or education is indicated;
- what your job history says about how often you change job, how likely you are to stay with the company, the kinds of work you have accepted in the past, and your career path. If there are unusual jumps from one job to another, employers may ask you the reasons for this at interview. For mature students, the employer will probably want to see a period of continuity within the work history (at least two years). It is expected that younger applicants may have a number of short-contract jobs. This is also true for certain types of work that are organised in short contracts.

You will be required to give information such as:

- employer names;
- employer addresses;
- contact details for the employer (telephone, fax, email);
- dates you began and finished work for each employer;
- your job title;
- your chief responsibilities;
- previous employers who can act as referees.

Contents of personal records file

Educational history

1. Record of education and training

2. Certificates for all qualifications

3. Degree transcript

4. Evidence of learning

Employment history

1. Record of employment history

2. Contract for current employment

3. Names, addresses, job titles and other contact details for at least three referees

4. References and testimonials (if any)

5. Your National Insurance number

6. P45 or P60

7. Pay slips

8. Pension details for all jobs

9. Analysis of learning through work

Other experience

1. Positions of responsibility in clubs, societies or organisations

2. Achievements (from sports, leisure, social life, etc.)

3. Travel

4. Languages

5. Voluntary and community work

6. Mentoring experience

7. Life experience that developed skills or personal qualities

8. Health and safety

9. Equal opportunities

Skills, competences and personal qualities

1. Personal profile (skills, experience, personal qualities)

2. Evidence of skills and personal qualities

3. Critical incident sheet(s)

4. Competence sheets for specific skills

5. Analysis of personal qualities

Personal development

1. Self-evaluation questionnaires

2. Reflective documents and activities

3. Extracts from reflective journal

4. Quotations that motivate or inspire

5. Drawings, photographs and personally relevant documents

Overview documents

1. Position statement

2. Personal action plan

3. Curriculum vitae (CV)

4. Analysis of knowledge and experience

Other materials

Anything else that you feel is relevant to you

Records of education and training

It is likely that every job you apply for, as well as any future courses, will ask about your education, qualifications and training. You may be asked to provide one or more of the following:

● Your highest level of qualification (e.g. a degree, a master's degree)
● To confirm that you have particular qualifications required for the job and, if you are offered the job, to provide the certficates
● Details of all your education from a certain age, such as from GCSE (or equivalent) onwards
● Details of training you have undertaken, formal courses and informal learning such as on-the-job training
● Evidence, either through your personal statement or at interview, of what you have learnt through your education, training and experiences, especially experiences of employment.

On the chart in the Resource Bank (page 274), record details of your educational history. Order these so that your most recent courses and qualifications are at the head of the list.

Record of your work history

You will need accurate records of your work history. This could be maintained as an up to date list within your CV. If you are not permitted to send in a CV, you can cut and paste these details either onto the form the employer sends or onto an attachment. If you do the latter, make sure that you include all the details that the employer requests. The information required varies from one job to another, and you may also need this for other purposes. For each job and period of employment keep a record of:

● the exact dates you start and finish;
● the employer name and address;
● the job title;
● key responsibilities of your role;
● the experience you acquired;
● your reason for leaving;
● details of anyone you may want to call on for a reference.

Employers tend to require details of the salary of your last job and any additional benefits provided by your employer. They may also ask you to account for any gaps in your work history.

Skills and personal qualities

It is likely that you will be asked to provide details of your skills and personal qualities on many different occasaions such as:

● applying for jobs;
● applying for promotions;
● applying for voluntary work, roles in the community;
● as part of annual review or appraisal;
● for skills sets inventories drawn up by businesses, community organisations, Boards of Governors and Trustees.

In general, you can expect to do more than simply list these. You may be asked to describe how you applied those skills in particular situations. It is easy to forget occasions when we applied particular skills well, so updating your records of these occasionally can be useful.

● The 'Personal Profile: Skills, Abilities and Personal Qualities' sheet in the electronic Resource Bank and on page 225 enables you to identify the range of skills and qualities you possess.
● The 'Evidence of Skills and Personal Qualities' sheet in the Resource Bank and on page 280 enables you to analyse one or more skills in more depth as preparation for when you need to call upon this information.

Critical incident

During job applications, employers often ask if you can give details of an important event or experience that had a major impact upon your life or work. This is sometimes referred to as a 'critical incident'. In particular, they are looking to see what kinds of things you regard as important (your values), how you managed transition and change, or how well you learn from experience.

Personal profile: Skills, Abilities and Personal Qualities

People

- [ ] Ability to get on with people from different backgrounds
- [ ] Ability to see and understand other people's points of view
- [ ] Dealing with the general public
- [ ] Team work
- [ ] Managing other people
- [ ] Teaching or training others
- [ ] Listening skills
- [ ] Communicating clearly
- [ ] Negotiating
- [ ] Helping others to arrive at decisions
- [ ] Being sensitive to others' feelings
- [ ] Caring for others
- [ ] Being able to read other people's body language
- [ ] Dealing with others by phone
- [ ] Being able to cope with 'difficult' people
- [ ] Speaking clearly and to the point
- [ ] Being able to take direction from others
- [ ] Having courage to speak out against injustice
- [ ] Others:

Activities

- [ ] Creativity, design and layout
- [ ] Being able to see the 'whole picture'
- [ ] Researching information
- [ ] Classifying and organising information, e.g. filing
- [ ] Applying theory to practice
- [ ] Being good at argument and debate
- [ ] Making decisions
- [ ] Managing change and transition
- [ ] Setting priorities
- [ ] Working out agendas

- [ ] Organising work to meet deadlines
- [ ] Facilitating meetings
- [ ] Reading complicated texts
- [ ] Word-processing
- [ ] Computer literacy
- [ ] Using the Internet
- [ ] Technical skills
- [ ] Number work
- [ ] Selling
- [ ] Problem solving
- [ ] Getting things done
- [ ] Fund-raising
- [ ] Practical things
- [ ] Seeing how things work
- [ ] Writing reports or official letters
- [ ] Others:

Personal qualities

- [ ] Recognising my own needs and asking for help
- [ ] Being able to learn from my mistakes
- [ ] Staying calm in a crisis
- [ ] Managing stress
- [ ] Being willing to take risks and experiment
- [ ] Demonstrating assertiveness
- [ ] Showing determination and perseverance
- [ ] Setting my own goals
- [ ] Maintaining a high level of motivation
- [ ] Taking responsibility for my own actions
- [ ] Trusting in my own abilities
- [ ] Honesty
- [ ] Commitment to values or ethics
- [ ] Showing attention to detail
- [ ] Others:

© Stella Cottrell (2003, 2010), *Skills for Success*, Palgrave Macmillan

It is useful to be prepared for this question, and the 'Critical Incident Sheet' in the Resource Bank, p. 281, outlines some of the main themes that are worth considering. Even if you are not applying for work, this is a useful exercise to work through from time to time, either using the same incident, or comparing your responses to different incidents.

Responding to competence-based questions

When you apply for a graduate job, you will receive a 'person specification' that outlines the qualities required for the post. Increasingly, employers are introducing competence-based applications. These ask you to give specific evidence of your competence under a number of headings that they provide. Whether or not you are asked details about competences at the application stage, it is typical for some or all of a job interview to be competence-based. Having a set of well-recorded competences can significantly boost your confidence in your performance during the application process. If you store these records electronically, you will find that you can save yourself a great deal of time in making each application.

What is a 'competence'?

To be competent means to be able to perform an activity reasonably well and on more than one occasion. To consider yourself competent at a task, you are likely to be able to do what is necessary to achieve a successful outcome without having to check continually what needs to be done, and without supervision. Competence is associated with the notion of repeated performance; simply doing something once is not usually a sign of competence. Competence is often associated with well-placed confidence. It requires proficiency in a set of relevant skills. If you can train or advise others in the area, this is usually a sign of competence.

Describing your competence

In interview, you may be asked to give evidence of your competence from one of a range of different perspectives (see Chapter 10). This can often catch people unawares so that they feel they have not done themselves justice. Similarly, when writing competence-based applications, it is easy to omit details for which the selection panel will be looking. This can make the difference between being selected or not.

The competences selected for analysis in the Resource Bank (pages 282–317) are those frequently asked of graduates and others when they apply for jobs. A set of competence sheets are provided. Select those that are relevant to your employment or the types of position that you are likely to apply for. Each sheet provides prompts to assist you to analyse your competence and identify details of your ability to meet the job requirements.

Your records should contain details of some or all of the following:

- The best example(s) of you demonstrating that competence;
- Brief contextual evidence of the occasion(s) when you best demonstrated that competence;
- Your level of responsibility (whether you were the manager with lead responsibility, or stepping in to cover in someone's absence, or part of a small or large team);
- Your personal role or actions: what you did or said.
- What was the outcome of your action?
- What would you do differently, if anything, in retrospect?
- What did you learn that you have been able to apply in other situations, or could in the position for which you are applying?

Selecting examples

For written applications, you are likely to be given a restricted word limit for listing skills or giving details of one example. In interviews, you may be given time only to describe one example in detail. It is not untypical to hear people say after an interview that the wrong example came to mind. For instance, they may have prepared to answer a question giving a 'recent example' and be asked for the 'best example in relation to the current job' – or vice versa. It is useful to update your records so that you are clear about:

- which is your *one* best example of the competence from your experience. Usually this will be a recent example but sometimes a significant event or achievement may not be recent;
- details of all aspects of that best example;
- two other good examples, in brief.
- What is the most relevant example for the job?
- What is a recent example?

Building your competence

If you find that you are not able to give good examples of competence in any area, you will need to decide:

- Is this a competence that is likely to be required for the kinds of jobs that interest you?
- What opportunities are open to you to develop that competence?

Most employers want to see that you have experience. It is a frequent complaint that people cannot gain experience because they cannot get a job and they cannot get a job they want because they cannot gain the experience. Students have many opportunities to develop experiences that are less easy to come by once student life is over. Again, this is often not appreciated until the chance has passed. Seize the opportunity while you are still a student – and ensure you have a good portfolio of skills and experience by the time you leave.

Completing the 'evidence of competence' sheets

The competence sheets in the Resource Bank, pages 283–317, can assist you in elaborating your personal competences. You may consider that very little space is provided for each answer. This encourages you to summarise the most salient points: it is unlikely that, in applying for jobs, you will ever have as much space as is provided by one of these sheets, nor time at interview to give fuller responses. You will be required to give very brief responses to each question, so your thinking must be clear, precise and succinct.

Employers are looking at your own personal involvement and the responsibility you take for your own actions. Anything which comes across as an excuse or appears to be blaming others for a poor outcome will sound unconvincing. Speak about your own role and take responsibility for what did not work. Identify what you have learnt about how you would do things differently in the future.

They will also be interested in knowing the level of operation: how high-profile was the work, how central were you to events, where did you stand in the hierarchy of people involved? Being able to contribute to projects led by others may be as important as being the leader, as both team work and leadership are prized qualities.

You may find it useful to copy the blank sheets before completing them, so that you can use them again in the future. Electronic copies are also available at www.palgrave.com/studyskills/pdp so that you can update them easily.

In completing the records, it is worth taking time to jot down all the occasions you can think of when you exemplified the competence in action. This will give you a full list from which to select your best examples. Make use of the responses you have made to activities in chapters earlier in this book or on your programme. It can help to have a friend or relation to prompt you if you struggle to find examples. You can call upon the same experience for more than one competence, but it is useful to refer to at least three separate experiences or examples overall.

Evidence of improvements in personal performance

When applying for a position, you may be asked questions about how you go about identifying areas for improvement, what you have done already to improve your performance and what the impact was of the action you took. It is likely that you will either be asked directly to provide one or more concrete examples of how you have drawn upon experience in order to improve performance, or that it will just be assumed that you will incorporate such examples in your applications and answers to interview questions. You may have to call upon such information as:

- A brief summary of the context.
- What needed to be done and why?
- What was your own role?
- How did you plan and prepare? (if relevant)
- How did you adapt your plan or strategy in the light of events?
- What was the effect of your action: what was different as a result of it? What could you have done even better?
- What did you learn about yourself and your own performance through this experience?

- What did you learn that has general applicability (such as to new skills, experience, insights, specialist knowledge) especially to the position for which you are applying?

The sheet in the Resource Bank on page 271 enables you to draw together your reflections of specific occasions where working on personal performance reaped rewards and provided insights that can be applied more generally.

Closing comments

This chapter provides guidance on developing personal resources that can assist in structuring your reflection about your experience. Experiences are more valuable when we are aware of their significance to our lives. They are our richest resource for learning, and yet we often resist slowing down sufficiently to examine what we have gained. It is much easier to move on to the next task – and even to repeat similar mistakes.

The main focus of this chapter has been reflecting on experience in order to be in a better position to move towards career goals. That is because the main aim of most graduates is to gain a job. However, the deepest learning is likely to come from our reflection about our broader life experiences – our vision, values and beliefs, the way we respond to other people, and how comfortably we live with ourselves. There is nothing to prevent you from using these resources to examine more personal questions, as and when you are ready.

These resources are not for use on a single occasion. As you move through your programme and as you gain wider experiences through life and work, you will find better examples to record. At the time, these experiences will appear very vivid in your mind but you will begin to lose the details over time. Write these down while they are still fresh. Reflect back upon those same events in a year's time. Often, you will find that you see much more significance in the same events after time has elapsed.

Chapter 10

Successful job applications

The more I want to get something done, the less I call it work.

Richard Bach

Work and play are words used to describe the same thing under different conditions.

Mark Twain

Learning outcomes

This chapter offers you opportunities to:

develop an awareness of what employers are looking for
consider what you want from an employer and your first job as a graduate
plan ahead towards the jobs you want
make use of progress files, personal records and personal statements
make a strong job application
write covering letters, CVs and competence statements when applying for jobs
understand the selection process
develop effective interview skills
use the application process to improve your performance.

Introduction

Applying for jobs is an art in itself. It is no longer sufficient to send a CV to a host of employers and hope that they will notice you. Whatever the application process and whatever the job, employers will be looking to see how well you present yourself and your experience in the light of their needs and interests.

For almost every job, you will have strong competition – other people will want that job just as much as you. This means that it pays, during your time as a student, to start developing the range of skills, qualities and experiences associated with the kinds of jobs that appeal to you. Such skills are not developed overnight, so the earlier you start thinking and planning towards a job, the more successful you are likely to be.

This chapter guides you through the processes of applying for your first job as a graduate, such as preparing for the interview so that it is a more predictable, manageable and successful event. You will gain an introduction to the general state of the employment market, and the kinds of skills employers want. It is worth remembering that almost half the jobs available to graduates are open to students of any discipline. This means that the opportunities open to you are very wide indeed – no matter what you have studied.

You will be a stronger candidate for a job if you can:

● talk about how the job meets your personal aims (see Chapter 1);
● come across as knowledgeable about the skills and qualities required for jobs that interest you;

- demonstrate you have taken steps to develop skills relevant to the workplace, either through your studies or outside of these;
- show you can make good use of opportunities when these arise;
- manage yourself, work well with others, and manage new tasks either in a team or by leading a team. Earlier chapters in this book address these skills.

What do employers want?

Minimum effort, minimum cost

Employers naturally want as easy a life as possible when it comes to taking on employees. They want to get the job done with least cost to themselves. They look for applicants who are, as far as possible, already skilled, confident, able to get on with a job with minimum direction and training, and who will understand what is needed in the context of that company. This formula will translate differently from one company to another. For some, it means they only recruit people with previous experience; for others, it may mean that new recruits are expected to read work situations well, learning quickly on the job, with minimum disruption to the work of colleagues and supervisors.

The employer's WIIFT

Bright and Earl (2007) recommend that when applying for jobs, candidates should always keep in mind 'an employer's WIIFT'. WIIFT stands for 'What's In It For Them?' If you simply 'sell yourself' you may come across as only interested in you. The more you know about the employer, the more you can identify how your own skills and experience will bring benefits to that company.

Rounded applicants, not subject specialists

Employers are likely to have much more interest in your broader development and its applicability to their workplace than subject knowledge. This can be quite difficult to acknowledge when a subject discipline has been the focus of your attention for several years. If you do nothing but study in that

time, you may find it more difficult to compete for jobs against students who have planned ahead towards a career whilst studying.

Soft skills

Apart from specialist skills and knowledge, employers consistently argue that they want graduates to have better 'soft skills'. Soft skills are those skills which are often hard to measure but which oil the wheels of any work situation. A survey by the Association of Graduate Recruiters (2009) found that the three skills most in demand were leadership, team work and communication skills. The list of most wanted skills does not change significantly over time. For example, in 1998, research by TMP Worldwide Research found employers valued, in order of importance:

1. oral communication;
2. team working;
3. listening;
4. written communication;
5. problem-solving;
6. relationship development;
7. adapting communication style;
8. time management;
9. sharing knowledge;
10. influencing others.

Recent surveys add to the list rather than removing skills previously found to be important, adding items such as 'cultural awareness'.

It is noticeable that most of these involve 'people' skills or 'problem-solving within teams'. This is not surprising as most jobs require employees to deal with others, whether colleagues, clients, customers, partners, pupils, patients, or the general public. Many work contexts are complex, requiring an understanding of how each person's contribution assists or hinders the work of others. This is very different from the way most school and university study is organised, which is normally on a very individual basis.

Skills in context

When employers refer to communication skills, time management or problem-solving, they are usually referring to a team or company context, not to an individual effort. Words such as 'written communication' can mean different things in a work or academic context. For example, whilst it is true that university does develop writing skills, employers usually want particular kinds of accuracy, speed, clarity, precision, style, layout and sensitivity to different audiences.

Employers do value the skills developed by a university education, but are frustrated when academic contexts are given as the only examples of skills. They like to see examples of those skills being used in work and 'real-life' contexts.

Students often cite 'presenting a seminar paper' as an example of 'oral communication'. Leading a seminar is a valuable experience and does develop public speaking skills. However, employers generally require employees to make formal presentations only on very rare occasions. They are more likely to appreciate that you fielded difficult questions from the seminar audience or contributed skilfully to class discussions.

Oral communication within the workplace tends to demand such skills as:

- establishing rapport;
- conveying information accurately;
- giving clear directions;
- making useful contributions to discussions and meetings;
- expressing yourself clearly and accurately;
- summarising what others say;
- dealing with difficult people;
- negotiating your position;
- offering criticism constructively;
- taking criticism constructively;
- adapting your communication style to suit varied circumstances.

📖 **Reflection**   Oral communication skills

- What could you do (or have you done) to develop oral communication skills suitable to work contexts?
- What skills have you gained from academic tasks involving oral communication that will be useful in a work context?
- Complete the oral communication competence sheet on p. 314.

Activity: Skills in context

Take at least seven different pieces of literature written for the public. Include two different types of newspaper, some leaflets on public information, advertisements, trade magazines, bank or building society information, or website marketing information. Browse through these, comparing the writing style with that used in higher education. What are the characteristics of such writing? What writing skills would it take to produce them?

Collect literature from the areas of work that interest you. Browse through these, comparing the writing style with that used in higher education. Consider, again, what are the characteristics of such writing? How do they differ from what is expected for academic writing?

- Where else do you develop your written communication skills outside of academic contexts?
- How could you develop skills in writing for a non-academic audience?
- What skills have you gained from your academic writing that will be useful to any context?
- Complete the written communication competence sheet on p. 312.

It is useful to build a 'rounded portfolio', developing skills in work or community contexts, such as through sandwich programmes, part-time work, projects for employers, voluntary work, helping in local schools or youth groups, running student groups, or helping in the Student Union.

I have made this letter longer only because I have not had time to make it shorter.

Blaise Pascale (1655)

The Careers Service and Student Union can give advice on local opportunities.

Employability skills

In 1998, the Committee of University Vice-Chancellors (the CVCP) commissioned research by Coopers and Lybrand to identify 'employability skills' for graduates. They produced the following list, which is still relevant today (CVCP, 1998):

1. Traditional intellectual skills
- Critical evaluation of evidence;
- the abilities to argue logically, apply theory to practice;
- to model problems qualitatively and quantitatively;
- to challenge taken-for-granted assumptions.

2. Core or key skills
- Communication;
- application of number;
- information and communications technology;
- improving one's own performance;
- working with others.

3. Personal attributes
- Self-reliance;
- adaptability;
- flexibility;
- 'nous';
- creativity.

4. Knowledge about how organisations work
The report points out that it is important that employability skills include this fourth area, and 'not just the first three'.

The 'personal attributes' section is worth noting. This refers to 'intra-personal' skills (see Chapter 4) and creativity (see Chapter 7). Intra-personal skills include the ability to manage oneself, one's attitudes and emotions, especially when working with other people. Personal and emotional self-management is expected as an individual responsibility. Employers want people who can use common sense ('nous'), creativity and initiative to resolve issues. As work contexts change very rapidly, employees are required to cope with and manage change. They need to be adaptable to changing circumstances, ready to move where the need is, and develop new skills as required. This is very different from workplaces of the past, where there was more of a 'production line', same-job-for-life mentality.

In March 2009, the CBI (Confederation of British Industry) and Universities UK released the report 'Future Fit – preparing graduates for the world of work'. Five hundred and eighty-one employers were surveyed, and identified 'employability skills' as the most important factor they considered in recruiting graduates. Whilst employers were generally satisfied with graduates' IT and numeracy skills they were less likely to be satisfied with graduates':

- Business and customer awareness;
- Self-management skills;
- Communication and literacy skills.

Managerial skills are expected of a wider range of employees and this trend is increasing. There is a growing demand for the following skills:

- *organisational skills*: knowing how to manage tasks, monitor performance and develop the business;
- *thinking and problem-solving skills*: strategic thinking, making decisions, conceptual skills, analysing information, solving problems;
- *people skills*: managing relationships in the workplace, team work, communicating with others.

Job advertisements

Advertisements for jobs usually list the most important features of the job, including skills that

---

Activity: Job advertisements

- Find at least 20 advertisements for jobs in career areas that interest you. Look at the Careers Service vacancy bulletin and main national newspapers. Alternatively, browse some of the websites given in the Useful Websites section at the end of the book (p. 321).
- Which skills are referred to the most often (count them)?
- Complete competence sheets (pp. 283–317) for the skills relevant to your career interests and place these in your personal records.
- What opportunities are available to you to develop these skills further?

are currently wanted. Browsing through the job advertisements associated with career areas that interest you will help you form a picture of the skills that are most valued by the kinds of employers you wish to work for. Use the activity on page 232 to get started.

What do you want from your first graduate job?

In Chapter 1, you considered what your vision and values were for the next ten years. You may have changed your mind about these as you worked through the book. Mature students may have a good idea of the job they want when they leave university, but it is not unusual for younger students to have only a vague notion of the kind of work they might want, especially if they have not yet tested out the workplace nor had the opportunity to build their confidence in skills such as leadership and team work.

Your first few jobs as a graduate may be traditional 'graduate' jobs. These offer reasonably good salaries and are often designed specifically for new graduates. They involve skilled work and recognise the value of a degree. However, graduates also enter into the wider workforce with the aim of gaining experience and building their skills. This is especially true of students in creative professions, where it is often expected that graduates will enter at a lower rung and plan for the longer term. Work experience is key to many jobs.

Your first step is to think about what it is you aim to gain from your first jobs after graduating, such as 'learning the ropes', personal projects, travel, trying out different occupational sectors, or developing expertise. You may prefer to work part-time on more than one job, or use agency work to build additional skills. If your plan is to walk straight into a particular job, make sure you have contingency plans in case this does not happen. What other jobs could carry your career or life plans forward?

Whatever job you choose, it is unlikely to be for life. Consider what there is to be gained from the opportunities available rather than panicking that the perfect career opening does not seem to be available to you straightaway.

Choosing a job

Know what is right for you

The Careers Service will have a wide range of paper and electronic resources, including psychometric tests, which will enable you to pinpoint the kinds of work that suit you. If you completed the activities in Chapters 1 and 2, you should have a good idea already of the general direction that you want to take in life. When applying for jobs, consider how far each job advances, in the short or long term, your life vision. Consider how far it is in line with your values and beliefs: it will be hard to come across well in interview if the job contravenes basic beliefs and values.

Consider the best route

Some jobs receive thousands of applications – they are very popular and the reality is that almost every applicant will be disappointed. That does not mean that it is impossible for you to be in a job that suits you.

Know all your options

Too many graduates select only the most obvious jobs. Talk to the Careers Service so that you have an idea of the range of jobs open to you. More than two out of every five jobs are open to any graduate. Identify which jobs have fewer applicants and whether any of these would suit you. They may provide easier entrance routes to the job you prefer over the longer term.

Plan long term

Consider unusual routes to your desired destination. Work experience, travel or gaining skills that are short in supply but relevant may all provide unexpected routes.

Starter posts

Companies tend to be loyal to their own personnel. It is worth thinking about entering at the bottom or in a less competitive post, and aiming to work towards the job you want from inside the company. Consider interim jobs that you could fill for a few years that would provide a sideways route into the job you want.

ⓔ Activity: What do I want to gain from my next job?

- On the table below, indicate with a tick or 'yes' if the item is something that you would like to gain or develop in the next (or first) job that you take. Put more than one tick if you feel this is very important.
- Then go through the items you have ticked and rate them in order of importance (1 for the most important, 2 for the next in importance, and so on).

From my next job, I want to . . .	Important to me?	Order of importance
1. gain work experience in a new field		
2. enhance career opportunities		
3. earn more money		
4. increase my job satisfaction		
5. work in accordance with my values and ethics		
6. work better hours		
7. work in better surroundings		
8. work near home		
9. work with people more like myself		
10. take on more responsibility		
11. broaden my mind		
12. give myself more challenge		
13. know myself better		
14. develop technical skills		
15. develop a wider range of skills		
16. work with a wider range of people		
17. develop problem-solving skills		
18. develop inter-personal skills		
19. develop a broader set of interests		
20. make friends		

Other things:

	Important to me?	Order of importance
1.		
2.		
3.		

📖 **Reflect**

In your reflective journal, consider:

- What do I really want from my next job?
- What would most persuade me to apply for a particular job?

Choose jobs you can do

Every employer receives a large number of applications from people who have not interpreted the job information correctly or have not addressed the person specification fully, generally because they are too inexperienced for the role. If you have very few of the qualifications, skills and experience required, you will not be short-listed. You could have spent your time making a stronger application for a job that is within your competence.

Consider smaller companies

Many students consider only the kinds of large companies that are invited to careers fairs at universities. However, many small and medium-sized companies also recruit graduates. These can provide very good opportunities to develop experience and to rise quickly within a company.

📖 Reflection   Routes into work

In your reflective journal, consider:

- What kinds of jobs are you most interested in?
- Broadly speaking, what are the statistical chances of you gaining that job as a first job? Your Careers Service will give you details of what to expect.
- Brainstorm alternative routes into that job. Which of these would you consider? Which are you most likely to succeed in gaining as your first job?

What do you want from an employer?

For your first job as a graduate you may want to look for specific characteristics in an employer – or you may just want to get a foot on the employment ladder. Local and personal circumstances will affect what kind of choice is available to you. However, the following points are worth considering.

Investors in People

A number of companies have gained Investors in People (IiP) status. This means that the company has demonstrated a commitment to the training and development of its employees. If an employer has IiP status, they are more likely to welcome questions at interview about how they develop their staff. They are very likely to ask candidates about what steps they take to further their own professional development.

Equal opportunities

Legislation on race, sex, disability, age, sexual orientation, and religion is aimed at protecting against unfair practices and discrimination. Many employers will make a reference to being an 'equal opportunity employer'. This means, usually, that they are keen to be seen making efforts in equal opportunities. It does not necessarily mean that all aspects of work at the company will affect all workers equally, nor that discriminatory practices do not take place. However, if equal opportunities matter to you, you may feel more comfortable at a company that has an equal opportunities policy that extends beyond the basic legal requirements. For more information, see www.equalityhumanrights.com

Career opportunities

Some companies expect their graduate employees to move very quickly from one post to another. This may mean travel, very varied work, and opportunities to gain a range of experience. Some provide opportunities to work or travel overseas. Larger companies will usually detail such opportunities in their graduate literature. It is reasonable to ask questions about this at interview. Smaller companies are not usually able to create such opportunities so this may affect the type of company that would suit you. However, a small company may be growing quickly and would offer a different kind of opportunity to employees who were with them from the beginning. For information about different kinds of companies, see:

- www.bloomberg.com (international and entrepreneur site);
- www.companieshouse.gov.uk (lists all UK public companies);
- www.bestcompaniesguide.co.uk (reports employee feedback on what it is like to work for named companies).

Graduate apprenticeships, internships and company schemes

Some companies offer programmes to bridge the time between university and work. Sometimes this is for an apprentice or intern, with training offered for a reasonable but relatively low salary (or no salary). These are useful for gaining experience of a new work context. Other companies offer outstanding opportunities to work on a particular project in a workplace but under supervision from the university. Your university Careers Service or Work-Based Learning Unit would have details of such programmes.

Your 'bottom line'

A first job can offer experience and training that will be of use in future applications. You are well advised to accept less than the ideal employment in order to gain that first step. However, you should be clear in your own mind about what is and what is not acceptable to you. This may relate to the level of pay, working hours, location, behaviours, being the only person of your sex or colour, lack of reliable transport, or something personal to you. You should be clear where you will not compromise on issues such as:

● personal safety;
● health and safety;
● disability access;
● unfairness, bullying or discriminatory behaviour;
● working hours you consider to be unreasonable.

Plan ahead

Make opportunities

You will see from the section below that career planning does not start with applying for jobs in your final year at university. Employers will want employees who know how to spot and use opportunities, think on a broad front, and can plan ahead for the good of the company.

They will look to see how you spotted, created and used opportunities on your own behalf. If you did not do this for yourself as a student, they will be less convinced that you could do this on behalf of their company. Ideally, your planning should start in your first year, so that you are in a strong position by the time you apply for jobs.

Develop a rounded portfolio

When people invest in stocks and shares, they are advised not to put all their money into one investment, but to develop a rounded portfolio that includes different kinds of investment. If one type of company fails, others may still provide returns on the investment.

Your time at university is a similar kind of investment. Your energy can be invested entirely in study or spread over a wider portfolio. Your degree is likely to be your most important investment at present, but it does not have to be your sole investment. Furthermore, there are 'smart' ways of putting a degree together so it counts for more.

A rounded student portfolio will contain 'investment' in at least three of the following:

● the degree subject;
● complementary subjects;
● a broad set of skills that could be transferred to the workplace;
● unusual technical expertise;
● work experience;
● volunteer activity;
● contributing to the community;
● a position of responsibility;
● general career awareness;
● awareness of the professional field or the companies where you want a job;
● evidence of taking responsibility for personal development needs or training.

When applying for a job, you need to consider:

● 'How have I used my time?'
● 'What have I done that makes my application stand out?'
● 'What will make this company consider me rather than somebody else?'
● 'What evidence have I got that I can deliver the skills they are asking for?'
● 'What experience can I offer?'

The subject and grade of degree are relevant, but are only a small part of the story for most jobs. You will not get a job simply because you have a 'first class' or '2.1' degree. That may be one of ten things the employer will consider, if at all, and is possibly the least important on their list.

When to use the Careers Service

The Careers Service can give you excellent advice from your first year at university, so that you can plan the best possible route towards the jobs that will interest you later.

The Careers Service should be able to guide you to put together a rounded portfolio. They can advise you on how to spend your time as a student so that you:

- choose an interesting but relevant selection of subjects and options;
- understand which skills are relevant to the field of work that interests you;
- know how to make the best use of work experience;
- plan and prepare well in advance for the areas of work that interest you;

- are aware of the range of opportunities available to you through the university, locally and further afield.

Many also have 'job shops' or similar, to help you gain student jobs whilst studying. You may find it helpful to browse websites that give career guidance for graduates. For example, see:

- www.prospects.ac.uk
- www.gradunet.co.uk
- www.careerplayer.com
- www.insidecareers.co.uk

Plan to stand out

Employers see hundreds of similar people, all wanting the same job for similar reasons, and all holding similar certificates and qualifications. This is one reason why Careers Services ask to see undergraduates early, so that they can give advice about planning ahead towards the job-application stage. You can prepare to 'stand out' from other applicants by various means:

- *Choose unusual subject options as electives or subsidiary subjects*
  Employers are likely to be interested in why you chose unusual options. They may appreciate that you have a broader outlook, or they may be able to use the subsidiary subject in some way. You should plan to choose companies that are likely to appreciate the subjects you selected. For example, you may choose to take a language as an option and look for companies that deal with overseas clients or have overseas branches. Be prepared to answer questions about what it was that interested you about the options you chose, and the links you can make between this, your subject and your career plans.

- *Choose smart combinations*
  Consider combining different subjects. For example, lawyers, accountants or designers

work for all kinds of businesses. A law student who has studied a module or two of sports science will look more appealing as a lawyer to the sports industry. Similarly, media industries or architectural firms might be more interested in business graduates who have undertaken some study in their own fields and therefore know something about these professions and their terms of reference.

● *Do something different*
An unusual interest, study abroad, travel, a curious combination of languages, success in a competition, holding an exhibition of your work, voluntary work and similar activities can spark an interest in employers. They are likely to ask you questions about these if they interview you.

Making use of personal records

Chapter 9, 'Personal records: reflection and recording achievement' provides a range of resources to assist you in recording the information you will need for applications and interviews. These cover most, if not all, of the material you need, to apply for almost any job. It is particularly important to focus on the section on personal competences and the competence sheets (see pp. 283–317). These resources are also provided electronically to help you build your electronic portfolio (see www.palgrave.com/studyskills/pdp).

📖 *Reflection*   Stand out from the crowd

In your reflective journal, consider:

● What is it about you that would make you stand out on an application form, increasing your chances of gaining an interview?
● What is it about you that would make you stand out in an interview so you will be remembered out of a large number of interviewees?
● What can you do now or during the year to develop your profile in this respect?

All of the chapters in this book have been designed to assist you to plan towards your future, develop personal insights, devise strategies for improving personal performance, and understand the skills that are required in many occupations. If you have worked through the activities in this and earlier chapters, you will have developed a good picture of yourself, and the kind of career that might interest you.

When completing your application or preparing for an interview, you will find your 'personal statement' (Chapter 8, pp. 213–14) is of particular value. In the context of applying for a job, a good personal statement will summarise your goals, achievements, and experiences in relation to the post you are considering.

Activity: Update personal records

● Put time aside to update your personal records this week. Which aspects need updating?
● Which three of the competence sheets on pp. 283–317 would you find most useful for the jobs that interest you? Your answers to competence-based questions need to be very brief and very specific.

Browse your personal records or progress file to prepare for the application process. These will remind you of what counts in your life, what you aim to achieve, what you have achieved and what you have to offer in a job.

Making the application

Read the documentation

First read the documentation you are sent. You will usually receive one or more of the following items.

General information
This will tell you more about the company, work conditions, and sometimes includes information about matters such as pensions, holidays, bonuses, and so forth. Check the company website or contact their Human Resources or Personnel department for further information. Research the company: large companies expect you to know something about them. All employers expect you to know something about their general area of work, whether from personal experience, from having talked to others or from some basic research. Ensure that you are happy with the work

ethos, the conditions on offer and the direction and ethics of the company.

The job description

This will outline the responsibilities of the post and what the post-holder is expected to do, building on information that was contained in the advertisement. Check that this does match what was said in the advertisement and that you are still interested. Tick all the responsibilities that you can manage successfully. It is unlikely that any candidates will be outstanding in all the areas that the employer requires, so do not be put off if there are one or two areas where you consider yourself to be weak. Consider what the essentials are and whether you could do these.

The 'Person specification'

The person specification will list the qualifications, experiences, skills and qualities that the employer is looking for. These may be divided into 'essential' and 'desirable'. If many candidates meet all the 'essential' specifications, employers will then look to the 'desirable' items and use these for making a short-list of people to interview. It is unlikely that many candidates will meet all the 'desirable' requirements; you need to make a judgement about your suitability for the job if you do not meet some of these. For example, some qualifications are very specific, such as for a qualified engineer, or an educational psychologist to administer tests closed to the public. If you lack those qualifications, it is not usually worth applying. However, sometimes relevant experience and skills can be considered as alternatives.

Ensure that your overall application refers specifically to ALL of the items on the person specification, usually in the order they are listed. Typically, an employer will tick off each specification that has been addressed successfully, and then add up the 'ticks'. If you merge two or three characteristics into a single paragraph or example of your experience, some items may not stand out clearly enough to show you meet the specification and this may cost you the interview.

Person specifications usually include:

- *a requirement for qualifications*: 'educated to degree level', 'preferably a degree in a business

subject', 'a degree in a care subject', 'preferably with a higher degree (MA)';

- *skills specific to the job*: 'experience and ability in managing a team', 'experience of working with the public', 'at least two years' experience of working in X';

- *general skills*: 'ability to work as an effective member of a team', 'excellent communication skills', 'ability to work independently', 'a good self-starter';

- *willingness to accept particular work conditions*: 'ability to work flexible hours', 'willingness to work across several sites', 'must be willing to travel'.

Information about how to apply

Read carefully to see whether the employer asks for a CV or other information to be sent in, and whether specific directions are given about completing the application form. Do exactly what is asked because if there are many applicants, the employer may choose to read only those applications that are completed correctly. Failure to follow instructions reflects poorly on applicants' ability to pay attention to details. If you are asked for a CV, send one; if you are asked not to, then don't.

Equal opportunities form

This form is usually for the personnel department and should not be available to the selection team. Large companies need to monitor that they are following equal opportunities policies, and to monitor for potential bias. If the form is not completed, it may make the company appear to be more successful at equal opportunities than they are, as the percentage of people they appoint from under-represented groups may appear to be a high percentage of those who actually apply.

An application form

Not all employers use these. If they do, you must complete it. If it has space for a long personal statement, you can usually provide this as a separate word-processed sheet, writing 'see attached' on the form. Forms are usually provided electronically now, but if they need to be hand-written, people with disabilities who cannot complete a form by hand can request other means of applying.

Complete the form

Complete the form, following the directions closely:

- Ensure the form is clean and neatly presented: good impressions do count.
- Be honest and accurate: the company is likely to check on information you give them, either immediately or at a later date.
- Be complete: do not leave gaps in work or recent educational histories as this suggests you have something to hide. Include all relevant training and give reasons for work breaks. Complete all requests for information.
- Refer clearly to all skills, qualities, qualifications and experience.

Qualifications

Provide the names of qualifications *in full*, either in the space provided or in your CV or covering letter. The employer may not know what is meant by abbreviations so avoid using these. This is

especially important if you are applying for a position overseas. Find out the local equivalent of your qualifications, and indicate these in the covering letter, so that the employer takes them into account.

If you have your degree results, you do not need to go into details about school history unless you are asked for this, or unless a particular school qualification is relevant to the job. However, if you have good A-level grades or equivalents, it is worth mentioning these. Also provide details of GCSE or equivalent in English, maths and, for jobs such as teaching, science.

Write the personal statement

This is an extremely important part of the application process and requires time and thoughtful consideration. Lay it out neatly and clearly so the main points can be found easily. If you were asked to send only a CV or letter of application rather than an application form, it is a good idea to include a personal statement to accompany these.

Good personal statements

In good personal statements for job applications, it is clear to the employer:

- ✔ that you know what the job will entail;
- ✔ that you understand what they are looking for as a new employee;
- ✔ that you know something about the organisation or company;
- ✔ why you want the job;
- ✔ how your skills, qualities and experience match what they have asked for, in ways that are relevant to the job that you will be doing;
- ✔ exactly where you are addressing each item in the person specification;
- ✔ that you have tailored your application to this particular job rather than sending a standard response;
- ✔ that you write well, clearly, and succinctly and can proof-read accurately (this is an example of your written communication so make sure it is perfectly presented);
- ✔ that, through the way you have laid out information so that key points are easy to find, you value the employer's time.

Refer to your personal records

If you maintain good records and competence sheets, such as those recommended in Chapter 9, it will be easier to select appropriate information to complete your personal statement. Read through your records to remind yourself of your strongest competences and the best examples of your experience.

Employers will want to know what you are capable of achieving, so it is important to identify which of your experiences and responsibilities can be described as achievements and successes. If you have held positions of responsibility, ensure that it is clear what your role was. If you held a post in a student society or have held down a job, identify your achievements during that time. For example, turn a sentence such as:

> As Social Secretary, I was responsible for organising social activities for the student body.

into a more detailed statement such as:

> As Social Secretary (2009–10), I was responsible for organising activities for a student body of 14,000 people. I successfully ran 10 events involving 3000 people. Satisfaction surveys were conducted and these received excellent feedback from 87% of respondents. I also increased income by six per cent over the previous year.

Write to the person specification

Go through the person specification and job specification in detail. Use each item in the person specification as a separate heading. Write a succinct paragraph to address each item, giving at least one good (but brief) example to illustrate each. For example:

Example

Specification: 'ability to work as an effective member of a team'

As part of my current part-time job, I am a member of a team of ten people. This requires me to work towards common goals to strict deadlines. The employer has provided two training days in team-work skills. I have been asked to stand in as deputy team leader on several occasions, which attests to my team-management skills. I feel I am a good team member as I am ready to listen and act upon other people's ideas and am confident in making my own suggestions. I also have extensive experience of problem-solving in small groups as part of my degree. I completed a successful group project, which received good feedback from tutors. My main roles in that group were as meeting co-ordinator and data researcher.

Refer to the job

In the statement, include a few sentences in which you clarify why you are interested in the job and what you have to offer to the employer. Select three or four skills or qualities that you think are particularly relevant and list these as benefits that you can offer to the company. This will indicate to the employer that you are serious about this particular job. It will suggest you have thought about its needs and have selected it on the basis of your own suitability.

Writing a covering letter

If you have included a personal statement, your covering letter can be brief (see page 242). If not, your letter should cover the points addressed in the 'personal statement' section above. Your covering letter should:

- be clear, to the point and businesslike – avoid waffle and anecdote;
- refer clearly to the job for which you are applying, including any reference number that was given;
- state where you saw the job advertised;
- be well-written and proof-read;
- demonstrate with confidence how you meet the requirements of the job – or state that this is outlined in your personal statement.

If the employer's form offers very little space for details about your employment history, use the covering letter to detail the relevance of previous roles, responsibilities and training. Mention any other personal qualities, skills and experience that are relevant to the post.

Example | A covering letter

Your name	Amit Evans
Your full address	1111 Apple Avenue Summertown, London
Your postcode	BB1 11B
Your contact details	Tel: 11111 0303030; Mobile phone: 22222 0303030 Email: agevans@freemail.happy
Date	31 August 2010
Employer contact name **Employer address**	Ms Samantha Browne Alpha Conferences 222–228 Olive Grove Berryfield BB1 XXX
	Dear Ms Browne
State the name of the post, its reference, and where and when you saw it advertised	I am very interested in the post of Assistant Conference Manager (ref. AAP/223/01) advertised in the *Guardian* on 27/8/2010.
Give brief details of your experience and suitability. Refer to your competence sheets	I have recently completed a degree in Business and Economics. As part of my degree, I undertook a project for an events company that mounted conferences for employers locally and nationally. As well as this providing me with experience of event planning, I thoroughly enjoyed the atmosphere and the opportunity to meet a wide range of people. I have worked in sales and with the public for many years. I hope my ability to speak and write several languages will be of additional benefit in the conference world.
Indicate that you know something about the company and why you feel it is the right appointment for you	I am particularly interested in working in a new and growing organisation with an international dimension such as *Alpha Conferences*. I would like to feel I had contributed to the development of a new company in its early stages. Your commitment to employee training is impressive and I would be keen to further my own professional development.
Indicate when you would be available for work	I live locally and would be ready to start work at short notice. I enclose my CV, as requested, and would appreciate the opportunity of an interview to discuss the post further. I look forward to hearing from you.
Use 'sincerely' when you address a named person	Yours sincerely
Sign the letter	*A E Evans*
Type your name beneath	Amit Evans

Competence-based applications

A number of employers are starting to use competence-based applications (see pp. 283–317). These are looking to see which candidates can demonstrate the best examples of the skills, qualities and experience needed for the job. Usually, such jobs are open to a very wide range of people. The employer is likely to take account of 'transferable' skills acquired in very different situations from the job under consideration. This can be an advantage if you have developed skills but wish to change your field of work. However, such jobs also tend to attract a very wide range of applicants, so care needs to be taken to select the best examples of your experience for each competence.

Typically, competence-based applications use an application form and allow very small, specific amounts of space for you to complete details about each competence. You will probably be told not to send additional sheets or a CV. This means that you must be very precise and succinct in summarising your competences in order to include the maximum amount of information about yourself in the space available.

The competence sheets on pp. 283–317 will help you to identify the relevant information and to develop skills in writing brief summaries of key information. Competence-based applications are time-consuming, so it is useful to keep good and updated personal records that enable you to identify information quickly.

Curriculum vitae (CV)

This used to be the most common form of document required by employers. However, it is less in demand than it used to be. Agencies often request CVs, and some employers respond to CVs even when they do not have a job on offer. There is a wide variety of acceptable CV formats. However, as an employer may spend less than a minute reading your CV, whatever format you choose needs to be pleasing to the eye and contain a few key details that will make the selector choose you for interview (see the two examples on pp. 244, 245).

Content

CVs must include:

- full name;
- date of birth;
- home address;
- contact details (phone, email, mobile, fax);
- educational history;
- qualifications;
- employment history;
- interests and other information (relevant training, languages, certificates, driving licence).

Incorporate, in the relevant sections, a few key details that indicate levels and breadth of responsibility and experience.

Layout and style

Presentation

Presentation is extremely important to CVs. Employers may receive hundreds of CVs and may conduct the first selection on the basis of presentation skills. If so, they are more likely to eliminate CVs that are too long, which clearly omit essential sections, are handwritten or poorly typed.

Your CV should be:

- divided into clear sections with headings;
- laid out in legible lists or tables for educational history and employment;
- easy to read and proof-read for errors;
- brief and concise;
- relevant to the job.

The whole document should be in the same font style. Use larger fonts and bold or underlining or italics for headings. Each main section should have the same level of heading (the same font size, style and format). Avoid colour, images, unusual or hard-to-read fonts. Avoid 'gimmicks' and special effects.

Amit Geraint Evans

Personal details

Date of birth: 10/10/1988   Nationality: British
Address: 1111 Apple Avenue, Summertown, London   Postcode: BB1 11B
Tel: 11111 0303030; Mobile phone: 22222 0303030   Email: agevans@freemail.happy

Educational history

2007–10	University College of England, Broad Street, Berryfield, BB1 22K
1999–2007	Albertina Sisulu School, Juniper Street, Hollyacre, YY1 22Y
1992–1999	Oak Primary School, Blethyn Avenue, Llanpwll, XX1 XX2

Qualifications

2010	BA Hons. Business and Economics	2.1
2007	A-level History	Grade A
2007	A-level Economics	Grade C
2007	A-level Business Studies	Grade D
2005	Seven GCSEs (five A*)	

Employment history

2005–2007	Phantom Books, College Street, Berryfield, BB1 33B	Part-time shop assistant	Two days a week; responsibilities for sales and dealing with the public; 2006 promoted to assistant supervisor.
2002–2007	Juniper Papers, Juniper Street, Hollyacre, YY1 22X	Newspaper round	Maintained the same job for five years.

Positions of responsibility

Dates	Position	Organisation	Achievement
2009–10	Student mentor	Holly FE College	Coached three pupils in maths. All successfully passed their GCSE Maths.
2008–09	Treasurer	University Rowing Club	Successfully managed accounts and increased profits by 15 per cent.

Skills and competences

As part of my degree, I undertook a team project for a local employer, Berryfield Employer Forum. We successfully set up a new processing system, which we devised to meet the employer specifications. This was adopted by the company. I took a lead in contacting the employers and encouraging them to take part. The project developed my team-building and negotiation skills, as well as familiarising me with events planning. I feel this experience will be of benefit to a post in your conferencing company.

Interests and achievements

I enjoy walking (British Isles; Germany) and rowing. I was a member of the rowing team that won the Community Shield (2009). I enjoyed working on a Mentoring Schools Programme organised by a local FE college, and felt a sense of achievement when pupils' number-skills improved.

Other information

I speak and write, fluently, in Punjabi and Welsh, have GCSE French, and communicate well with a wide range of people. I am used to dealing with the public. I am computer literate and familiar with most business and project software. I am a good self-starter, and enjoy working to tight deadlines. I am keen to develop my expertise in the conference and events business.

Anna Leroy

Personal details

Date of birth: 10/10/1968

Address: 1112 Apple Avenue, Summertown, London

Tel: 11111 0303031; Mobile phone: 22222 0303031

Nationality: British

Postcode: JJ1 11K

Email: aaleroy@freemail.happy

Educational history

2007–2010	University College of England, Broad Street, Berryfield, BB1 22B
2005–2007	Hilier College, Beckham Road, Oakfield OO2 1DD
1979–1987	Gotama School, Blossom Street, Oakfield, OO1 22Y
1972–1979	St Ann's RC Primary, Super Road, Ashby, AA1 2AA

Qualifications

2010	BA Hons. Psychology, Grade 2.2
2007	Access to Higher Education (Hilier College, Social Science Foundation Course)
2005	GCSE English, Grade B
1984	"O" Level Maths, Grade B
1984	1 "O" Level and four CSEs (grade 1)

Employment history

Dates	Employer	Post	Responsibilities
1998–present	Berry Lawyers, Sharpe Street, Berryfield, BB1 3BB	Part-time legal assistant	Assisting solicitor prepare cases for court; dealing with clients.
1992–1997	Accomb Solicitors, Tailor Road, Oakfield, OO1 22B	Part-time legal assistant	Assisting solicitor prepare cases for court; dealing with clients.
1986–1992	J. J. Field, Solicitors, Tailor Road, Oakfield, OO1 22X	Full-time Administrator/PA	Managing all aspects of a legal office; dealing with the public.
1985–1986	H. Smith Associates, Ash Road, Oakfield, OO1 22P	Administrative assistant	General office duties.

Positions of responsibility

Dates	Position	Organisation	Achievement
2008–2009	Volunteer tutor	University Volunteer Bureau	Tutored a deaf student on a local Access programme. Student has been offered a university place.
2008–2009	Chair	Mature Student Association	Worked with a team to organise 30 meetings and events.
2000–2002	Secretary	Oakfield Playgroup, Ash Road, Oakfield.	Established a thriving playgroup involving 40 families; it still exists. Co-organised meetings and events.
1995–1999	Chair	Oakfield Residents Association, Alder Street, Oakfield OO1 22A	Successful management of an association of 2000 residents; chaired over 50 meetings.

Skills and competences

My work and life history demonstrates that I am a natural organiser. I can see where there are opportunities and will take the lead in creating new groups. I am used to multi-tasking, and have managed to study and maintain family life without taking absences from work. I am very determined and highly motivated. My work in legal companies helped me to develop a wide range of analytical skills and people skills, which I have developed further through my programme and in the organisations that I have helped to run.

Interests and achievements

I enjoy playing an active part in community events and am generally good with people. I am keen to work in a profession related to the caring professions, where I can make use of the knowledge and skills gained through my Psychology degree.

Other information

I have a full driving licence and the European Computer Driving Licence. I am ready to start work at short notice. I am currently taking a course in basic counselling skills.

Language

Use words that emphasise action (verbs). Look for opportunities to include words such as:

> achieved, contributed, co-ordinated, organised, established, demonstrated, accomplished, applied, implemented, initiated, created, set up, developed.

Use words and phrases that demonstrate qualities that employers will value, such as:

> attention to detail, positive outcome, achievement, success, effectively, efficiently, care, creativity, team work, meeting deadlines, co-operation, value for money, time-saving, problem-solving, self-starter, coping strategies, negotiating, networking, flexibility, versatility, creativity, innovation, entrepreneurship, profits, leadership, decision making, priority setting, competitiveness, commercial awareness, communication skills.

Product

The completed CV should be:

- word-processed;
- printed on A4 paper;
- unfolded and sent in an A4 envelope;
- on good-quality paper;
- of 'top copy' quality.

CVs for different purposes

You may need more than one CV. The basic CV should be brief, fit on one side and contain standard information. Academic CVs tend to be longer. If you are looking for an academic job, then include conferences and seminars to which you contributed a paper or workshop, all research projects with details of who funded these, and all your publications. When applying for a job, adapt your basic CV to fit what you know about the company and the requirements of the person specification.

Competence statements in CVs

Traditionally, a CV fits on a single page. If you have a large number of qualifications or jobs, the information may need to fit onto more than one page. In either case, use only a few words to list the responsibilities associated with each item.

Bright and Earl (2007) argue that candidates who include a brief competence statement within a CV have a good chance of being short-listed. They found that there was no particular place on the CV where it was better to position the competence statement. When you have elaborated your competences (see Chapter 9), you may wish to use short competence statements in your CV.

Sending uninvited CVs

Some employers do file and use CVs sent to them when they have not advertised for a post. Many will not, as those using equal opportunities practices usually will advertise all posts. If you have rare and marketable specialist skills, such as high-level IT skills, then the opportunistic CV can be particularly useful.

If you do send CVs on an opportunistic basis, include additional information relevant to the post, either in the CV or in a covering letter. The employer will need to know, for example:

- the kinds of job that interest you – using job titles if possible;
- whether you wish to work full- or part-time;
- an indication of the salary level you expect;
- which parts of the country you are willing to work in;
- the size and kind of company you are interested in working for;
- what your ideal job would be.

These CVs may be slightly longer – but do aim to stay under two pages. Include more details about your skills, experience and what you can offer. Your enthusiasm and interest should radiate from the CV in order for it to be considered.

Using the Internet

Ultimately, I think the internet will become the primary means of advertising and looking for work. The enormous size of the audience and specificity of positions that it offers makes the traditional media forms (e.g. newspapers) seem obsolete and vastly over-priced.

Tom Campbell, futurologist,
New Media Knowledge, in Chapman (2001)

A source of jobs and advice

Graduate jobs will normally be advertised through the Internet. There are several hundred job sites on the web, such as www.monster.co.uk and www.gradunet.co.uk. In addition, there are career advice resources on the net, some aimed at students. Some employers will send job details and accept applications and CVs by email. A list of such resources is given in the 'Useful Websites' section at the end of this book.

Activity: Newspaper sites

Find out which quality or trade papers run advertisements for jobs that interest you.
Enter their website address, and check whether they run the jobs on-line too. Most do. Alternatively use www.jobhunter.co.uk. You can check for jobs on a weekly basis even if you forget to buy the paper.

Put your CV on-line

Large recruiters may provide their own facilities for you to create a CV using a 'wizard'. This is not simply a question of putting up the CV as you have already typed it as, if you do that, you can lose most of the presentational features such as font style and layout: it may look fine on your screen but look messy or bizarre when viewed on the employer's. You will usually need to write in your details for each website. This takes time so it is worth researching the best recruitment sites for the jobs that interest you. Use a plain-text version to 'cut and paste', using the same font throughout and without using tables or formatting. This will save you time. Leave at least half an hour to do this for each site.

Some employers may simply ask you to send a CV as an attachment. If so, use a rich-text format so that you increase the chance of it printing with the desired layout and presentational features on the employer's printer.

Email cover letters

If you send an application by email, include a covering letter. This should follow the same general principles as any other cover letter. In other words, it should be brief, relevant, to the point, summarising your interest and what you have to offer to the company. Email responses can be signed off as 'Best wishes' rather than 'yours faithfully'.

Assessment centres

What is an assessment centre?

Assessment centres provide a series of extended selection procedures which are used by many companies during recruitment. Sessions typically last one or two days. They may be used either as an initial selection tool or for additional information in between first interviews and final selection.

What would I have to do?

Selection tasks vary. You may be asked to sit a set of written papers or you could spend time in a relatively small group of 6–8 people with 2–4 assessors. You can expect to be assessed through a combination of the following.

Group exercises
These are used to assess how effectively you can work in a team, and your communication and problem-solving skills.

In-Tray exercises
These assess your ability to manage complex information quickly, make decisions and manage your time. They are based on realistic work scenarios.

Presentations
These assess your ability to structure information and convey this to other people. You may receive details of the presentation topic in advance of the assessment centre or on the day itself.

Psychometric assessments
These are carried out by licensed professionals and provide a structured and standardised way of assessing how you might perform on a given task or within a given context. Assessments may be either ability tests or personality assessments.

1. *Ability Tests*
   These look at specific skills and knowledge within categories such as cognitive ability, e.g. memory, verbal reasoning, hand-eye co-ordination.

2. *Personality Assessment*
   These are usually questionnaires that you fill in. There are two main types:

   ● Trait instruments: these focus on behaviour and what you are likely to do in a given context. Your scores are likely to change over time as your skills and experience change. A typical test is the OPQ32.
   ● Type instruments: these focus on our preferences for thinking, interacting, learning and working. These preferences tend to be more stable and less likely to change over time. A typical test is the Myers Briggs Type Indicator.

How to prepare for an assessment centre

Some aspects of assessment preparation are very similar to how you would prepare for a standard job interview. You can prepare by:

● researching the company website and taking note of any information on recruitment;
● thinking about your strengths and potential areas for development;
● planning your journey to the assessment centre to make sure that you get there on time.

You are not usually being assessed on what you know, so you do not need to learn specific information in advance. There are a number of websites that can help you prepare for specific aspects of the assessment centre by giving you more information about the types of task that may be given and opportunities to complete test questionnaires. Some of these are listed at the end of the chapter (page 258).

Assessment centres can be quite daunting but it is important to bear in mind:

● As a range of areas are being assessed, it is likely that you will find some assessments easier than others and that you will perform more effectively on some than on others. Try not to

panic if you feel you have performed poorly on one task – you may well perform well in other areas and it is your overall performance that is being assessed.
● Focus on your own performance and avoid becoming over-concerned about the performance of other candidates. You are being assessed against pre-determined criteria rather than your performance in relation to other people.
● Stay focused through the sessions. Even though assessment centres can be very tiring, your motivation levels are being assessed and you need to maintain these.

Referring to disabilities

Many students with disabilities are unsure whether they should mention a disability at interview or not. In Britain, legislation should protect your rights if you have a disability, but employers are still not always aware of what to do when faced with a candidate with a disability.

Should I tell the employer?

There is no easy answer to this. If you need particular help for the application process, the interview or the job, then you will need to disclose the disability. If you do not, then it may not be relevant and it would be an individual decision whether you say anything. You must ensure that you would not leave employers in a position where they could not meet their health and safety responsibilities to you or the public if you do not disclose.

How should I bring up the subject in interview?

If you have not needed to change the interview in any way because of the disability, then the employer may not be aware of the disability. Personnel usually keep this information confidential. It is probably best to assume that the employer may know little about what the disability means in terms of how you might do the job, and may even hold erroneous, very confused or exaggerated ideas about what different disabilities are.

Choose a positive way of introducing the disability. For example, identify the additional skills and qualities you have acquired because of the disability. It is likely that you will have developed additional skills and personal qualities to manage the disability alongside study, work and other people's attitudes. This may have become such a way of life that you underestimate how many skills you have developed in this respect. For example, you may have:

- IT skills (awareness of different ways of making electronic material accessible, which the company might need in order to meet disability legislation);
- people skills (familiarity in dealing with other people's discomfort, embarrassment or rudeness; familiarity with a wider range of people; awareness of how people respond to 'outsiders'; greater ease in dealing with people with disabilities, who form a large minority of the population);
- creativity and problem-solving skills (you will probably have had to find new ways of performing a range of tasks, some of which called for ingenuity);
- self-management skills (disabilities usually call for greater application, determination, self-motivation and endurance).

No two people are alike

Your disability and your strategies for dealing with it, as well as your individual characteristics, will mean that you are different from any other person with a disability that the employer has met. However, the employer may have had a bad experience employing a person with a similar disability. Even though it should be obvious, it is worth your mentioning that no two people with the disability respond in the same way, so that the employer starts with a cleaner slate in considering your application.

Be clear about your abilities

The employer may have very mistaken ideas about what a person with your disability can do. They may underestimate your capabilities. Outline, briefly, your achievements. For example:

I gained excellent feedback from my work placement, where I helped to design a new door operation system. I was able to call upon the design and IT skills that I had developed through my degree, and feel these would be very useful for this job too.

I worked as a volunteer technician for three years for a local theatre group. This brought me into contact with a wide range of people. Many community groups used the theatre. I feel this experience has developed my expertise in finding technical solutions at very short notice and on a tight budget. It also showed me that I enjoy working with older people. These skills and qualities should stand me in good stead for this post.

Outline briefly how the disability does affect you

If possible, present this in the context of what you can do, or the strategies you have developed in order to achieve a result. For example:

My writing skills are good when I use speech-to-text software. I am very familiar with X software. I work quickly and I have a clear writing style. I proof-read well but it is useful if someone else checks the final version.

I organise my time so that I change between tasks every few minutes if I can, so as to change the groups of muscles I am using. I tend to keep two or three different tasks on the go at any one time. This is usually very efficient because I do not get bored and it fills in the natural pauses that occur when you wait for responses from clients.

Mention ways that the disability will affect you at work and what your needs will be.

- 'I need to jot down verbal instructions and then I can work through them.'
- 'The wheel chair requires a width of X cm.'
- 'I am sensitive to light and will need to work in dimmed light or wear glasses with tinted lenses, which I will provide.'

Preparing for the interview

Mental preparation

If you have made a sensible job choice, were able to meet the 'person specifications' and have thought through answers to likely questions, you should feel confident that you have a reasonable chance of being considered for the job. The majority of applicants do not receive an interview, so if you have been offered one, this is already a success. Focus on being calm, and on the questions you can answer. Remind yourself of your interest in the job and of what you have to offer the employer. Make sure you sound convincing to yourself. It is natural to feel anxious, but avoid feeding your anxiety by negative thinking.

Prepare for likely questions

Preparing for the more obvious questions will help you to feel confident about answering at least some questions well. This gives you more room for error on other questions. The section below gives an indication of the kinds of questions that you can expect.

Two-minute answers

When preparing your answers, aim to complete any answer in one to two minutes. The interviewer may wish to ask between six and ten questions, as well as using time to ask the question and make comments of their own. It is unlikely the employer will wish the question stage to last more than 20–30 minutes. If your answers are long, they may not be able to ask all their questions, which means you will be disadvantaged if they award points for each answer.

Identify your strong points for each question

Before the interview, identify what are the strongest points you can make for each likely question. A strong answer will refer to experience, achievement and success. It will also be specific: give at least one example, with reference to the scale or importance of the achievement, including one or two key pieces of data if relevant.

Prepare points to include in the interview

Use the interview to bring out your strongest points. Be very clear what these are in advance so that you bring them in when an opportunity arises. Before the interview:

● List your strongest five achievements, qualities or attributes;
● sum these up in fewer than 20 words;
● think of which questions you may be asked where you can bring in these five points;
● be ready to bring them in elsewhere if they do not arise naturally.

Sense of time

Practise speaking aloud and timing yourself so that you develop a sense of what two to three minutes feels like. You should build up a sense of how much you can say within that time, without

---

Activity: Speaking time

Look at the example below. How long do you think it would take to deliver? Read it aloud at a reasonable speed, with expression, and time yourself.

Q: 'Have you worked in a caring post before?' (The candidate has not done so.)

A: 'My most relevant work experience has been in acting as a student tutor to three young children in a local school. Those children were very vulnerable, and I had to develop skills which are typical of those needed in care posts. For example, I focused on building a rapport with the children, watching for non-verbal cues, and being sensitive to their feelings. I had to be prepared to wait and work at their speed. I also had to consider the wishes of the teacher and other parties. I feel I achieved a good relationship with the children and their teachers. I negotiated work schemes with the teacher and each child. The teacher said that they all made an improvement and I received very good feedback, so it seems to have worked well. I think that gives me a good foundation for this post, and I particularly look forward to working with children and parents.'

● What do you think are the strong points about this answer?

---

sounding rushed. You can cover a number of relevant details in two minutes if you are precise and to the point. The activity on page 250 should help.

Presentation

Employers expect candidates to be smartly dressed and presentable: you may need to act as the public face of their company at some stage. Pay attention to details such as clean hands and fingernails, polished shoes, and a smart bag. This is true even if you will not be expected to dress smartly in the job.

In the interview

First impressions

Although the whole interview is important, you can make the interview run more smoothly if the first minute is well managed. This requires only a few simple actions.

- Look clean and smart.
- Be on time.
- Ensure your right hand is free in order to shake hands.
- No matter how you feel, smile and appear relaxed.
- Look pleased to meet the interviewers. Shake hands firmly, look them in the eye, and listen when they say their names.
- Move calmly so that you do not crash into furniture.
- Sit upright, alert and interested for the interview.

During the interview, avoid apologies and regrets. Work with the situation as it is, not with what might have gone better. Tell yourself that the interviewers' questions are interesting and manageable – keep considering what it is they are looking for in an employee and what examples you can give them to reassure them that you can meet their needs.

You do not need to be magical, a super-brain, or word-perfect. Everybody stumbles on some words and questions. Avoid gimmicks, 'hard sell' and theatrics. Be natural. If possible, imagine you are being interviewed by an interested relation of one of your friends or colleagues. Although this advice seems obvious, many candidates do not come across as genuinely interested in the job, easy to get on with, honest or natural.

Keep it simple

It is not unusual to ruin a potentially good interview by trying too hard to impress. If you demonstrate a reasonable degree of calm, interest and enthusiasm, you will already be well placed.

Employers may take a number of approaches to selecting a candidate. They will usually look for a 'good fit' between what they want and what the candidates can offer. This is partly a question of skills and experience. However, the majority of candidates short-listed for interview will probably be well matched for skills and experience. Possibly, none may meet all the requirements. All will meet about 75–95 per cent, with different kinds of strengths. If the employer needs very specific skills which are in short supply, the person with the best skills will get the job.

However, the probability is that the choice will come down to inter-personal skills and behaviour demonstrated in the interview. The interview is about meeting you and seeing what you are like: the employer already has information about your skills and experience. The employer or interview panel will want to choose someone who:

- can do the job with minimum training and supervision;
- seems like a reasonable, sensible person, with common sense, whom colleagues could work with;
- answers their questions, rather than delivers a sales pitch;
- will 'fit' the post; who seems to suit the work temperamentally;
- looks as though they will 'fit in' generally.

Team work and supportive working climates are important so it is understandable that interview panels will favour people who seem to have the right characteristics to suit their work environment. This is usually a question of apparent personality. Under equal opportunities legislation, interviews should not discriminate on the grounds of sex, race, disability, etc. However, personality and other characteristics can become confused in people's minds. If you suspect discrimination, you have legal rights.

It is important to project yourself as mature, reasonable and friendly. It may help to focus on this rather than struggling to make 'perfect answers'. Many people come across as very stilted, and even bizarre, in interview because they are nervous. Focus on the needs of the panel – what they are looking for – rather than on 'selling' yourself.

During the interview

Put yourself in the employers' position. They are likely to interview at least four people during a period of two to three hours. They may be interviewing dozens of people over several weeks. Even four interviews in a row can be tiring. It will be appreciated if you:

- provide brief answers which are to the point;
- provide clear examples;
- provide exactly the information you are asked for;
- are ready for predictable questions so that you can answer promptly.

Avoid

- long, winding answers that go off the point;
- 'interesting anecdotes';
- giving several examples if you are asked only for one;
- giving a long background to your answers.

Opening questions

Employers tend to start interviews with one or two questions to settle the interviewee. Here are some typical questions.

'Have you had a good journey?'
This is politeness. Answer very briefly.

'Tell me a little about your programme'
Two or three sentences will suffice. Draw out unusual features as these may reflect well upon you.

...traffic on Old St... dreadful... temporary lights on Windsor Road... and don't get me started on the contraflow!!

'Why do you want this job now?'
Be as specific as you can. Include reference to something about the company that appeals to you. The employer wants to know why you want to work at this company, and that you have done some homework about the company, not that you are desperate for a job. Indicate what you think you can offer to the company.

'Where do you see yourself in 3/5/20 years' time?'
The employer is looking to see whether you are realistic and whether you are a good match for the job. They may be checking to see whether you are likely to leave within a few months or weeks of appointment. You may not know your plans five years into the future but give a strong answer that indicates you have an idea of what you want to achieve. Refer to the kind of experience you hope to achieve from this job that will further your own aims in a few years' time. Your answer should suggest there is benefit to yourself as well as the employer in you being offered this post.

'What attracted you to this job?'
Candidates are unlikely to be interviewed and/or appointed unless they show interest in the specific job and work context, unless they possess very highly valued skills in short supply. Find out about the occupational area or industry and the employer – at least enough to hold a conversation for a few minutes.

'Tell us about yourself'

This can be the most difficult question as there is so much to choose from. It is, therefore, a question for which you should prepare. Play safe by referring to your career ambitions and why you think these suit your personal characteristics and experience. Keep it very brief. The employer may be looking to see how aware of your audience and how concise you are, rather than being interested in your life.

Person specification and competency questions

Most questions will relate to the person specification. Although you will have given this information already when you applied, employers may ask similar questions to ones you believe you have answered. This may be for several reasons:

- The panel may not have been involved in the short-listing process and may have received your details at the last moment.
- The panel is seeing many people. They are likely to remember what they hear rather than what you have written.
- Do not assume that just because you have given the answer in the paperwork, the panel will have read it. Give a full answer in case they have not.
- The panel is looking at your people skills. They know you know the answers to most questions, but want to see how well you communicate information to other people.
- They are 'double-checking' to compare your verbal answers with those on paper.

Competence questions

For competence-based applications, most questions usually relate to the competences in the person specification. This means you can prepare for these with reasonable confidence. Think of unusual angles for the question. A competence question may be phrased in very different ways. For example, a question on dealing with difficult people might be phrased as:

- 'From your life and work so far, give the best example of a time when you had to deal with a difficult member of the public.'
- 'Can you give us two or three examples of a time when you . . .'

- 'Think of an example when you dealt badly with a member of the public. What did you learn from that occasion and how has this affected the way you would approach a similar situation now?'
- 'What kind of advice would you give a new member of staff who had not dealt with the public before?'
- 'What professional development have you undertaken in recent years to improve your capability in dealing with members of the public?'
- 'What is the worst example of you dealing with a member of the public? What did this teach you?'

Catch-all questions

A number of questions tend to appear in many job descriptions, and mean different things depending on the type of job.

'Team work' may be used to mean:

- good at people skills;
- easy to get on with;
- takes on board colleagues' needs;
- has specific skills in negotiating with others;
- has experience of working in project teams.

'Leadership' could be used to refer to:

- willingness to speak on behalf of the group;
- a strong vision that carries other people – such as directing plays or setting up student groups;
- a tendency to be the person chosen to act as group chair;
- experience of running a project;
- experience of running a major project.

'Good self-starter' may mean:

- enjoys working on their own;
- will accept a job that offers little support;
- works well independently;
- can start a new job without supervision;
- has good problem-solving skills;
- can take on major projects in almost any area;
- is a responsible worker.

'Flexibility' may mean willingness to:

- fit in;
- work with a wide range of people;
- work unusual or long hours;

- change schedule at short notice;
- respond quickly to crises;
- work at different locations;
- travel;
- help out different departments in emergencies;
- change department, role or workload;
- find solutions to a wide variety of problems.

It is important to work out, from the level and nature of the job, what kind of interpretation to use. It is also important to gain a balance, so that you can show that you are able to work with and listen to others, but are also able to work alone, take responsibility, and give direction to your own and others' work.

Anticipating questions

For each element of the person specification, consider how you would respond to the following questions, bearing in mind the requirements of the job for which you are applying:

- Your best example. What is good about it? What worked well? What was your own contribution?
- Two or three brief examples. What do these suggest about the breadth of your experience?
- An example from which you learnt something that improved your current performance. If you are asked for your 'worst experience', this may be a useful example as you can emphasise what you learnt that benefits your current performance.
- How would you advise somebody else to perform this competence?
- What professional development have you undertaken in relation to this competence?
- What skills and personal qualities were involved in an example of this competence?
- How regularly do you demonstrate this competence? (This is to check whether your example is a 'one off' or represents your everyday experience.)
- At what level of responsibility do you demonstrate this competence? (This is to check your ability to take responsibility for tasks that involve this competence.)

Other typical questions

Other favourite questions are variations on the following themes.

An example of a highlight from your life or career so far

Be prepared to describe briefly what happened and why you consider this to be a highlight. For example, it may have developed particular skills that would be useful to the company. It may have been an occasion where you took on a challenge or worked at a higher level of responsibility than previously and proved your capability.

An example of your worst mistake

Use this as an opportunity to show how you are willing to learn from mistakes and to put that learning to good use. Avoid using an example that would make the employer worry about employing you. Select the kind of mistake that anybody could make. The employer will also want to see that you are willing to take responsibility for your own actions, rather than trying to lay the blame on others (even if it was someone else's fault, in your opinion). See the Competence Sheet on p. 310.

Examples of your commitment to personal development

You can expect this kind of question from employers who have 'Investors in People' status, professional organisations and posts related to public office.

What contribution do you think you can make? What have you got to offer?

Refer to specific experience and skills that you have gained and which are likely to be of benefit to the company. Relate your contribution to what has been described in the job specification and to what you have found out about the company. Include personal qualities. If possible, refer to feedback that you have received from employers or from colleagues or team members.

What personal qualities do you possess that would be of benefit in this work?

Select two or three qualities upon which you can

focus. Give one or two sentences to sum up where you demonstrated this quality and why you consider it relevant to the current post. List briefly three to five other qualities that you also possess. Leave it to the interviewer to ask you more details about these. Be prepared to give examples if questioned further. See pp. 225 and 280.

A critical event in your life or work that you have coped with

This may be another way of asking about 'worst mistakes' or 'highlights', depending on how it is phrased. You are unlikely to receive all three questions, so you should be able to use the same material to prepare for at least two of these questions. This question is looking for such features as evidence of levels of responsibility you have held, coping and problem-solving strategies, ability to reflect upon and learn from experience and apply learning to new areas. For caring professions, it may be used to explore your ability to describe and work with emotions and feelings; in creative fields, to see how you use experience as inspiration for your artwork; for management posts, to see how well you manage complex and difficult situations.

What you learned from . . .

You may be asked why you chose a particular study option or job, and what you learned from these. For example, you may have learnt to be flexible, to work with difficult people, to maintain high levels of concentration when working with numbers, to think analytically, to be a stronger person emotionally, to deal with the unexpected. Indicate how the subject or experience drew out your natural strengths and abilities. Focus on those aspects that are relevant to the job for which you are applying.

Closing questions

General interest questions

Sometimes employers ask about your general interests at the end of an interview. These usually seem to be easier, and so candidates may relax and let down their guard, revealing a different side to themselves. For example, the employer may ask:

Q: 'I see you are keen on Mexico. What is the interest there?'

It is important to remember that you are still being interviewed. The employer is still looking to see what it is you have to offer the company. Your answer should reflect this. Keep your reply brief: this is not an opportunity to tell the employer all about your pet interests. Your answer might bring out personal qualities or an ability that is useful to the company. For example (depending on the circumstances):

A: 'I am keen to develop my Spanish.' (*Useful if the company has Spanish-speaking offices or customers.*)

A: 'I wanted to find out about a different culture and have always been interested in Mexican art.' (*This suggests you have a breadth of interests and the confidence to go and find things out for yourself.*)

Do you have any questions you would like to ask us?

You do not have to have a question, especially if the information is available in the literature that was sent to you, or is available from Personnel or on the Internet. Avoid unnecessary questions: they may suggest you have not done your homework. The employer will not want the interview to go on too long, so keep to one or two essential questions. Reasonable questions to ask are, for example:

- related to something that was reported recently in the trade papers about the company, especially if it allows them to make a positive response;
- genuine questions that determine whether you want the job. Now is the time to ask these;
- questions about training and professional development;
- whether there is a mentoring scheme for new employees;
- what would the employer consider to be a sign of your success after two years with the company? What are their expectations of you as a new employee?
- who you will be reporting to;
- opportunities for travel, or for secondment;
- what the next step will be. When are you likely to hear the outcome of the interview?

Questions to avoid

Avoid asking questions:

- where the information is provided already in the paperwork or on the company website;
- that you could have checked with HR/Personnel before the interview;
- that you should have checked before applying in order to make sure this was the right job;
- about whether advertised terms and conditions can be changed just for you;
- questions that start with 'Will I have to . . . ?' (Use: Will the job involve . . . ?)
- that your common sense should be able to answer.

Activity: Sabotage the interview

1. List all the things you can think of to really mess up an interview so that the employer is convinced you are unprepared and unsuitable. You may include comments related to:

   - your clothing;
   - your punctuality;
   - not knowing anything about the company;
   - asking silly questions when given the opportunity.

2. Give yourself advice!
   What advice would you give to somebody else who said they sabotaged interviews in this way? The advice may seem obvious to you – but many people forget the basics. If you are uncertain about how to prevent the sabotage you suggest, speak to a careers adviser at the university.

3. Write a preparation list for yourself in order to ensure you are ready for your interview.

Is there anything you feel we should know that you have not yet had a chance to tell us?

- Some employers are aware that candidates are anxious and may not have given their best answers. If you really feel that you have let yourself down on an answer, this is an opportunity to return to it, if you feel you can now give a better response.
- Before the interview, you may have rehearsed

skills and qualities that you feel are important to this kind of job or company. If these have not been referred to in the interview, raise these now.

If we offered you the job, when would you be able to start?

Ensure you are clear about your personal arrangements so that you are in a position to answer this.

Activity: Practise the interview

- Find one or preferably two other people with whom to practise your interview techniques. This may be embarrassing, but it is better to get feedback before the interview rather than after.
- Give details of the kind of job for which you are applying. The other person(s) can use and adapt the questions in this chapter to conduct an interview for your job.
- Give at least 15 minutes for each person's interview.
- Ask for (or give) feedback that is constructive. The feedback should give clear guidance on what is good about your interview performance already, as well as what could be even better.
- Note down the feedback you receive and decide what you will do to improve your performance.

After the interview

After the interview, you will probably remember all the things you wish you had said. It is not always easy to tell whether you were successful. Use the experience to learn more about your performance so that it was not a waste of time, no matter what the outcome is.

Analyse the questions

Jot down all the questions you were asked.

- Which ones were unexpected? Were any of these similar to questions that you had prepared, without you realising? Note the different ways that employers can word questions aiming at similar information.

- Note how many questions you were asked. How long was your interview supposed to last? Take ten minutes off that time and divide the remaining time by the number of questions. How long did the employer expect each answer to be?
- Were your answers too long? If so, practise punchier responses for the next interview.
- Were your answers too brief? If so, think of a good example of your experience that you could use to develop that answer more fully.

Analyse your performance

- Which examples did you use? Were these your best? Remind yourself of your best example so that this stays in your mind next time.
- Did you include all of your best points?
- What went well about the interview? Jot this down and read it before the next interview.
- What could have been better? How would you deal with this next time? Write this down and read it before the next interview.

Ask for feedback

Some companies will give brief feedback to unsuccessful candidates. It is worth asking for this. However, be prepared for very general comments such as 'the candidate we selected was the most successful in meeting the criteria'. Some companies refuse to give any feedback, in order to avoid legal repercussions.

> ### Reflection   Learn from the job application
>
> - Select one job interview that you attended, whether successful or not. If you have not applied for a job interview, now is a good time to practise with a friend.
> - In your reflective journal, go through the 'After the interview' section above. Jot down ten things you did well.
> - Jot down the three things which are most important to improving your performance at job interviews.

Closing comments

This chapter has covered the basics of applying for work as a graduate student. There is a very wide range of materials available to help with specific aspects of the process. If you are very anxious about certain aspects, such as answering interview questions, or writing CVs for the Internet, then there are books to help with every detail.

However, in most cases, the basics are enough. If the employer wants someone with more experience or particular skills, they will employ on that basis, no matter how good your application. The important basic rules are:

- Apply a problem-solving strategy to finding a job. Good preparation is similar to the 'problem elaboration' referred to in Chapter 5.
- Research your options and look for opportunities that carry you towards your long-term goals.
- Choose well. Unrealistic and unsuitable applications may be a waste of your time.
- Rather than sending out hundreds of applications, select a few applications, research the companies and fine-tune the personal statement or competences so that they are precise, informative, clear and relevant to the job.
- Ensure you keep your personal records or progress file up to date so that you can make a good application at short notice.
- Prepare for the interview. Use the competence sheets in your progress file.

Finally, aim to learn from the experience. You may pass the majority of courses or exams that you take in your life, but it is unlikely that you will be successful in gaining a job for each application. You will benefit enormously if you view each application and interview as a chance to gain experience, develop application skills, and learn something about employers or yourself. Reflect on the experiences and keep records so that you can benefit in the future.

Further reading

Bright, J. and Earl, J. (2007) *Brilliant CV: What Employers Want to See and How to Say It*, 3rd edn (London: Prentice Hall). (Useful if the jobs you apply for are mostly CV-based rather than form-based.)

Chapman, A. (2001) *The Monster Guide to Jobhunting* (London: Financial Times/Prentice Hall). (Detailed guidance on using the Internet. Useful if you are not already comfortable using the Internet.)

Hodgson, S. (2007) *Brilliant Answers to Tough Interview Questions*, 3rd edn (London: Prentice Hall). (One of a number of books that are useful to focus the mind when preparing for an interview.)

Jackson, T. and Jackson, E. (1997) *The Perfect CV: How to Get the Job You Really Want*, revised and updated edition (London: Piaktus).

Popovich, I. (2003) *Teach Yourself Winning at Job Interviews* (London: Hodder Education). (Traditional but sensible advice on job interviews.)

Resources on assessment centres

www.prospects.ac.uk/links/AssessmentCntrs   General advice on exercises and how to prepare

http://targetjobs.co.uk/general-advice/assessment-centres.aspx   General advice

www.psychometric-success.com/assessment-centers/assessment-and-development-center.htm   Advice and practice tests

www.shl.com/TryATest/Pages/CandidateHelp.aspx   Practice tests

Chapter 11

Drawing it together

Even if you're on the right track, you'll get run over if you just sit there.

Will Rogers

Learning outcomes

This chapter offers opportunities to:

- recognise personal changes and achievements
- review your reflections on personal planning
- update your profile of skills and qualities
- identify your 'learning edge'
- identify emerging personal responsibilities
- plan your next steps.

Introduction

Personal planning is not simply about making a 'plan' and following it. It is a developmental process that each individual moulds to suit their own needs and interests over time. It is about getting to grips with issues such as:

- who you are and the kind of person you want to be;
- the life you want to lead and what you want from life;
- what matters to you and what you want to achieve;
- the steps you will take to achieve your goals;
- recognising changes in your interests and charting out a new plan in line with those changes.

Good planning involves taking steps to ensure you have the information you need at your fingertips when you need it. It involves thinking about possibilities, some of which may seem far-fetched, and starting to put the support and skills in place now that might be useful later.

This chapter offers structured opportunities to review your current position, referring back to activities undertaken in previous chapters, and looking forward to your next step. It looks at the process of managing personal development planning once you are already embarked on the journey of self-discovery and life planning.

Recognising personal changes

Goal inertia

Chapter 1 encouraged you to form a strong vision of what you wanted to be or to achieve. However, your views may already have changed. Each day, our experiences shape us anew. Over time, our aims and goals may become out of touch with who we have become: this is 'goal inertia'.

The 'newer you' is inspired by fresh ideas, moulded by experiences, changed by the knowledge you are acquiring, living in an environment that also changes each day. Is this 'newer you' still inspired by plans made one, three or five years ago?

◻ Activity: Recognising personal changes

Take ten minutes to brainstorm all the differences you can detect between yourself now and yourself three years ago.

	Me three years ago	Me now
Appearance		
Clothes		
Friends		
Interests		
Tastes in music		
Life aims or vision		
Attitudes		

	Me three years ago	Me now
Inspiration		
Personal qualities I want to develop		
People I admire		
People who support me		
Job taken		
Career interests		
Other significant changes		

Review your goals

You may be inspired by the same vision or aims all of your life. However, if you feel that your goals are not inspiring you anymore, you have probably outgrown them. It is worth reviewing your goals from time to time. For example:

- Complete the 'Dream' or 'Long-term vision' activities again (pp. 20–22). Compare your current and previous responses.
- Talk to someone about your goals. Ask them to press you into really exploring what you want.
- Take a journey to somewhere you have never visited before. The change of scene can generate new ideas about what you really want.
- Speak to other people about their goals and interests. Broaden your perspective on the options open to you.

Success is a very personal thing. For you, success may mean reaching the stars or it may mean a particular source of happiness that other people would not appreciate.

Success is associated with happiness. Does your vision of your life leave you with a feeling of relative happiness? If the goals you set for yourself are unappealing, or make you feel that you are making more hurdles for yourself in life, or seem to be setting you off on paths towards places that you no longer find attractive, it is probably time for a rethink.

Review your values

Your vision will be strongly influenced by your values – either in what you view as successful, or in the behaviours and lifestyle you find acceptable and desirable.

Using the reflective process

Monitoring personal progress

Progress can be measured against your personal goals or against objective criteria such as exam marks. In the grand scheme of life, marks given by others count for much less than:

- the depth of your personal awareness;
- your ability to monitor your own progress; and

- your ability and motivation to take action to improve performance without being told to do so.

In order to monitor performance and personal change, you need records. A reflective journal, maintained for your own purposes, is a key tool for monitoring change. If you haven't read through your reflective journal for a while, now is a good time to do so.

📖 **Reflection**   Reviewing your reflective journal

Read through ten pages of your reflective journal, preferably from at least six months ago.

- What do you notice about your state of mind at the time? How does it differ from now?
- What things had you forgotten were in the journal that you are pleased to find?
- What things did you mean to do but have not yet got round to doing?
- What else strikes you as interesting from your journal?

Identifying change

Keeping a reflective journal provides material to help you monitor changes in yourself over time. The following activity invites you to look back over your reflection and identify themes and changes in your responses.

Activity: Has your thinking changed?

- Select three activities from anywhere in this book. Include one you enjoyed and one that you found difficult or resisted.
- Do these again now.
- Compare your responses with those you made previously.
- How do you account for any differences in your responses?

Being a reflective practitioner

Reflective practice is very similar to making New Year resolutions. It is easy to start well, but by mid-year the resolutions are often long forgotten. Similarly, reflection on our goals, performance and personal development may start out well. However, reflection is often an early casualty when there is pressure on our time. You may find that this has been true of you. If so, just take up from wherever you left off. If you keep doing this, you will find that reflective practice becomes a habit.

📖 **Reflection**   Developing skills in reflective practice

In your reflective journal, jot down your responses to the following.

- What did you gain from taking a reflective and self-evaluating approach to your academic, personal or professional development?
- How well do you feel you have developed and maintained a reflective approach?
- What steps could you take to improve your reflective practice?

Activity: Building from personal expertise

In your reflective journal, jot down *one* skill or area of expertise which you feel is your strongest point. This could be a sub-skill such as organising space or drawing up timetables or planning a piece of writing.

- Take two minutes to brainstorm ways this skill or area of expertise might be helpful to your future study.
- Take two minutes to brainstorm ways this skill or area of expertise might help in work contexts.
- Take two minutes to brainstorm ways this skill or area of expertise might be helpful to your life more generally.

Once you have completed this for one skill, go through the same questions with at least two other personal strengths. You may find it useful to update your competence sheets once you have completed this activity.

Improving performance

Working with our strengths

One way of improving performance is to identify current strengths and to build upon these. Chapter 2, for example, identified ways of using expertise in one area to develop understanding in another area. Look back through the competence sheets and other evaluations of your skills and qualities in Chapter 9 to remind yourself of your current strengths. Look back over your learning goals and the areas that you have worked on to improve personal performance. Consider how well you drew on your personal strengths in order to achieve your learning goals.

Identifying 'transferable skills'

To transfer skills from one context to another, it is usually necessary to:

- be aware of the skills (and especially sub-skills) you already use;
- identify which of those skills can be adapted to fit the new context.

The sub-skills are especially important as it is usually these that transfer to new contexts. For example, if you are good at working with numbers, the sub-skills might include paying attention to details, sequencing, seeing patterns, logical skills, seeing how numbers relate to words, having the patience to retest all the subsequent stages in a problem in order to identify an error, a good memory for formulas, etc.

If you are good at working with people, the sub-skills and personal qualities involved might include listening skills, coping with other people's anger, seeing things from another person's point of view, being very sensitive to your own feelings and the impact these have on others, taking responsibility for your own mistakes, being able to ask for what you need, etc.

> **Activity: Transferring skills**
>
> - Select one of your skills or strengths.
> - Where did you develop this skill?
> - What are the sub-skills and qualities you have developed as part of the overall skill?
>
> Now select one context or situation from the following list. Choose the context with which you are least familiar:
>
> Working with children;
> Setting up an arts exhibition;
> Designing an office;
> Counselling others on a phone line;
> Raising money for a charity;
> Making a video;
> Designing a Web page for a company;
> Being the first on the scene of a serious accident;
> Organising a conference;
> Opening a restaurant.
>
> - Take five minutes to brainstorm all the ways that the sub-skills you identified could be of any use at all in the new context you chose. There will be ways that are not immediately apparent.
> - In what ways would you need to adapt those sub-skills so that they fit the new context?

Make the link!

Interconnections between areas of expertise

Very few skills are gained in isolation from others. Our development is usually a complex web of newly emerging strengths and relative weaknesses. When we develop one area of expertise, we usually enhance performance in others, even if this is not visible.

For example, people who sing in choirs develop their voices and their musicality. However, they also tend to acquire a good sense of timing in their 'response' to others, which can contribute to their people skills. A vast array of other skills can be linked to this one activity, such as developing confidence in performing in front of others, team work, taking direction, following a sequence, attention to detail, sensitivity to mood, etc. The same is true of most other areas of expertise.

The converse is also true. If we are weak in one skill or area of expertise, the ramifications of this will be felt in a wide range of contexts. For example, if we hate sport, this could impact upon our health, our stamina, our opportunities to mix with others, our ability to join in certain conversations, the number of connections we can make with other people, the range of metaphors we have to call upon, our understanding of other people's interest and motivations, etc.

Because of this, the root of difficulties we experience in one area of our lives may lie in a completely different area. For example, poor organisational skills may originate in one of a number of areas, such as poor time-management skills, low motivation, unhelpful attitudes, an inability to say 'No' to too many requests for help, or a lack of responsibility for our own actions. Unless we work on the root cause, the difficulties may not go away.

Raising the game

Recognising your achievements

It may be tempting to feel at times that your personal development could now 'come to an end'. That is usually a good signal for raising your game, setting new challenges, finding a new aspect to stimulate your interest.

One boost to motivation is reviewing your successes. Note what you have achieved so far with your own development and consider the benefits this has brought you.

> 📖 **Reflection**   Linking skills and expertise
>
> - What is the area where you have developed most expertise?
> - What are the wider range of sub-skills and qualities that have developed as part of that expertise? List at least 20.
> - Which one skill, personal quality or area of expertise do you feel you need to improve?
> - How would improving this one area also lead to improvements in other skills, qualities, attitudes or areas of expertise?
>
> What do you think is at the root of this area of weakness? What can you do to address this?

> **Activity: Making the connections**
>
> Make a list of 3–5 themes that you are working on at the moment. Then identify various sections of the book that can develop relevant skills for improving your performance. For example:
>
> *Your goals and how to achieve them*: Chapter 1, 'The vision', and Chapter 5, 'Successful problem-solving and task management'.
>
> *Managing your responses when working with difficult people*: Chapter 4, 'Successful self-management', and Chapter 6, 'People skills'.
>
> *Working on problems and looking for creative solutions*: Chapter 5, 'Successful problem-solving and task management', and Chapter 7, 'Thinking outside the box'.
>
> - Identify the ways that skills and insights developed in one aspect of your life can have an effect upon performance in other areas.

> 📖 **Reflection**   Note success
>
> Browse through your reflective journal for the last year – or since your last review. In your journal, note:
>
> - What goals did you work on during that time?
> - Which ones have you achieved?
> - What are the benefits of having achieved these?
>
> Consider what the effects of these achievements are. These may be changes in your life, successes in your study, the ability to manage a particular situation, or a feeling of accomplishment. Don't be modest. Make sure you include a list of all the sub-skills you developed and your minor achievements as well as the more noticeable ones.
>
> Have you celebrated your achievements? If not: make sure you do!

Working at your 'edge'

Once you have built your confidence in your own success, you are ready to set yourself greater challenges. This can also mean looking at your approach to challenge itself. Do you welcome challenge? Are you prepared to take on goals that will stretch you?

Activity: Attitude to challenge

Indicate how important each of the following is to you achieving well.

(a) I achieve best when I . . .	Very important	Important	Quite important	Not very important	Not at all important
● can see some results quickly	☐	☐	☐	☐	☐
● have feedback from others so I know how well I am doing	☐	☐	☐	☐	☐
● receive guidance or suggestions from other people	☐	☐	☐	☐	☐
● know I am heading in the right direction	☐	☐	☐	☐	☐
● have planned out the whole process in advance	☐	☐	☐	☐	☐
● set short-term targets that I know are achievable	☐	☐	☐	☐	☐
● set goals that I am certain I can achieve	☐	☐	☐	☐	☐
● plan each step closely so as to avoid setbacks	☐	☐	☐	☐	☐
● have a clear vision of where I am going	☐	☐	☐	☐	☐
● have a safety net to fall back on if things do not work out.	☐	☐	☐	☐	☐

Indicate how far each statement below is typical of you.

(b) I am able to motivate myself to work towards a goal even if . . .	Very typical	Typical	Sometimes the case	Not very typical	Not typical at all
● I have to wait a long time to see the results	☐	☐	☐	☐	☐
● it takes years to reach the ultimate goal	☐	☐	☐	☐	☐
● nobody else is available to tell me what to do	☐	☐	☐	☐	☐
● there is a really difficult challenge	☐	☐	☐	☐	☐
● it is not clear that the outcome will be successful	☐	☐	☐	☐	☐
● the eventual goal is rather vague	☐	☐	☐	☐	☐
● the plan has to evolve slowly over time	☐	☐	☐	☐	☐
● I have to work hard for something that I may not achieve	☐	☐	☐	☐	☐
● there are many setbacks	☐	☐	☐	☐	☐
● other people think I am aiming too high.	☐	☐	☐	☐	☐

Attitude to challenge

The greatest barriers to success are usually those that derive from our attitudes and fears. The challenge may simply be too great for us at that time. The challenges we set ourselves should be appropriate for our current coping skills, support networks, and emotional well-being. The activity on p. 266 gives an indication of the ways in which you currently cope with challenge.

📖 Using your responses for (a)
- Highlight all the answers to which you responded with a 'Very important' or 'Important'.
- Write these out in your reflective journal, starting: 'To cope with a new challenge, it is important for me that . . .'.
- As you write, add details or examples from your experience to illustrate how you know this is really true of you.

📖 Using your responses for (b)
- Highlight all the answers to which you responded with a 'Not very typical' or 'Not typical at all'.
- Write these out in your reflective journal, starting: 'I am unlikely to keep going with a new challenge if . . .'.
- As you write, add details or examples from your experience to illustrate how you know this is really true of you.

Interpreting your responses

Your answers to (a) provide you with a summary of the approaches that increase your chances of success with new challenges. For example, you may have indicated that you need support in order to achieve. If this is true of you, you are more likely to be successful if you remain open to guidance from others, plan carefully and set manageable targets. However, see 'The comfort zone' below.

Your answers to (b) provide you with a summary of how highly motivated you are likely to remain even in high-risk contexts. If you indicated many 'Very typical' and 'Typical' replies here, your responses suggest you are likely to respond well to challenge and risk. You appear to be highly motivated and able to manage your own path to success very well. However, see 'The comfort zone' below.

If your responses to (b) were mostly 'Not very typical' or 'Not typical at all', set yourself challenges that avoid most of those circumstances. Your 'edge' is likely to be working on developing your motivation so that you can achieve your goals even when conditions are not ideal.

The comfort zone and 'the working edge'

When we only work to our strengths and preferences, we run the risk of not setting sufficient challenges for ourselves. The 'comfort zone' is where we operate when we are running no risks, setting ourselves no challenges, ensuring we always have a very strong and wide safety net, ensuring we always have more than enough support. A good personal development plan will include areas for improvement that challenge us to work at our 'edge'.

'The edge' is the boundary between the comfort zone and unnecessary or inappropriate risks. It is different for everybody. For one person it might be learning to take advice from others; for another person it may be learning to work more independently of others. For people who avoid risk, the 'edge' might be in learning to set more adventurous challenges. This might entail developing related skills, qualities or attitudes such as managing change, seeing mistakes as opportunities to learn, developing emotional coping strategies, and so forth. For those who take high-risk strategies, the 'edge' might be in developing ways of coping with stress, or developing trust in other people, or in living without high excitement.

> 📖 **Reflection**   Working at the 'edge'
>
> - What do you feel is the 'edge' you need to work at next?
> - What makes you feel that this is your 'edge'? Who could you speak to about this?
> - How will you take on this new challenge?
> - What support or guidance do you need?

Sometimes it is hard to acknowledge where the edge lies. For example, the kind of advice we dislike the most is often an indicator of where our personal 'edge' lies. We may need guidance on how to work at our edge. As with the 'edge' of a cliff or precipice, we should approach our personal limits with due caution and the right support. It is good to set challenges – but not to go over the edge without a rope.

Closing comments

Congratulations on reaching this stage of the book. If you worked through most of the chapters and activities, you will have a very strong sense of yourself, your strengths and what you need to do to achieve your goals.

It is likely that you used the book selectively, picking out activities that seemed most relevant or to which you were directed by your tutors. If there were aspects of this process that you at first resisted, found uncomfortable or absolutely hated but worked through, you have really achieved something. What exactly that 'something' is, is for you to judge.

We are always a 'work in progress':

● there is always more that we can understand about ourselves;
● the range of our knowledge and expertise can always be extended;
● there is always an area of our performance that can be improved.

Our personal development is as dynamic a process as we choose to make it. If we use a reflective approach on a regular basis, we will know ourselves more fully, be more aware of our needs and wants, and more able to achieve what we really desire.

Seek out that particular mental attitude which makes you feel most deeply and vitally alive, along with which comes the inner voice which says, 'this is the real me', and when you have found that attitude, follow it.

William James

Resource Bank

Full contents of the Resource Bank

1. Tools for evaluating performance

Improving personal performance

Date:

Example of where I took action to improve my performance.
What needed to be done?
What were the issues?
What made this a priority or a good area to address?
The preparation and planning I undertook.
My strategy (plan) for improving my performance.

Improving personal performance

What I did. Any changes or adaptations that I made to the strategy.
What worked?
What changed?
What else could I have done or could I try on a future occasion?
What did I learn about my own performance through this experience?
The ways this knowledge is more generally applicable to my study, work or life.

Evaluating progress on learning goals

Current learning goals
(*see Action Plan*)

Targets and milestones.

Action taken to achieve the goal ('What have I done so far?')

Evaluation of performance so far ('How well am I meeting my targets? How sensible were the targets? Do they need to be changed?')

What feedback have I received from others?

How have I made use of this feedback?

Things I have learnt about myself, other people or the task so far.

Strong points about my attitude, approach and performance.

Things I could improve about my attitude, approach and performance.

How have I changed?

Next steps?

Other comments

Signed _____   Date _____

2. Personal Records

 # Record of education and training

Education

On the chart below, record details of your educational history, excluding short courses.

Secondary school (ages 11–16; focus on qualifications after age 14)					
Dates (from . . . to . . .)	Name and address of institution or provider	Subjects studied	Qualification achieved (and grade where relevant)	Year of the qualification	Topics covered and skills acquired

Post-16 education (before degree level)					
Dates (from . . . to . . .)	Name and address of institution or provider	Subjects studied	Qualification achieved (and grade where relevant)	Year of the qualification	Topics covered and skills acquired

Copy and complete for additional qualifications

University education					
Dates (from . . . to . . .)	Name and address of institution or provider	Name of course or programme	Qualification achieved (and grade where applicable)	Year qualification was awarded	Topics covered and skills acquired

Short courses, programmes and training

On the chart below, record details of other training you have undertaken at college, through work, or through private agencies.

Dates (from . . . to . . .)	Institution or provider	Name of course or programme	Qualification achieved, if relevant, and year	Topics covered	Skills acquired

Copy and complete for additional training and qualifications

Informal learning

Other learning developed through work experience, informal training by peers and 'away-days', etc.

Year	Where learning took place	Other people involved	Reason for undertaking the learning	What was learnt? Topics covered and skills acquired

Other qualifications, experience and assets

Driving licence, additional languages, familiarity with other countries or cultures.

1.
2.
3.
4.
5.

Copy and complete for additional information

Evidence of learning

Qualifications are one way of providing evidence of learning. However, employers are often interested in seeing what you have valued about your learning, or hearing what you think you have learnt, in order to find out how you demonstrate and apply your skills and intelligence. It is useful to be prepared for such questions.

What has interested you most about your programme?

What do you feel has been the most important thing you have learnt from your programme?

What do you think you have learnt on your programme that could benefit you in the world of work?

In what way is your subject relevant to the world outside of university?

What advice would you give to other students embarking upon your programme?

Record of work history

Starting with your earliest work experience after the age of 16, give details of all work that you have undertaken. You will then have a complete record of the essential information most commonly required when completing application forms.

Dates (from . . . to . . .)	Employer and employer address	Job title	Responsibilities	Experience acquired	Reason for leaving

The most important things I have learnt through my work history that are of benefit to me in other jobs (or in life more generally) are:

1.

2.

3.

4.

5.

Copy and update

Place and date Incident (*basic details*).
What I did.
Responsibility involved.
What others did.
What I learned.
Skills I acquired.
Feedback from employer.
Feedback from clients.
Feedback from others.
How I made use of feedback.

Evidence of Skills and Personal Qualities

Skill, quality or attribute

1. How and when I developed this skill or quality.	
2. Examples of occasions when I demonstrate this skill.	At university At work In life
3. Evidence that I possess this quality or skill (e.g. reliable feedback from others; qualifications, testimonials, etc.).	At university At work In life

Copy and complete for other skills and personal qualities

Critical incident sheet

1. Context: brief details of the critical incident. What happened, where, and when?	
2. My role in the incident. What I did.	
3. My immediate response to the incident. How I coped.	
4. How I made use of advice and feedback from other people.	
5. The longer-term impact of the incident upon my life or work. How important this incident was in the grand scheme of my life. What changed?	
6. Positive outcomes for me or for other people.	
7. What lessons I learned from this occasion.	
8. How I applied what I learned to new situations.	
9. The impact of the incident upon my values, beliefs, attitudes and motivation.	
10. Personal considerations and comments.	

3. Competence Sheets

(e) (1) Evidence of competence in team work

1. The best example.	
2. The purpose of the team, the nature of the team activities and membership.	
3. Context: brief details of the circumstances, event or activity when I showed good team skills.	
4. Level of responsibility in this team. The scale and scope of the work or event.	
5. Personal contribution: what I did; the role(s) I played in the team.	
6. Example of leadership: (e.g. planning, negotiating, persuading).	
7. Example of ability to work with others (e.g. accepting others' views, following directions, working out a compromise, etc.).	
8. What worked well on this occasion?	

9. The lessons I learned from this occasion.	
10. What would I do differently on another occasion?	
11. How typical is this example for me (a daily occurrence/ weekly/occasionally/rarely)?	
12. Brief details of a recent (or second) example.	
13. Brief details of a third, preferably contrasting, example.	
14. How do I measure my success for this competence?	
15. How could this competence be applied to other situations?	

(2) Evidence of competence in working independently

1. The best example.	
2. Context: brief details of the work undertaken, for whom and where it was undertaken.	
3. Level of responsibility for the work in question. The scale and scope of the work.	
4. Size or scope of the work undertaken.	
5. Outcomes: what I achieved.	
6. Contribution of this work to any larger project or team work. How this work linked to the work undertaken by other people.	
7. How I organised my work in order to motivate myself and meet targets.	

8. What worked well for this example of independent work?	
9. What lessons did I learn from this example of independent work?	
10. How would I manage independent work differently on another occasion?	
11. How typical is this example for me (a daily occurrence/ weekly/occasionally/rarely)?	
12. Brief details of a recent (or second) example.	
13. Brief details of a third, preferably contrasting, example.	
14. How could this competence be applied to other situations?	
15. How do I measure my success for this competence?	

1. The best example.	
2. Context: brief details of the circumstances, event or activity.	
3. Level of responsibility on this occasion. The scale and scope of the work or event.	
4. Personal contribution: what I did.	
5. Who else was involved – and what they did.	
6. Skills I exercised.	
7. What worked well on this occasion?	

8. What lessons did I learn from this occasion?	
9. What would I do differently on another occasion?	
10. How typical is this example for me (a daily occurrence/ weekly/occasionally/rarely)?	
11. Brief details of a recent (or second) example.	
12. Brief details of a third, preferably contrasting, example.	
13. How could this competence be applied to other situations?	
14. How do I measure my success for this competence?	

(4) Evidence of competence in leadership

1. The best example.	
2. What I believe is meant by 'leadership'.	
3. Context: brief details of the circumstances, event or activity when I gave leadership to others.	
4. Level of responsibility on this occasion. The scale and scope of the work or event.	
5. Personal contribution: what I did.	
6. Who else was involved – and what they did. How I involved other people, such as delegating authority, or seeking opinions.	
7. Example of leadership skills I exercised.	
8. How I took on board the opinions and feelings of other people.	

9. The outcomes. What happened.	
10. What worked well on this occasion?	
11. What lessons did I learn from this occasion?	
12. What would I do differently on another occasion?	
13. How typical is this example for me (a daily occurrence/ weekly/occasionally/rarely)?	
14. Brief details of a recent (or second) example.	
15. Brief details of a third, preferably contrasting, example.	
16. How could this competence be applied to other situations?	
17. How do I measure my success for this competence?	

1. The best example.	
2. Context: brief details of the circumstances, event or activity. Why was it necessary to exercise persuasion?	
3. Level of responsibility on this occasion. The scale and scope of the work or event.	
4. Personal contribution: what I did.	
5. Example of leadership skills involved on this occasion.	
6. Who else was involved – and what they did. How I involved or worked with others on this occasion.	
7. Skills I exercised and qualities I demonstrated.	
8. The outcomes.	

9. What worked well on this occasion?	
10. What lessons did I learn from this occasion?	
11. What would I do differently on another occasion?	
12. How typical is this example for me (a daily occurrence/ weekly/occasionally/rarely)?	
13. Brief details of a recent (or second) example.	
14. Brief details of a third, preferably contrasting, example.	
15. How could this competence be applied to other situations?	
16. How do I measure my success for this competence?	

ⓔ (6) Evidence of competence in negotiating a compromise

1. The best example.	
2. Context: brief details of the circumstances, event or activity. Why was it necessary to negotiate a compromise?	
3. Level of responsibility on this occasion. The scale and scope of the work or event.	
4. Personal contribution: what I did.	
5. Example of leadership skills involved on this occasion.	
6. Who else was involved – and what they did. How I involved or worked with others on this occasion.	
7. Skills I exercised and qualities I demonstrated.	

8. The outcomes.	
9. What worked well on this occasion?	
10. What lessons did I learn from this occasion?	
11. What would I do differently on another occasion?	
12. How typical is this example for me (a daily occurrence/ weekly/occasionally/rarely)?	
13. Brief details of a recent (or second) example.	
14. Brief details of a third, preferably contrasting, example.	
15. How could this competence be applied to other situations?	
16. How do I measure my success for this competence?	

(7) Evidence of competence in problem-solving

1. The best example.	
2. Context: brief details of the circumstances and the problem to be solved.	
3. Level of responsibility on this occasion. The scale and scope of the work or event.	
4. Personal contribution: what I did.	
5. The problem-solving approach I took – my strategy, the alternatives I considered.	
6. Who else was involved – and what they did. How I involved or worked with others on this occasion.	
7. The outcomes. What was achieved?	

8. What worked well on this occasion?	
9. What lessons did I learn from this occasion?	
10. What would I do differently on another occasion?	
11. How typical is this example for me (a daily occurrence/ weekly/occasionally/rarely)?	
12. Brief details of a recent (or second) example.	
13. Brief details of a third, preferably contrasting, example.	
14. How could this competence be applied to other situations?	
15. How do I measure my success for this competence?	

(8) Evidence of competence in project or task management

1. The best example.	
2. Context: brief details of the circumstances, project or task selected.	
3. Level of responsibility on this occasion. The scale and scope of the work or event.	
4. Personal contribution: what I did.	
5. The approach I took – my strategy, the alternatives I considered.	
6. Who else was involved – and what they did. How I involved or worked with others on this occasion.	
7. The outcomes. What was achieved?	

8. What worked well on this occasion?	
9. What lessons did I learn from this occasion?	
10. What would I do differently on another occasion?	
11. How typical is this example for me (a daily occurrence/weekly/occasionally/rarely)?	
12. Brief details of a recent (or second) example.	
13. Brief details of a third, preferably contrasting, example.	
14. How could this competence be applied to other situations?	
15. How do I measure my success for this competence?	

1. The best example.	
2. Context: brief details of the circumstances or situation.	
3. Level of responsibility on this occasion. The scale and scope of the work or event.	
4. Personal contribution: what I did to resolve the conflict.	
5. The approach I took – why I adopted the techniques or strategy that I did.	
6. Who else was involved – and what they did. How I involved or worked with others on this occasion.	
7. The outcomes. How far the conflict was resolved for the short or long term.	

8. What worked well on this occasion?	
9. What lessons did I learn from this occasion?	
10. What would I do differently on another occasion?	
11. How typical is this example for me (a daily occurrence/ weekly/occasionally/rarely)?	
12. Brief details of a recent (or second) example.	
13. Brief details of a third, preferably contrasting, example.	
14. How could this competence be applied to other situations?	
15 How do I measure my success for this competence?	

▣ (10) Evidence of competence in managing a difficult situation

1. The best example.	
2. Context: brief details of the difficult situation: where it took place, and why it arose.	
3. Level of responsibility on this occasion. The scale and scope of the work or event.	
4. Personal contribution: what I did to manage the situation and resolve the difficulty.	
5. The approach I took – why I adopted the techniques or strategy that I did.	
6. Who else was involved – and what they did. How I involved or worked with others on this occasion.	
7. The outcomes. How far the conflict was resolved for the short or long term.	

8. What worked well on this occasion?	
9. What lessons did I learn from this occasion?	
10. What would I do differently on another occasion?	
11. How typical is this example for me (a daily occurrence/ weekly/occasionally/rarely)?	
12. Brief details of a recent (or second) example.	
13. Brief details of a third, preferably contrasting, example.	
14. How could this competence be applied to other situations?	
15. How do I measure my success for this competence?	

(11) Evidence of competence in working under pressure or to tight deadlines

1. The best example.	
2. Context: brief details of the circumstances that created the pressure or tight deadlines.	
3. Level of responsibility on this occasion. The scale and scope of the work or event.	
4. Personal contribution: what I did.	
5. What action I took to help me cope with the pressure and stress.	
6. Who else was involved – and what they did. How I involved or worked with others on this occasion.	
7. Evidence of ability to work with others under pressure.	

8. The outcomes. The extent to which deadlines were met or the work completed.	
9. What worked well on this occasion?	
10. What lessons did I learn from this occasion?	
11. What would I do differently on another occasion?	
12. How typical is this example for me (a daily occurrence/ weekly/occasionally/rarely)?	
13. Brief details of a recent (or second) example.	
14. Brief details of a third, preferably contrasting, example.	
15. How could this competence be applied to other situations?	
16. How do I measure my success for this competence?	

(12) Evidence of competence in equal opportunities

1. The best example.	
2. What I understand by the term 'equal opportunities'.	
3. Context: brief details of the circumstances and issues involved.	
4. Level of responsibility on this occasion. The scale and scope of the issue.	
5. Personal contribution: what I did.	
6. Who else was involved on this occasion – and what they did. How I involved or worked with others.	
7. The outcomes (long term or short term).	
8. What worked well on this occasion?	

9. What lessons did I learn from this occasion?	
10. What would I do differently on another occasion?	
11. How typical is this example for me (a daily occurrence/ weekly/occasionally/rarely)?	
12. General awareness of equal opportunities issues and legislation. Experience of working with people from a wide variety of backgrounds.	
13. Brief details of a recent (or second) example.	
14. Brief details of a third, preferably contrasting, example.	
15. How could this competence be applied to other situations?	
16. How do I measure my success for this competence?	

(13) Evidence of competence in managing change

1. The best example.	
2. Context: brief details of the circumstances where change was introduced and why it was needed.	
3. Level of responsibility on this occasion. The scale and scope of the issue.	
4. Personal contribution: what I did. How far I initiated the change, or managed my own or others' response to change.	
5. Who else was involved on this occasion – and what they did. How I involved or worked with others. How I supported others through a time of change.	
6. The outcomes of my actions or involvement.	
7. What worked well on this occasion?	

8. What lessons did I learn from this occasion?	
9. What would I do differently on another occasion?	
10. How typical is this example of my life or work experience?	
11. Brief details of a recent (or second) example.	
12. Brief details of a third, preferably contrasting, example.	
13. How could this competence be applied to other situations?	
14. How do I measure my success for this competence?	

(14) Evidence of competence in taking calculated risks

1. The best example.	
2. Context: brief details of the circumstances.	
3. The nature of the risk involved; the factors that needed to be weighed in the balance.	
4. Level of responsibility on this occasion. The scale and scope of the issue.	
5. Personal contribution: what I did.	
6. Who else was involved on this occasion – and what they did. How I involved or worked with others.	
7. What I did to manage the pressure and stress for myself and others.	

8. The outcomes of my actions or involvement.	
9. What worked well on this occasion?	
10. What lessons did I learn from this occasion?	
11. What would I do differently on another occasion?	
12. How typical is this example of my life or work experience?	
13. Brief details of a recent (or second) example	
14. Brief details of a third, preferably contrasting, example.	
15. How could this competence be applied to other situations?	
16. How do I measure my success for this competence?	

(15) Evidence of competence in learning from my own mistakes

1. The best example.	
2. Context: brief details of the circumstances.	
3. The mistake(s) that I made on this occasion. What circumstances led to the mistake/error of judgement? How I discovered the mistake.	
4. Level of responsibility on this occasion. The scale and scope of the issue.	
5. Personal contribution: what I did.	
6. Who else was involved on this occasion – and what they did. How I involved or worked with others.	
7. What I did to manage the pressure and stress for myself and others.	

8. The outcomes of my actions or involvement. How I took responsibility for my own actions.	
9. What, if anything, was positive about my contribution?	
10. What lessons did I learn from this occasion?	
11. What would I do differently on another occasion? How I acted differently on a second occasion.	
12. How typical is it for me to use a reflective approach to improve my performance?	
13. Brief details of a recent (or second) example.	
14. Brief details of a third, preferably contrasting, example.	
15. How could this competence be applied to other situations?	
16. How do I measure my success for this competence?	

(16) Evidence of competence in written communication skills

1. The best example.	
2. Context: brief details of the circumstances.	
3. Level of responsibility on this occasion. The time-scale, word limits and importance of the task.	
4. The nature of the audience.	
5. Personal contribution: what I did, including how the writing was suited to the audience.	
6. Who else was involved on this occasion – and what they did. How I involved or worked with others on this occasion.	
7. Outcomes. The extent to which deadlines were met or the work completed. What feedback I received.	

8. What lessons did I learn from this occasion? How I used feedback.	
9. What would I do differently on another occasion?	
10. What skills have I acquired through academic writing?	
11. Awareness of differences between academic writing and that for the career area which interests me.	
12. How typical is this example for me (a daily occurrence/ weekly/occasionally/rarely)?	
13. Brief details of a recent (or second) example.	
14. Brief details of a third, preferably contrasting, example.	
15. How could this competence be applied to other situations?	
16. How do I measure my success for this competence?	

(17) Evidence of competence in oral communication skills

1. The best example.	
2. Context: brief details of the circumstances.	
3. Level of responsibility on this occasion. The time limit, scale and scope of the work or event.	
4. The nature of the audience and how I took this into consideration.	
5. Personal contribution: what I did.	
6. Who else was involved on this occasion – and what they did. How I involved or worked with others on this occasion.	
7. Outcomes. The extent to which deadlines were met or the work completed. Feedback I received.	

8. What worked well on this occasion?	
9. What lessons did I learn from this occasion?	
10. What would I do differently on another occasion?	
11. How typical is this example for me (a daily occurrence/weekly/occasionally/rarely)?	
12. Brief details of a recent (or second) example.	
13. Brief details of a third, preferably contrasting, example.	
14. How could this competence be applied to other situations?	
15. How do I measure my success for this competence?	

Pro-forma for mapping other competences

🖳 (18) Evidence of competence in: _____

1. The best example.	
2. Context: brief details of the circumstances.	
3. Level of responsibility on this occasion. The scale and scope of the issue.	
4. Personal contribution: what I did.	
5. Who else was involved on this occasion – and what they did. How I involved or worked with others.	
6. The outcomes of my actions or involvement.	
7. What worked well on this occasion?	

8. What lessons did I learn from this occasion?	
9. What would I do differently on another occasion?	
10. How typical is this example of my life or work experience?	
11. Brief details of a recent (or second) example.	
12. Brief details of a third, preferably contrasting, example.	
13. How could this competence be applied to other situations?	
14. How do I measure my success for this competence?	

(19) Health and safety

Date:

My general understanding of health and safety issues and legislation.

Examples of specific health and safety issues that I needed to be aware of in one place I have worked or studied.

Health and safety training I have received.

An incident that demonstrates my management of health and safety issues.

Copy and update

References

Association of Graduate Recruiters (2010) 'Graduate Recruitment Survey', www.agr.org.uk/Content/Graduate-Recruitment-Survey (downloaded 24 January 2010).

Atkins, S. and Murphy, K. (1994) 'Reflective Practice', in *Nursing Standard*, **8** (39), pp. 49–54.

Beaver, D. (1998) *NLP for Lazy Learning* (Shaftesbury, Dorset, and Boston, MA: Element).

Belbin, M. R. (1996) *Management Teams: Why They Succeed or Fail* (London: Butterworth-Heinemann).

Belbin, M. R. (2010) *Team Roles at Work*, 2nd edn (London: Butterworth-Heinemann).

Benson, J. F. (2009) *Working More Creatively with Groups*, 3rd edn (London: Tavistock).

Boud, D., Keogh, R. and Walker, D. (1985) *Reflection: Turning Experience into Learning* (London: Routledge).

Bright, J. and Earl, J. (2007) *Brilliant CV: What Employers Want to See and How to Say It*, 3rd edn (London: Prentice Hall).

Butterworth, G. (1992) 'Context and Cognition in Models of Cognitive Growth', in P. Light and G. Butterworth (eds), *Context and Cognition* (London: Harvester).

Buzan, T. (2006) *The Mind Map Book* (London: BBC Active).

Chapman, A. (2001) *The Monster Guide to Jobhunting* (London: Financial Times/Prentice Hall).

Chase, W. G. and Simon, H. A. (1973) 'Perception in Chess', *Cognitive Science*, **13**, 145–82.

Cottrell, S. (2001) *Teaching Study Skills and Supporting Learning* (Basingstoke: Palgrave Macmillan).

Cottrell, S. (2005) *Critical Thinking Skills: Developing Effective Analysis and Argument* (Basingstoke: Palgrave Macmillan).

Cottrell, S. (2007) *The Exam Skills Handbook: Achieving Peak Performance* (Basingstoke: Palgrave Macmillan).

Cottrell, S. (2008) *The Study Skills Handbook*, 3rd edn (Basingstoke: Palgrave Macmillan).

Cottrell, S. (2010) (new edition annually) *The Palgrave Student Planner* (Basingstoke: Palgrave Macmillan).

Covey, S. R. (2004) *The Seven Habits of Highly Effective People: Powerful Lessons in Personal Change*, 15th Anniversary edn (London: Free Press).

Committee of Vice-Chancellors and Principals/Department for Education and Employment (CVCP) (1998) *Skills Development in Higher Education, Short Report* (London: Committee of Vice-Chancellors and Principals)

Davidson, J. (2000) *The Ten-Minute Guide to Project Management* (Indianapolis: Alpha Books).

Dearing, R. (1997) *The Summary Report of the National Committee of Inquiry into Higher Education* (London: HMSO).

De Bono, E. (1996) *Teach Yourself to Think* (London: Penguin).

De Bono, E. (2006) *De Bono's Thinking Course*, revised and updated (London: BBC Active).

Dilts, R., Hallbom, T. and Smith, S. (1990) *Beliefs: Pathways to Health and Well-being* (Portland, OR: Metamorphous Press).

Donaldson, M. (1978) *Children's Minds* (London: Fontana).

Dryden, W. and Gordon, J. (1993) *Peak Performance: Become More Effective at Work* (Didcot, Oxon: Mercury Business Books).

Dunn, R., Griggs, S., Olson, J., Beasley, M. and Gorman, B. (1995) 'A Meta-analytic Validation of the Dunn and Dunn Model of Learning Style Preferences', *Journal of Educational Research*, **88** (6), 353–62.

Egan, D. and Schwartz, B. (1979) 'Chunking in Recall of Symbolic Drawings', *Memory and Cognition*, 7, 149–58.

Ellis, A. (1994) *Reason and Emotion in Psychotherapy*, revised and updated (New York: Birch Lane Press).

Fennell, M. (2009) *Overcoming Low Self-esteem: A Self-help Guide using Cognitive Behavioural Techniques* (London: Robinson).

Goleman, D. (1995) *Emotional Intelligence* (London: Bloomsbury).

Graham, R. J. (1989) *Project Management as if People Mattered* (Bala Cynwyd, PA: Primavera Press).

Greenfield, S. (2001) *The Human Brain: A Guided Tour* (London: Phoenix).

Hallows, J. (1997) *Information Systems Project Management* (New York: Amacom).

Heerkens, G. R. (2002) *Project Management* (New York: McGraw-Hill).

Heron, J. (1992) *Feeling and Personhood* (London: Sage Publications).

Hodgson, S. (2007) *Brilliant Answers to Tough Interview Questions*, 3rd edn (London: Prentice Hall).

Honey, P. and Mumford, A. (1992) *The Manual of Learning Styles Questionnaire* (Maidenhead, Berks: Peter Honey).

Jackson, T. and Jackson, E. (1997) *The Perfect CV: How to Get the Job You Really Want*, 2nd revised edn (London: Piaktus).

Kolb, D. A. (1984) *Experiential Learning: Experience as the Source of Learning and Development* (Englewood Cliffs, NJ: Prentice Hall).

Kozubska, J. (1997) *The 7 Keys of Charisma: The Secrets of Those Who Have It* (London: Kogan Page).

Lawrence, G. (1993) *People Types and Tiger Stripes*, 3rd edn (Gainesville, FL: Centre for Applications of Psychological Type).

Lazarus, R. S. (1999) *Stress and Emotion* (London: Free Association Books).

Luft, J. (1984) *Group Processes: An Introduction to Group Dynamics*, 3rd edn (Mayfield, CA: Mountain View).

McCormick, R. and Paechter, C. (1999) *Learning and Knowledge* (London: The Open University).

McGill, I. and Beaty, L. (2001) *Action Learning: A Practitioner's Guide*, 2nd revised edn (London: Routledge).

Mezirow, J. (ed.) (1990) *Fostering Critical Reflection in Adulthood: A Guide to Transformative and Emancipatory Learning* (San Francisco, CA: Jossey-Bass).

Mingus, N. (2002) *Alpha Teach Yourself Project Management in 24 Hours* (Indianapolis: Alpha Books).

Moon, J. (2004) *A Handbook of Reflective and Experiential Learning: Theory and Practice* (London: RoutledgeFalmer).

Neenan, M. and Dryden, W. (2002) *Life Coaching: A Cognitive-Behavioural Approach* (New York: Brunner-Routledge).

Neill, J. (2004) *Experiential Learning Cycles*, viewed at www.wilderdom.com/experiential/elc/Experiential L e a r n i n g Cycle.htm (July 2009).

Nolan, V. (ed) (2000) *Creative Education: Educating a Nation of Innovators. Papers by Members of the Synetics Education Initiative* (Buckinghamshire: Synetics Education Initiative).

Palmer, S. and Dryden, W. (1995) *Counselling for Stress Problems* (London: Sage).

Perry, W. G. (1970) *Forms of Intellectual and Ethical Development in the College Years: A Scheme* (New York: Holt, Rinehart and Winston).

Piaget, J. (1952) *The Origins of Intelligence in Children* (New York: International Universities Press).

Piaget, J. (1975) *The Development of Thought: Equilibration of Cognitive Structures* (Oxford: Blackwell).

Popovich, I. (2003) *Teach Yourself Winning at Job Interviews*, new edn (London: Hodder Education).

Project Management Institute (2000) *A Guide to the Project Management Body of Knowledge* (Newtown Square, PA: Project Management Institute).

Qualifications and Curriculum Authority (2000) *Improving Your Own Learning and Performance*, Key Skills Unit (London: QCA).

Qualifications and Curriculum Authority (2000) *Problem Solving*, Key Skills Unit (London: QCA).

Quality Assurance Agency for Higher Education (2000) www.qaa.ac.uk/Heprogressfile (30/5/2000).

Ribbens, G. and Thompson, R. (2002) *Understanding Body Language* (Abingdon: Gower).

Rossett, A. and Sheldon, K. (2001) *Beyond the Podium: Delivering Training and Performance to a Digital World* (San Francisco, CA: Jossey-Bass/Pfeiffer).

Sapadin, L. (1997) *It's about Time* (New York: Penguin).

Saven-Baden, M. (2000) *Problem-based Learning in Higher Education: Untold Stories* (Buckingham: SRHE and Open University Press).

Schon, D. A. (1983) *The Reflective Practitioner* (New York: Basic Books).

Schon, D. A. (1989) *The Reflective Practitioner: How Professionals Think in Action* (London: Temple Smith).

Siegler, R. S. (1991) *Children's Thinking* (Englewood Cliffs, NJ: Prentice Hall).

Skills and Enterprise Network (2001) *Update: A Digest of Recent Labour Market, Research and Evaluation Reports and Developments*, no. 1, February (Sheffield: Skills and Enterprise Network).

Stordy, J. B. (2000) 'Dark Adaptation, Motor Skills, Docosahexaenoic Acid and Dyslexia', *American Journal of Clinical Nutrition*, 71 (supplement), 323–6.

Taylor, R. and Humphrey, J. (2002) *Fast Track to the Top: Skills for Career Success* (London: Kogan Page).

Thompson, S. and Thompson, N. (2008) *The Critically Reflective Practitioner* (Basingstoke: Palgrave Macmillan).

TMP Worldwide Research (1998) *Soft Skills: Employers' Desirability and Actual Incidence* (32, Aybrook St, London, W1M 3JL).

Universities UK and CBI (2009) 'Future Fit – Preparing Graduates for the World of Work' (London: CBI).

Van Oech, R. (2008) *A Whack on the Side of the Head: How to be More Creative*, revised and updated edn (New York: Grand Central Publishing).

Useful websites

Assessment centres

www.prospects.ac.uk/links/AssessmentCntrs
general advice on exercises and how to prepare
http://targetjobs.co.uk/general-advice/assessment-centres.aspx
general advice
www.psychometric-success.com/assessment-centers/assessment-and-development-center.htm
advice and practice tests
www.shl.com/TryATest/Pages/CandidateHelp.aspx
practice tests

Career guidance

www.prospects.ac.uk	advice and jobs for graduates
www.gradunet.co.uk	advice and jobs for graduates
www.agcas.co.uk	advice and information for graduates
www.hobsons.com	guidance and jobs for school leavers, young people and graduates
www.insidecareers.co.uk	guidance and jobs for graduates

Employment companies

www.bloomberg.com	international and entrepreneur site
www.companieshouse.gov.uk	lists all UK public companies
www.vault.com	what it is like to work for named companies

Employment: job hunting

www.paler.com/uk	list of job sites
www.totaljobs.com/graduates	graduate jobs
www.jobsite.co.uk	general
www.eteach.com	teaching
www.fish4jobs.co.uk	regional jobs
www.careers.lon.ac.uk/ijo	international jobs
www.jobhunter.co.uk	adverts that appear in newspapers
www.monster.co.uk	job adverts and career advice
www.planetrecruit.com	IT, engineering and telecom jobs

Employment rights

www.equalityhumanrights.com	Equality and Human Rights Commission
www.emplaw.co.uk	employment law
www.adviceguide.org.uk	Citizens' Advice Bureau
www.hse.gov.uk	health and safety
www.i-resign.com/uk/home	leaving your job

Disability issues

www.ability.org.uk	disability charity
www.skill.org.uk	disability charity
www.direct.gov.uk/en/DisabledPeople	government's disability issues site
www.adult-dyslexia.org	Adult Dyslexia Organisation
www.bdadyslexia.org.uk	British Dyslexia Association

Index